IMAGES
of America

MYRTLE BEACH PAVILION

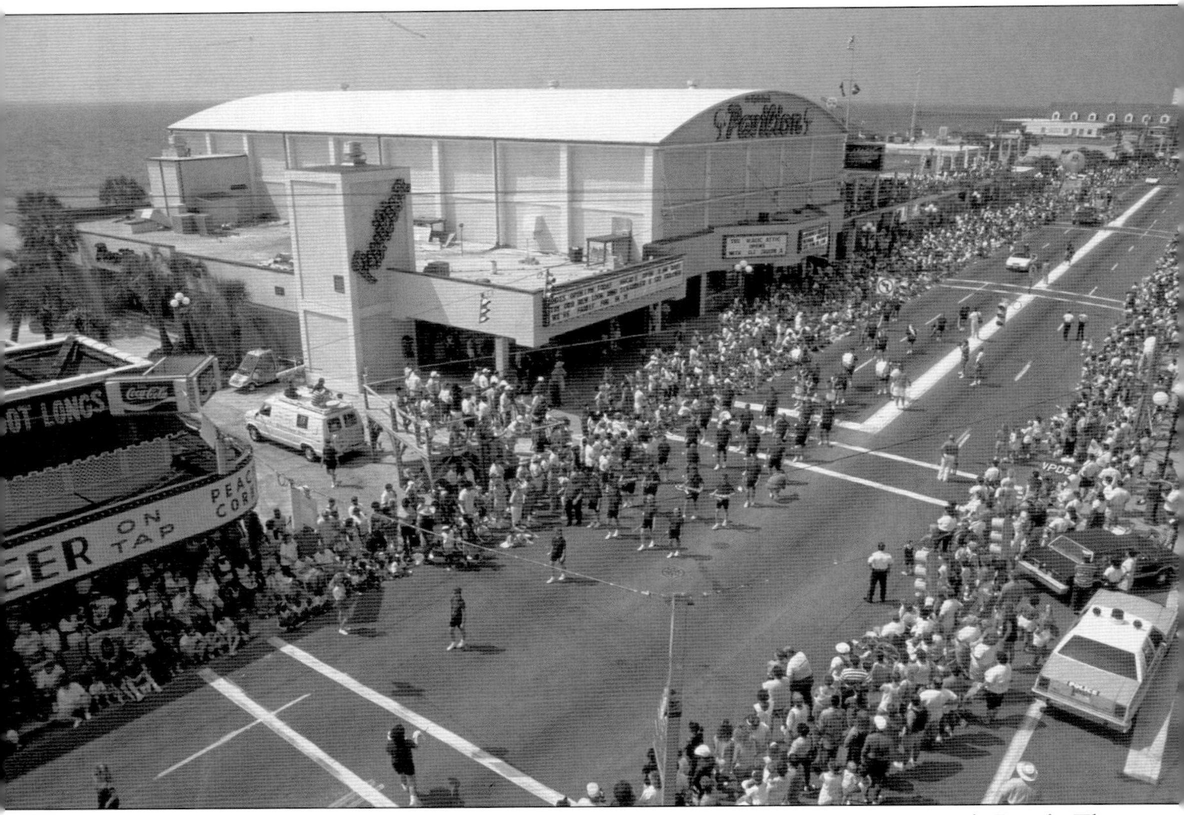

The Sun Fun Festival was created in 1951 in an effort to lure more tourists to Myrtle Beach. This 1991 photograph was taken from atop the Ripley's Believe It or Not building, looking south on Ocean Boulevard at the Pavilion and the parade. The Sun Fun Parade was always routed past the Pavilion, making the area around the Pavilion a prime area for viewing. (Photograph by Tim Ribar.)

On the Cover: Tanning and people watching were just two of the favorite pastimes for sunbathers parking their blankets on the Myrtle Beach Pavilion's beachfront. With showers, refreshments, and entertainment just a sand dune away, the Pavilion's beach remained the place to be from the time the Pavilion opened its doors in 1948 until it closed in 2006. (Courtesy Burroughs and Chapin Company, Inc.)

IMAGES
of America

MYRTLE BEACH PAVILION

Lesta Sue Hardee and Janice McDonald

ARCADIA
PUBLISHING

ISBN 978-0-7385-8601-4

Published by Arcadia Publishing
Charleston, South Carolina

Printed in the United States of America

Library of Congress Control Number: 2009943886

For all general information contact Arcadia Publishing at:
Telephone 843-853-2070
Fax 843-853-0044
E-mail sales@arcadiapublishing.com
For customer service and orders:
Toll-Free 1-888-313-2665

Visit us on the Internet at www.arcadiapublishing.com

We would like to dedicate this book to our families who taught us how to love the Pavilion and to those who shared that love.

Contents

ACKNOWLEDGMENTS

Writing this book together has been an adventure and a true treasure hunt for both of us. We have reconnected with old friends and made wonderful new ones. We have found fabulous resources that lay hidden behind closed doors, in attics, in boxes, in scrapbooks, and in the memories of everyone who has been touched by the Myrtle Beach Pavilion. Everyone that we spoke to gladly opened their hearts, shared their photographs, their stories, their laughter, and sometimes even their tears.

This book could not have been possible without the help of our editor at Arcadia, Lindsay Harris (thank you for making our dream a reality!), and everyone who lent us pictures and gave us names of people who might know someone who knows the aunt of the cousin that has the grandmother's pictures. They include Jimmy Lathan; "Deacon" Dawson; Mickey Brafford; Lauchlan McKay; Dorothy McDonald; Mary Catherine Hardee; Sandra K. Hardee; Diane Moskow-McKenzie and Mark Kruea of the City of Myrtle Beach; Allison Hardin, Glenn Broach; Kori Hippe of the Myrtle Beach Area Chamber of Commerce (MBCC); the Mark Garner Collection at the Chapin Memorial Library (CML); Carolyn Savage and Laura Fazekas; Christi Blanton and Julie Pinkney from the Horry County Museum; Horry County Historical Society (HCHS); Curt Teich Postcard Archives; Jack Thompson, Ray Hobbs, and Mike and Jean Hussey; Greg Stalvey; Tempe Oehler; Susan Nuckles Williams; Janice Cooney; Emily Ann Skews, Sarah Bryan, South Caroliniana Library; Lynn Livesay; Robert Montgomery; Virginia Blake Oyster; Robin Able Chapman; Beck Smith Williams; and lastly Brad Faircloth and Burroughs and Chapin Company, Inc.

Unless otherwise noted, all images appear courtesy of the authors.

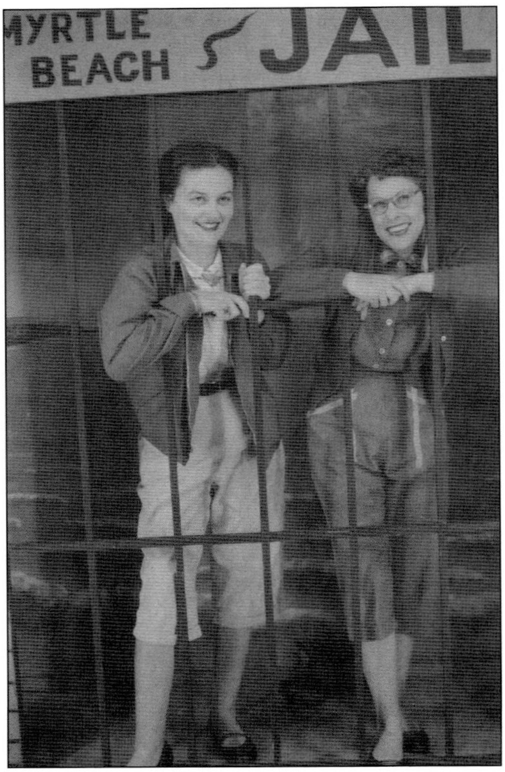

Mary Catherine Hardee (left) and a friend do "jail" time at the Myrtle Beach Pavilion in 1952.

INTRODUCTION

The Myrtle Beach Pavilion stood both figuratively and literally at the center of South Carolina's premier resort community for almost 60 years. Overlooking the ocean at the site where the town's first structures were erected in the late 1800s, the Pavilion stood as a monument to Myrtle Beach's founding as a place for people to get away from it all. Old-fashioned and sometimes a bit hokey, it was a reminder of simpler times. When people thought of Myrtle Beach, they thought of the Pavilion. Any hotel inquiry began with, "How far are you from the Pavilion?" Any direction started with, "If you're facing the Pavilion."

While most remember the large golden-bricked structure that stood between Eighth and Ninth Avenue North for almost six decades, there were actually a few other Pavilions along the way, starting as early as 1902. Each was designed to help entertain the town's guests. And each was grander than the next, as more and more people began to recognize the Pavilion as the central gathering point in Myrtle Beach. Cumulatively, the structures and the amusements that grew up around them helped establish the Grand Strand as one of the top family destinations in the United States. The people of Myrtle Beach and the tourists who came to visit adored the Pavilion and all it symbolized. They thought it would last forever. They were wrong.

Myrtle Beach was founded on land purchased in the 1890s by partners F. A. Burroughs and Benjamin Grier Collins. F. A.'s son F. G. Burroughs erected the first Pavilion as an annex for the area's very first hotel, the Sea Side Inn, built in 1901. Built specifically for entertainment, the Pavilion was the local hub of activity until 1920, when it burned to the ground.

Three years later, a two-story replacement was built, and it was here that people began coming in droves to be a part of a dance that would evolve into something called the Shag. By the time it was rebuilt and expanded again in 1927, the Pavilion was known as a location for shaggers. Those early dancers' children and their children's children would come to get some "sand in their shoes" on the dance floor.

When fire claimed that building in 1944, Burroughs and Chapin, now operating under the name Myrtle Beach Farms, made plans to construct something sturdier. They turned to local architect James Cooney, who drew up plans for a reinforced concrete structure that could withstand anything, including winds up to 150 miles an hour.

The building that would become the beloved Myrtle Beach Pavilion was completed in 1948 and was the first structure of its kind along the Grand Strand. This was the Pavilion that endured and saw Myrtle Beach grow to an international tourism destination. It was this Pavilion that withstood hurricanes and the onslaught of thousands of tourists who descended upon it each season. There were face-lifts and expansions, but it stood virtually unchanged for almost six decades before a wrecking ball demolished it in 2006.

Amusements had become a central part of activities surrounding the Pavilion. While the new building was going up, Myrtle Beach Farms bought out a traveling carnival that had been operating in Conway at the Tobacco Festival and placed it on the land across the boulevard. The rides were up and running by the time the building opened.

To attract more tourists, the city started the Sun Fun Festival in 1951 as a summer season kick-off. The Miss South Carolina Pageant was held at the Pavilion in 1952, and author Mickey Spillane came in to judge. He fell in love with the area and never left.

Hurricane Hazel in 1954 proved a turning point for the Pavilion and Myrtle Beach. The Category 4 storm wiped out almost everything on the beachfront except the Pavilion, and as the community rebuilt, the structure stood as a testament to the town's determination to endure.

It was during this time that two of the most recognized features of the Pavilion Amusement Park were added: the Baden band organ and the Herschell-Spillman carousel. More rides and more events began drawing larger crowds to the area. The music venue on the second floor of the Pavilion became the place for up-and-coming bands. Beach music reigned supreme.

Human checker games, air shows, parades, and the world's biggest sand castle (twice) were only some of the fun that found its way here. For more than a few Sun Fun Festivals, it was "against the law" to wear anything other than a bathing suit or shorts. Violators would find themselves thrown into jail in a makeshift structure at the Pavilion. Of course, a donation to charity would get them out.

The dance hall upstairs packed them in for dancing and concerts, regularly selling out its capacity (2,000 seats). In addition to beach music bands, many internationally known groups played here, including Jerry Lee Lewis, the Temptations, Journey, and for one song on one memorable night in 1978, even the Rolling Stones.

For decades, it was a given that driving by the Pavilion on Ocean Boulevard on any summer night would likely take someone at least 30 minutes to travel the six-block arcade region; this was the ultimate cruise zone. Teenagers would hang from the rails of the Pavilion deck and shout to those below, while others would sing out from the Ferris wheel, which was positioned so that its riders could see across the boardwalk and to the ocean. (By bribing the attendant, a couple could get a moment or two at the top while new riders boarded.) No summer was complete without throwing a few skee balls in the Pavilion Arcade or taking at least one tour through the fun mirrors with cotton candy or corn dog in hand.

The Pavilion was a place where every visitor to the beach made at least one stop on every stay and a place where every local brought their guests. Sometimes the national media would show up to document the fun. It was like an old friend who everyone felt would always be there.

When there were signs that the friend was getting a little tired, most thought it was just a phase. Then word came in 2006 that it would all come to an end. The outcry over plans to demolish was enormous but not enough to reverse the decision of the Pavilion's owner, the Burroughs and Chapin Company, Inc. (formerly Myrtle Beach Farms).

The Pavilion's demise left an enormous hole in the community. Time cannot be reversed, but a new boardwalk has been constructed in the area where the Pavilion stood. Meanwhile, the small Pavilion Nostalgia Park at Broadway at the Beach is one of the center's most popular features.

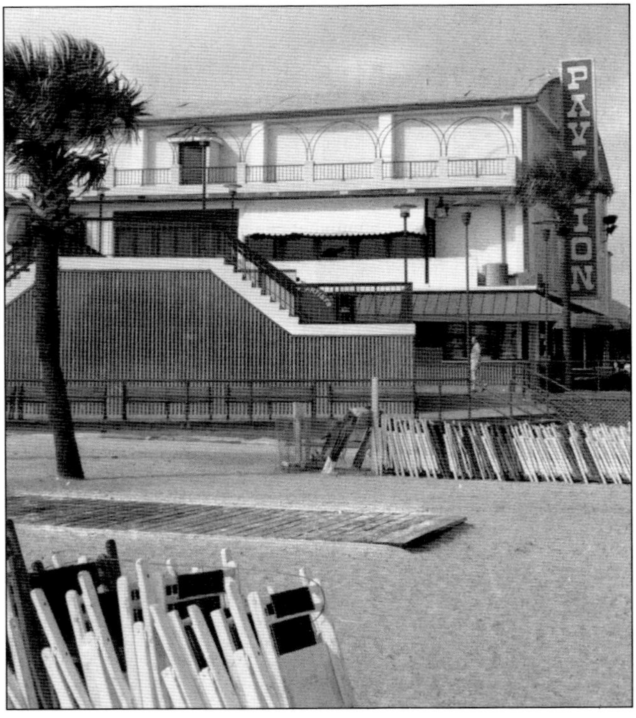

The Myrtle Beach Pavilion was a Myrtle Beach landmark for nearly 100 years.

One

The Birth of the Myrtle Beach Pavilion

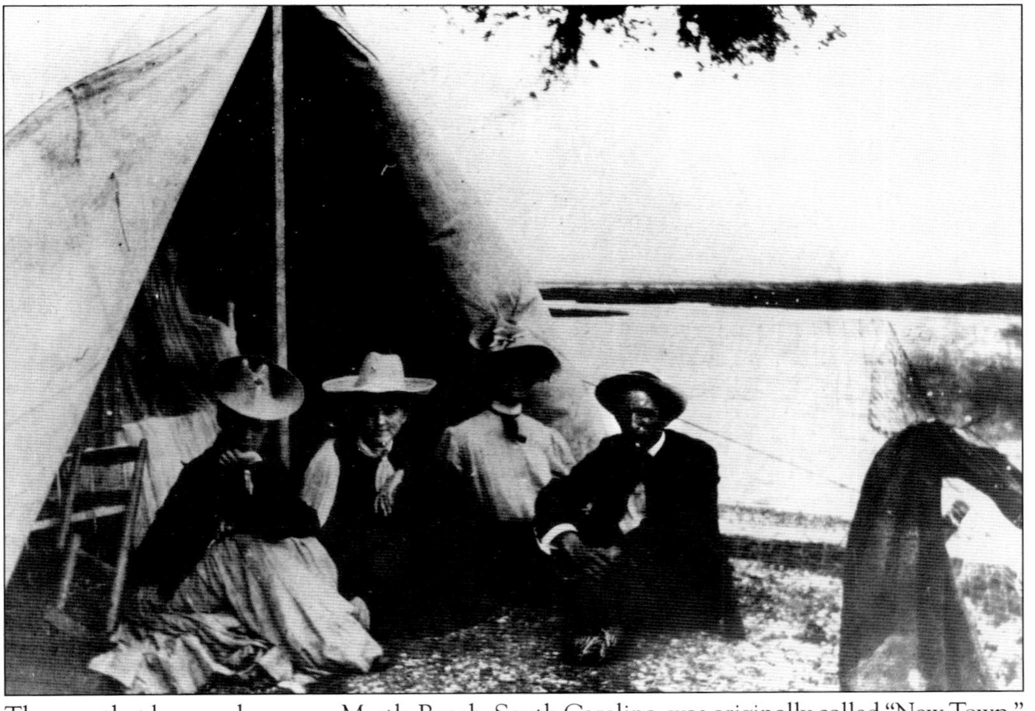

The area that became known as Myrtle Beach, South Carolina, was originally called "New Town," distinguishing it from "Old Town" or Conway, the Horry County seat. A popular stopover for coastal travelers since Colonial times, visitors did not start coming to the beach for recreation in earnest until Burroughs and Collins Company's Conway and Seashore Railroad began daily service in 1900. Anyone choosing to overnight at the beach had to camp.

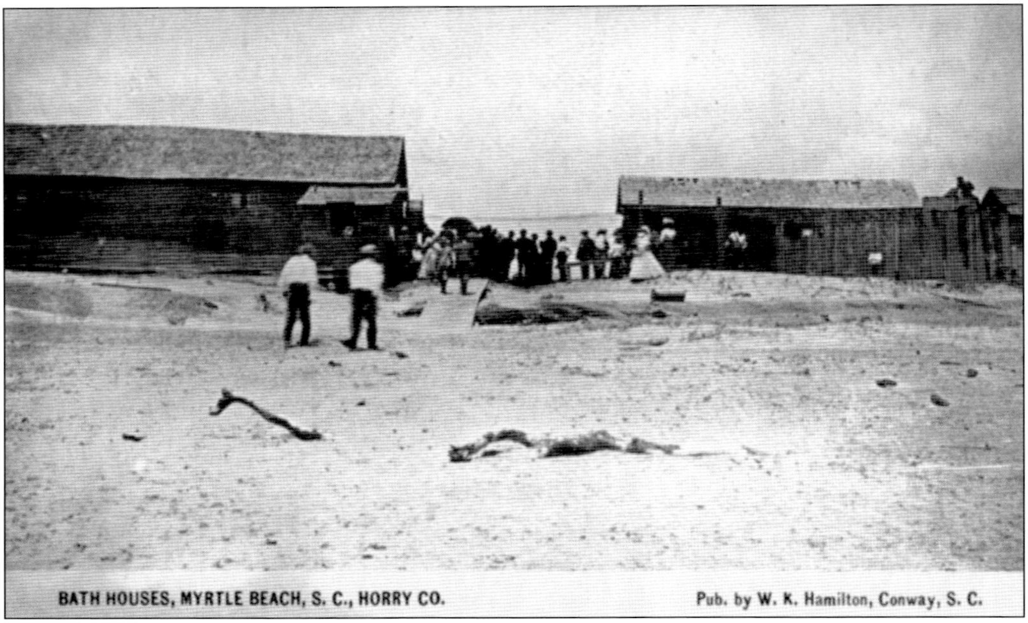

These wooden bathhouses were erected around 1902 to help draw visitors to the beach. Decorum of the day did not permit beachgoers to ride back to Conway on the train covered in salt and sand. The baths allowed "surf bathers" to freshen up before making the journey home. Damaged by weather and fire, the buildings were eventually removed in 1920 and replaced by a more sturdy bathhouse.

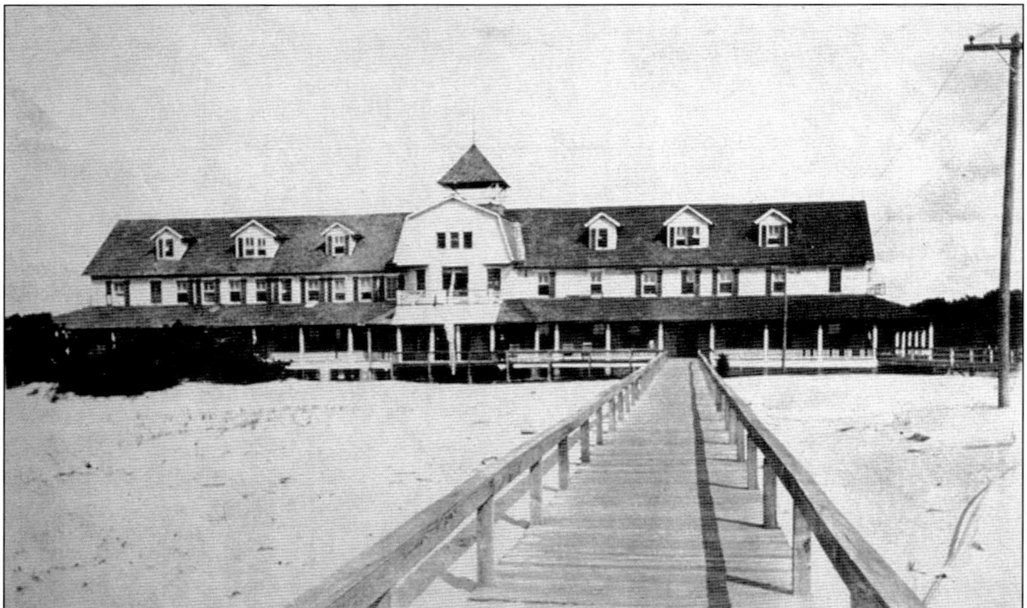

Myrtle Beach's first lodging opened its doors May 23, 1901. Owned by F. A. Burroughs, the Sea Side Inn was built to accommodate some of the "hundreds of visitors who come each year to spend some time on our pleasant beach," according to the *Horry Herald* newspaper. The two-story structure had 23 large rooms. Screens on the windows and canopies over beds helped protect guests against voracious mosquitoes. (Courtesy Burroughs and Chapin Company, Inc..)

The *Horry Herald* ran this advertisement for the Sea Side Inn on May 30, 1901, a week after it opened. Dining room offerings included fresh seafood and vegetables from the Burroughs's farm. Electricity replaced gas lamps in 1909. The Conway and Seashore Western Railroad was virtually the only way to reach the beach before 1914 when a new dirt road made it possible for automobiles to make the 14-mile, 45-minute journey from Conway.

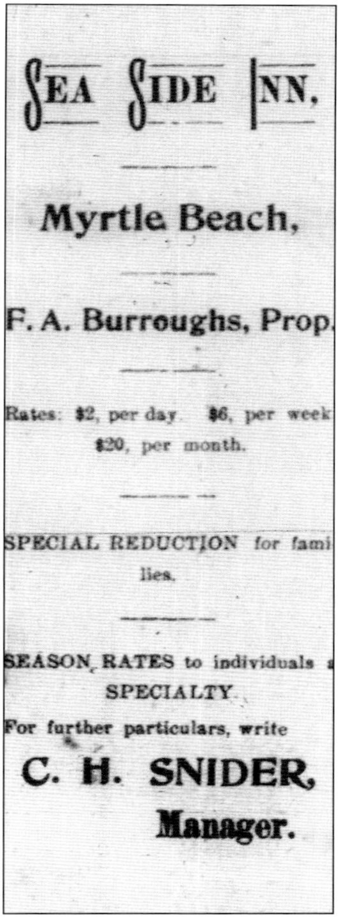

SEA SIDE INN,

Myrtle Beach,

F. A. Burroughs, Prop.

Rates: $2, per day. $6, per week $20, per month.

SPECIAL REDUCTION for families.

SEASON RATES to individuals a SPECIALTY.

For further particulars, write

C. H. SNIDER,

Manager.

This Pavilion set the trend in 1908 by becoming the gathering place for anyone coming to Myrtle Beach. It was built specifically for dancing and entertainment and was attached to the Sea Side Inn by a boardwalk. Multisided and surrounded by porches, it had a red-shingled roof, grey walls, and white windowsills. Music was provided by a Victrola and sometimes by what Annette Epps Reesor described as "a marvelous string band of Negro musicians."

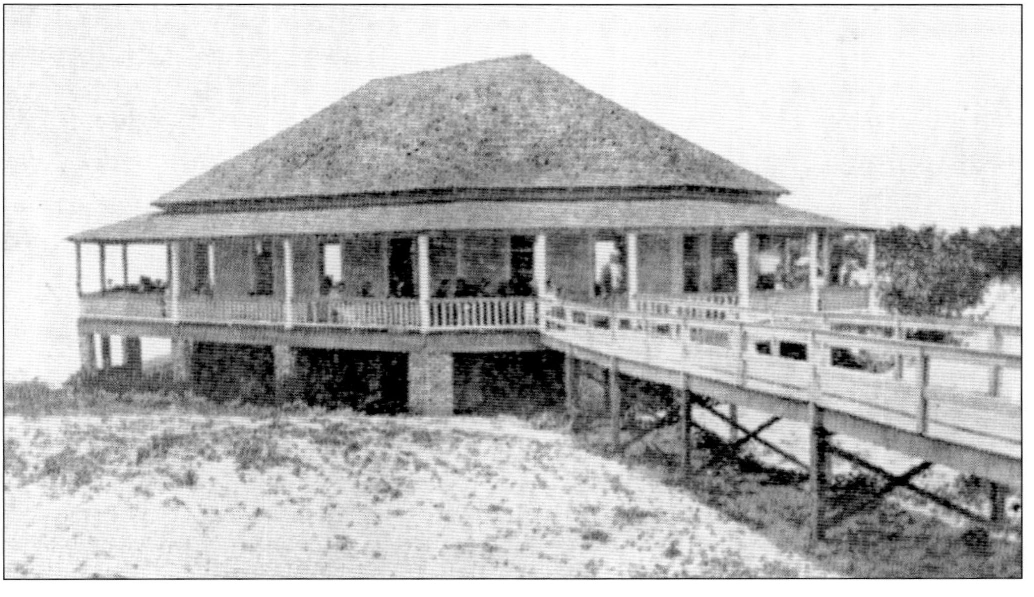

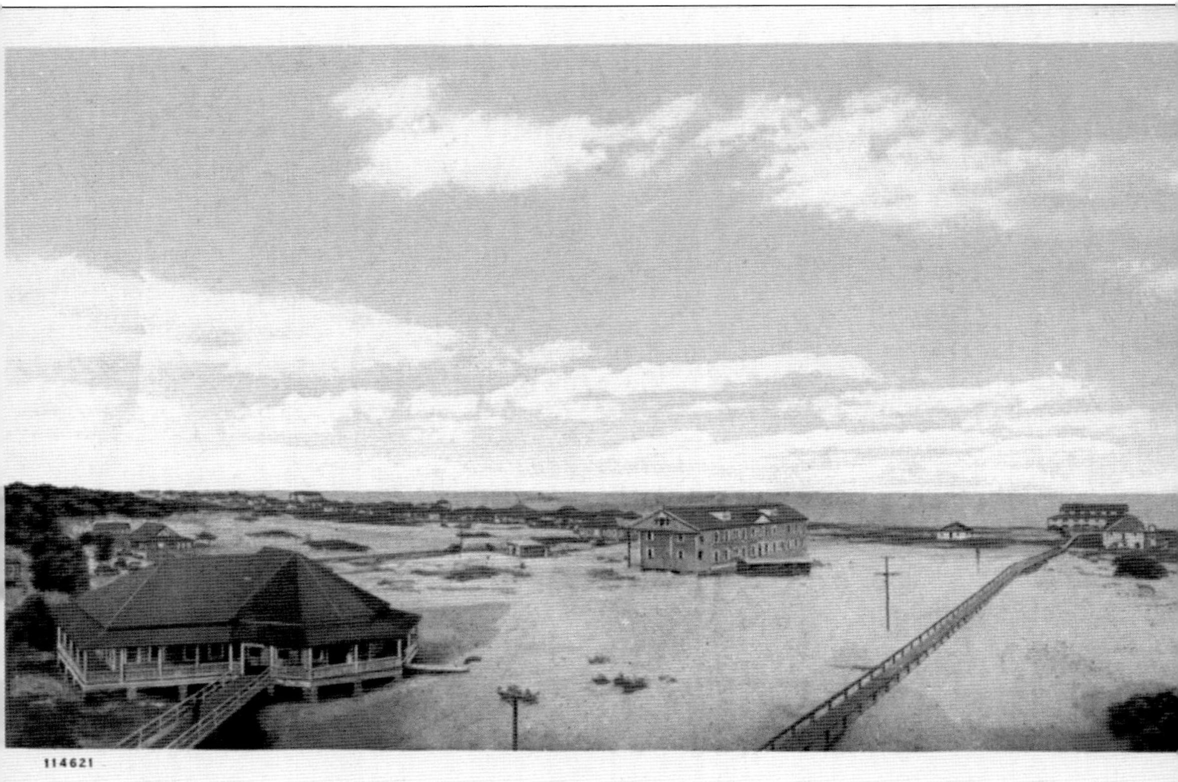

This 1924 panorama of Myrtle Beach was likely taken from the cupola on top of the Sea Side Inn. The photographer, Warren C. Johnson, was from Conway and a nephew of F. G. Burroughs. He became known for photography that helped chronicle the development of the region. In addition to the seafront cottages, in this image, the new Pavilion and the Annex stand at the end of the long boardwalk. A new hotel, still under construction, is just to the left of the boardwalk. The photograph helps depict just how sandy and devoid of vegetation this area was at the time. The

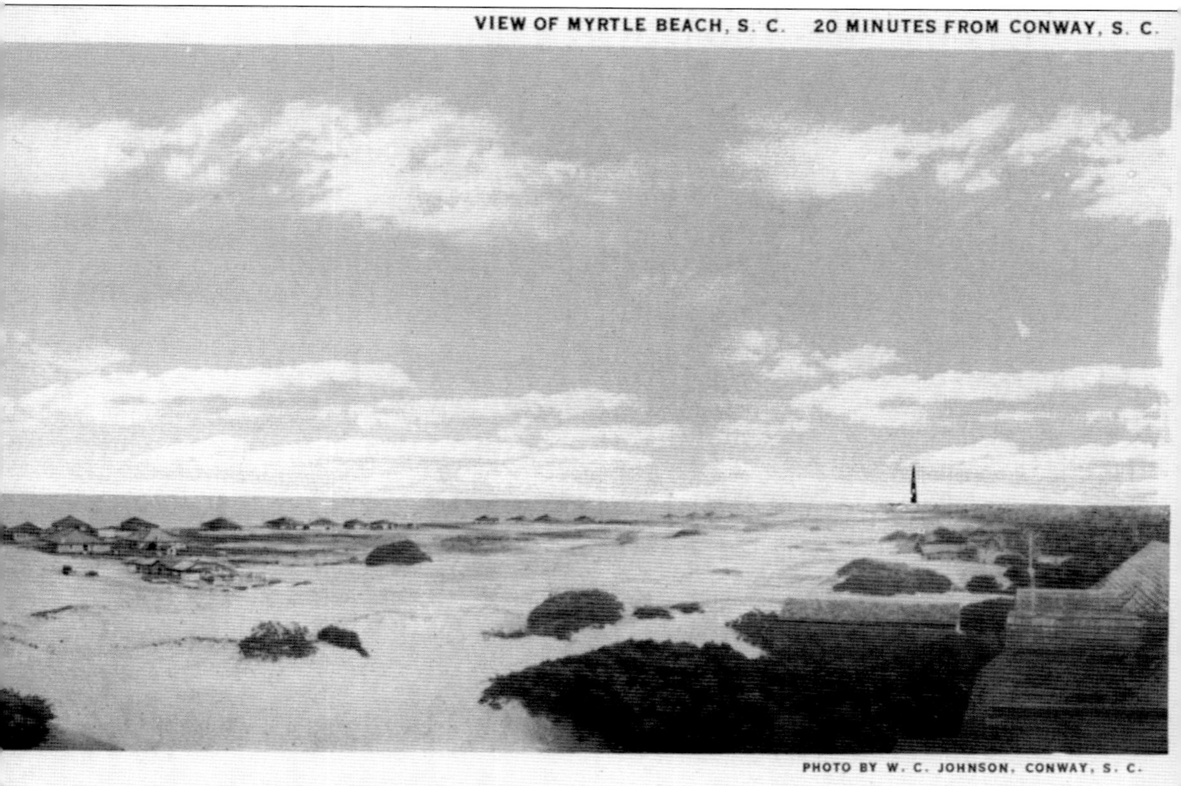

photograph also shows the exact area that would one day house the Pavilion Amusement Park as well as the Pavilion. The lighthouse in the upper right corner was an embellishment and never existed. There is some confusion about when the second oceanfront Pavilion was built. Some reports have the first Pavilion burning in 1920 and being replaced in 1923 by a larger two-story building on the oceanfront. Still other accounts have the first being burned and or torn down in 1925. This panorama supports the latter timeline. (Courtesy of Curt Teich Postcard Archives.)

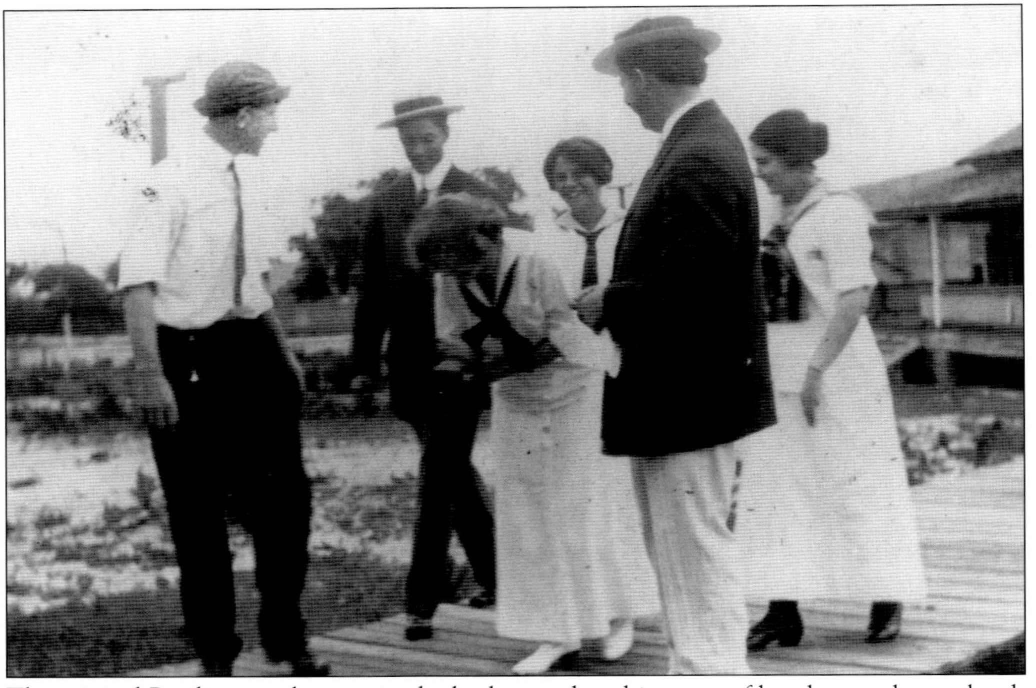

The original Pavilion can be seen in the background as this group of beachgoers share a laugh on the boardwalk, which connected the building to the Sea Side Inn. The Pavilion was closer to the beach than the inn, which was located 300 yards from the water in the area that would later become the Pavilion Amusement Park. Everyone dressed up to go to the Pavilion. No bare feet were allowed.

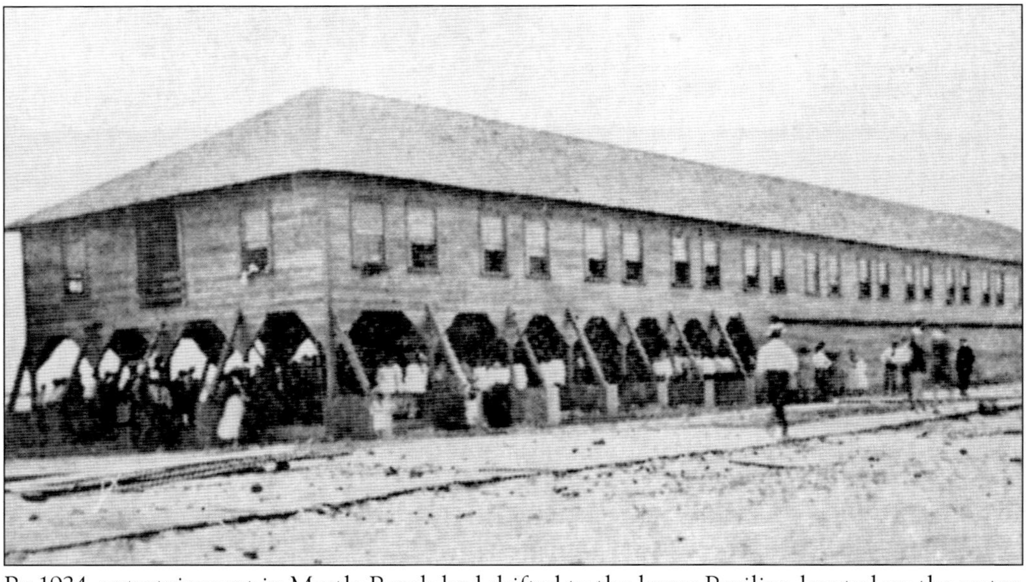

By 1924, entertainment in Myrtle Beach had shifted to the larger Pavilion located on the water. The lower floor had large archways to allow the sea breeze to circulate. A portion of that floor was used for dancing, and there was a concession area. By now, the daring dancers would try the Shimmy, a precursor to what would eventually become the Carolina Shag.

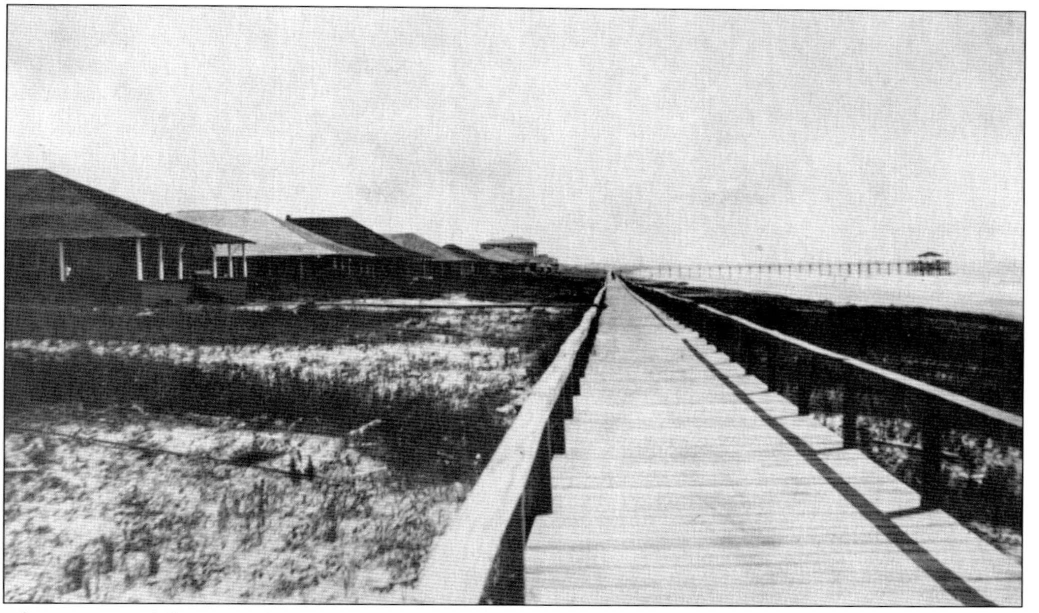

The terrain of dunes and windblown oaks along Myrtle Beach was difficult to navigate on foot. Elevated boardwalks were constructed to connect the Sea Side Inn, the Pavilion, and the growing number of cottages. Around 15 to 20 cottages were built on the oceanfront between 1900 and World War I.

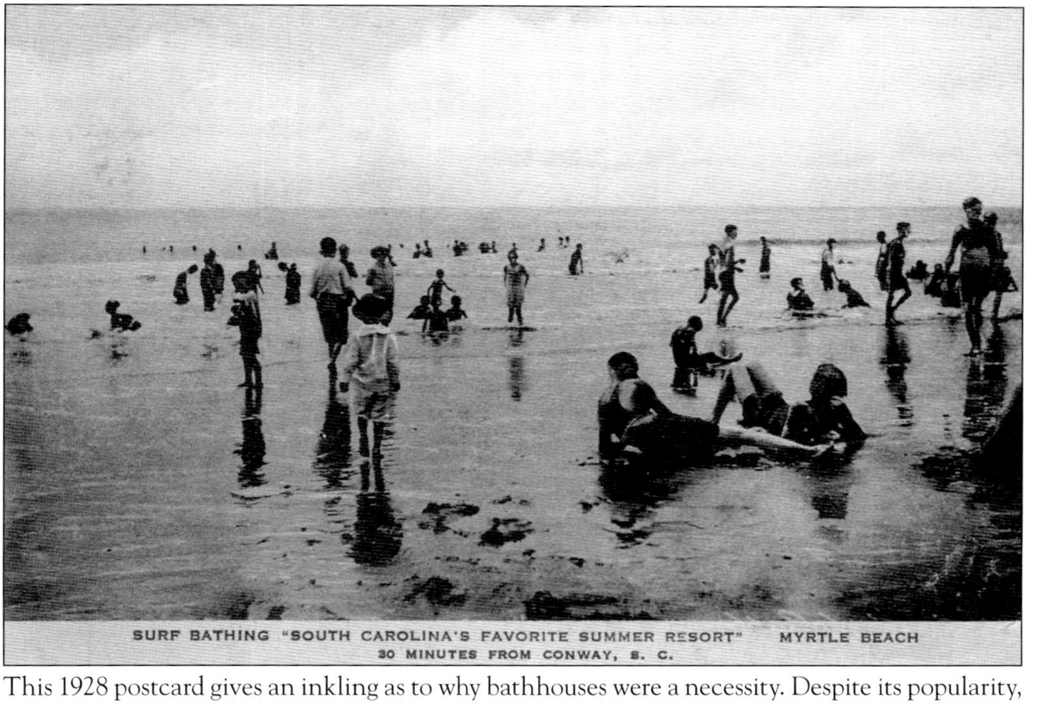

This 1928 postcard gives an inkling as to why bathhouses were a necessity. Despite its popularity, Myrtle Beach still only had two hotels. Beachgoers would make the trek from Conway for a day of "surf bathing" and would need to refresh themselves at the bathhouse before retiring to the Pavilion for an evening of music and entertainment.

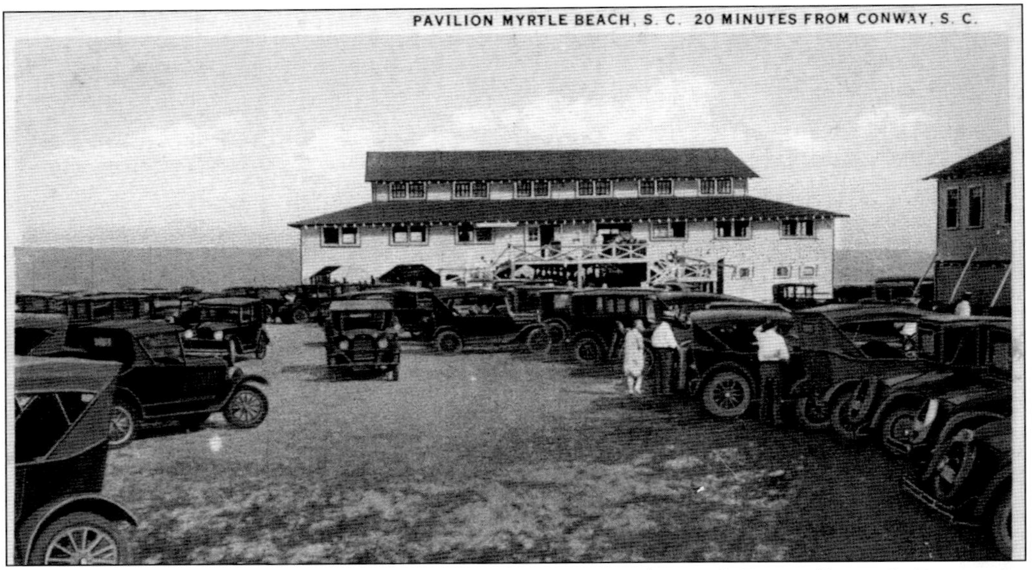

The second Pavilion did not weather well, and by 1925 Myrtle Beach Farms (formerly Burroughs and Collins) opted to tear it down and build a larger one that looked similar to the company's many tobacco warehouses. Despite its utilitarian external appearance, the third Pavilion was designed for optimum entertainment value; larger bands were being booked to play bigger crowds. Musicians could stay next door at the adjacent bathhouse and dormitory known as the Annex.

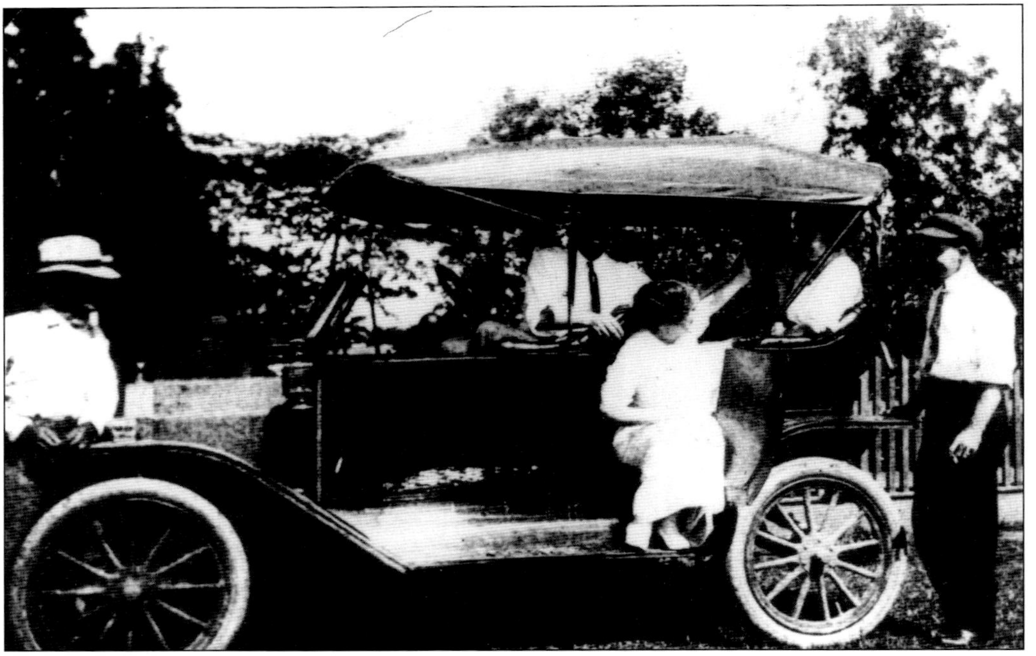

Getting to Myrtle Beach could be an adventure. Visitors traveled sandy roads through the pine forest and across rivers. The opening of a dedicated road between Myrtle Beach and Conway meant fewer people had to rely on the railroad to get to the beach. This photograph labeled "Beach Goers" by the Horry County Museum shows just how enthusiastic people were about their outings. Bus service between Conway and Myrtle Beach began in the 1920s.

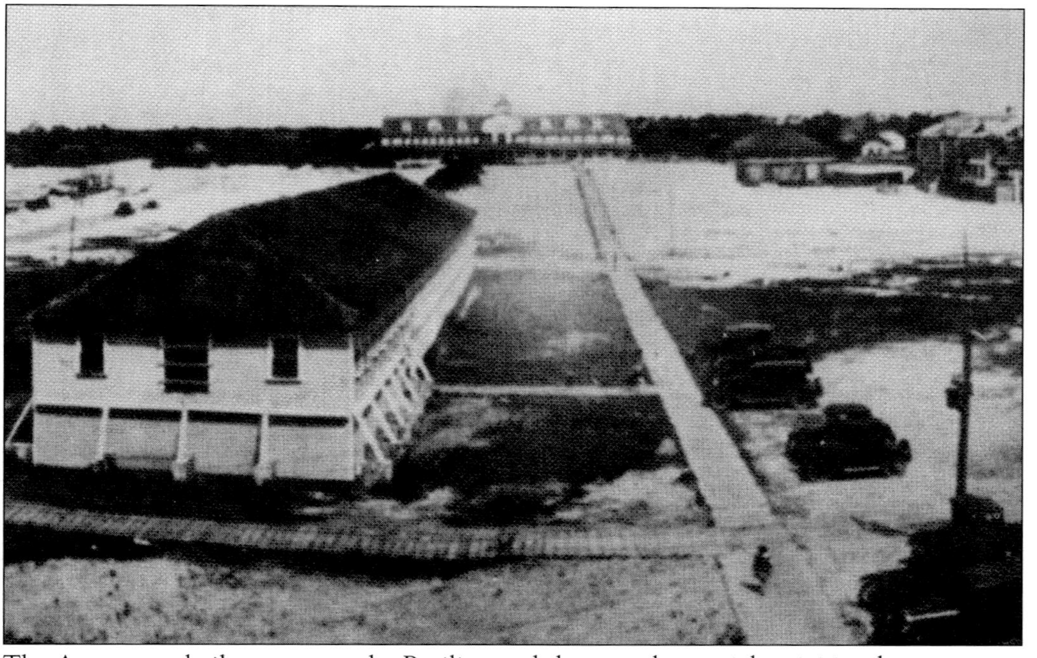

The Annex was built to support the Pavilion and the countless social activities that were now taking place there. The Annex's dorm not only housed the entertainers who would work at the Pavilion, but it provided rooms for the lifeguards. Lifeguards have been present in Myrtle Beach ever since the first recorded drowning in 1902— that of Ruth Burroughs, the 27-year-old daughter of Franklin Burroughs, the man who first envisioned Myrtle Beach as a resort.

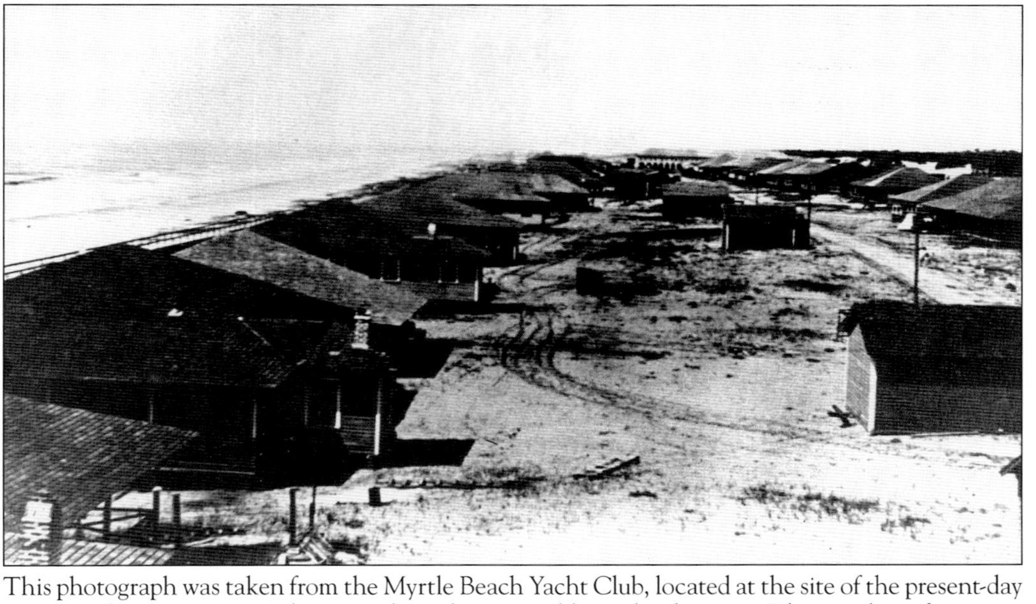

This photograph was taken from the Myrtle Beach Yacht Club, located at the site of the present-day Fourteenth Avenue Pier. The second Pavilion is visible in the distance. The number of cottages increased after 1909 when Burroughs and Collins began offering oceanfront lots for $25 each. Two-for-one purchases were available if the owner built within a year. Properties were measured by using a 30-foot-long cow chain.

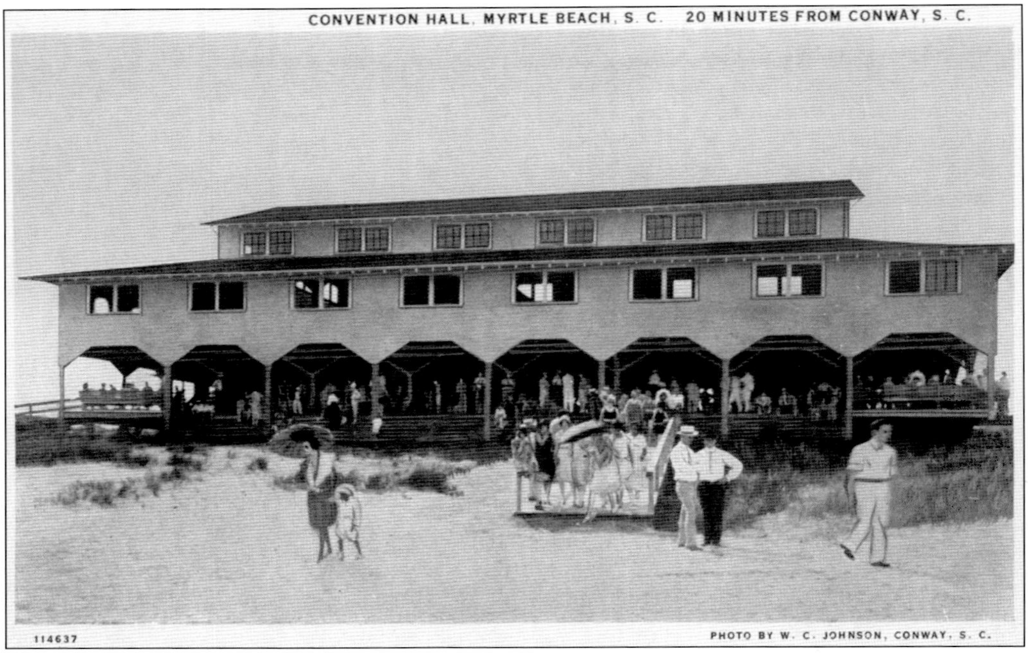

The Pavilion had truly become the center of activity in Myrtle Beach. In addition to still being the place to listen to music and dance, it also now doubled as a convention hall. Conferences held here helped increase tourism to the area. The Press Association, the Methodist Training Institute, and Group Six of the South Carolina Banking Association were among those who booked their conferences at what was now being billed as a convention hall and pavilion. This photograph, taken looking north from the beach, shows a Ferris wheel that had been added to the lot adjacent to the Pavilion. It was one of a handful of rides that had become permanent fixtures. During the off season, the Pavilion was used for community activities. The Parent-Teacher Association (PTA) held their annual Halloween Carnival here for more than 20 years. (Above, "Convention Hall and Pavilion" courtesy of Curt Teich Postcard Archives; below, CML.)

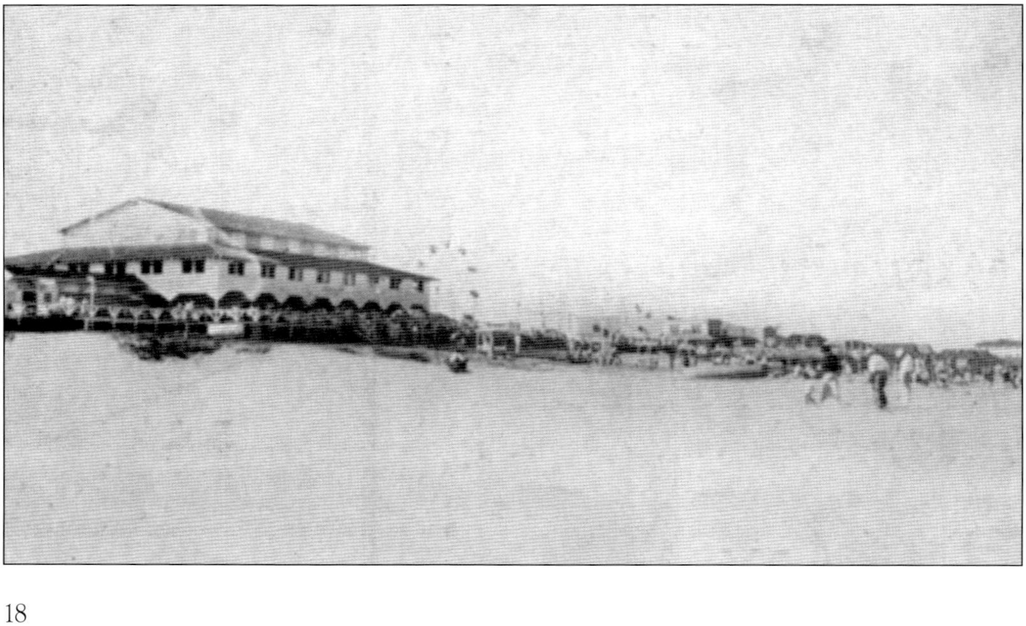

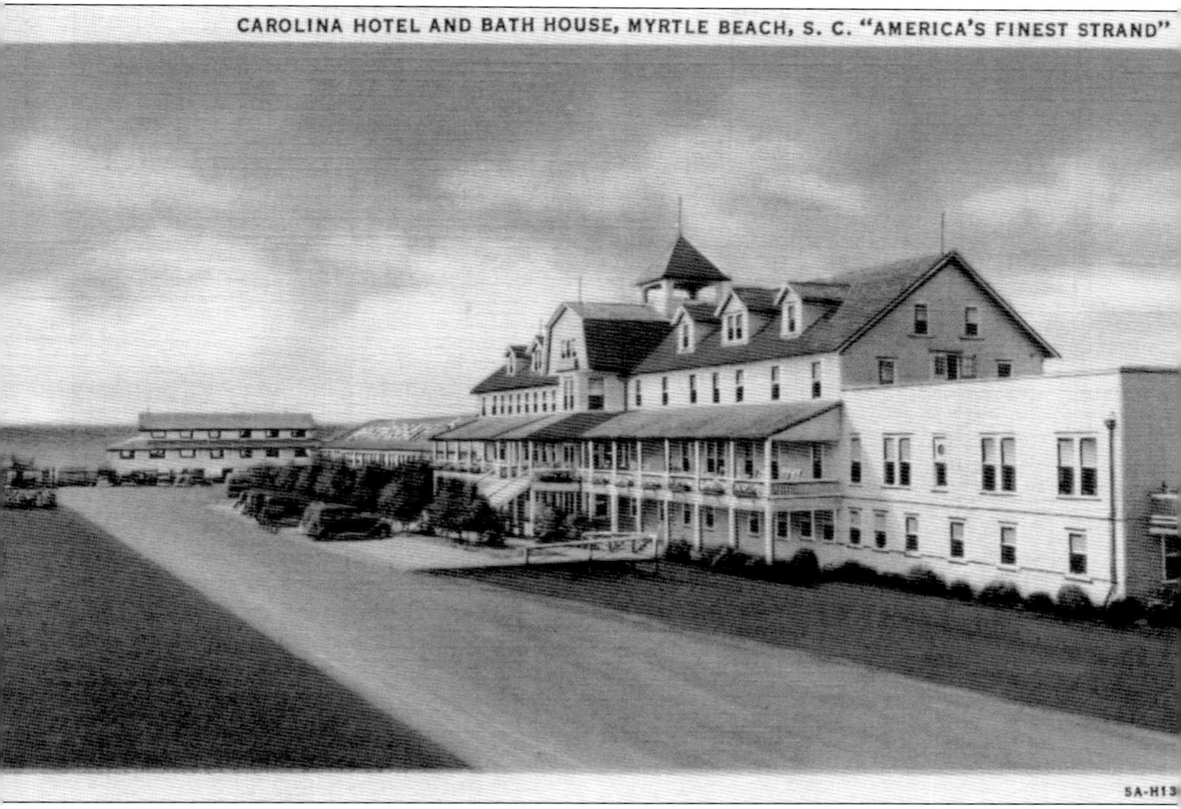

In 1930, the Sea Side Inn was jacked up and physically moved by rolling it on large logs so that it would be closer to the Pavilion and the ocean. After the move, it was connected to the Annex and renamed the Carolina Inn and Bath House. Remodeling of the Inn included the addition of bathrooms in every room of the Inn section. This postcard from 1931 shows just how much the entire Pavilion and inn complex had grown to accommodate the increasing number of tourists coming to Myrtle Beach. The Carolina Inn had been renamed the Strand, and by now it also included tennis courts for its guests. During the big band era, concerts were held every afternoon at 3:00 p.m. Speedy Spears managed the dance hall.

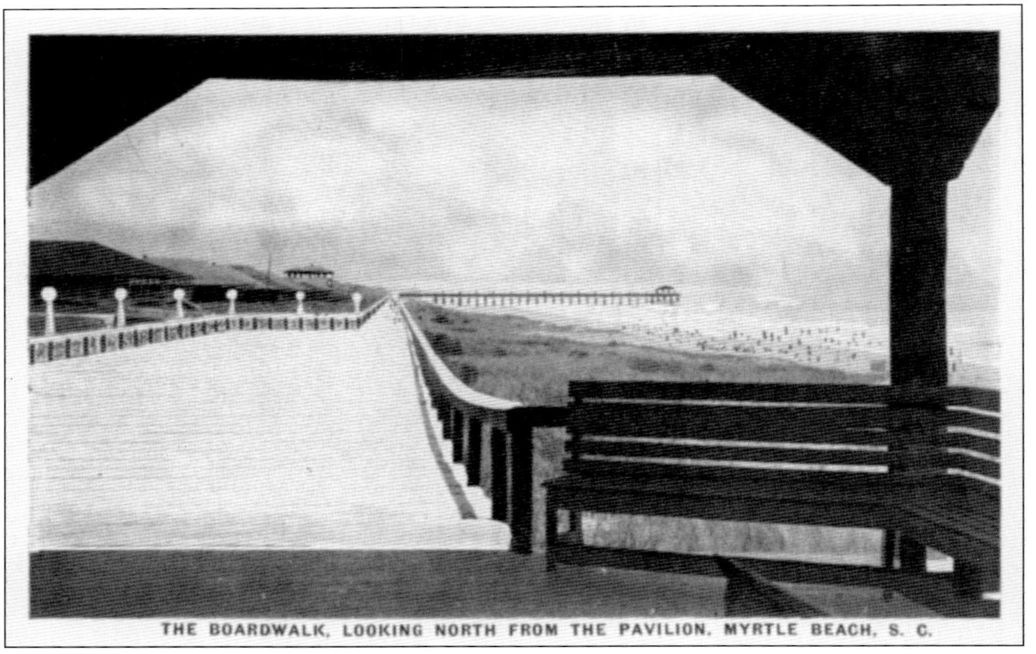

This postcard from 1930 was taken from just in front of the Myrtle Beach Pavilion looking north towards the Yacht Club and its pier. It illustrates the ever-expanding landscape of cottages that lined the boardwalk. By now, Myrtle Beach Farms had built a 4-mile-long boardwalk along the sand dunes overlooking the ocean.

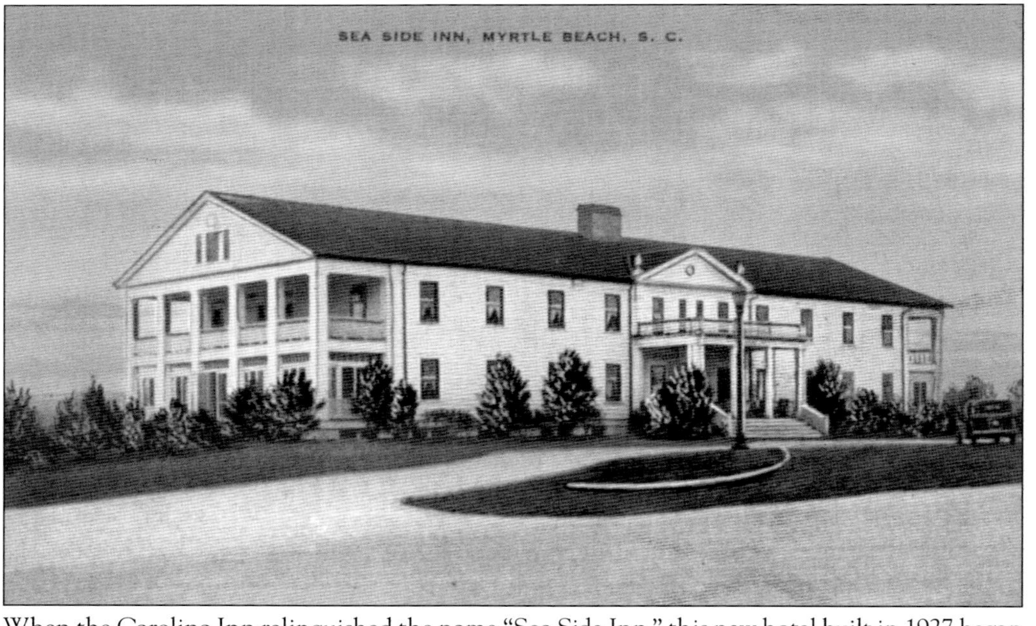

When the Carolina Inn relinquished the name "Sea Side Inn," this new hotel built in 1927 began calling itself the Seaside Inn. This postcard from 1928 shows the Seaside soon after it opened its doors to what advertisements referred to as a select clientele.

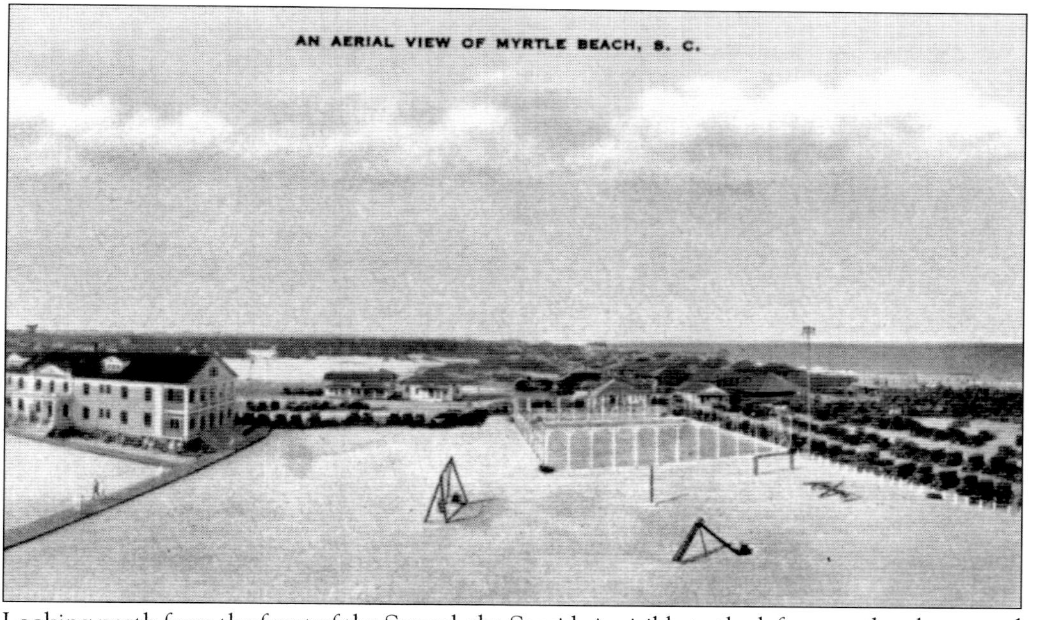

Looking north from the front of the Strand, the Seaside is visible to the left as are the playground and tennis courts for the guests. The crowded parking lot is for the Pavilion and its bathhouse and reflects how popular the destination has become. It is also apparent from the number of cottages in the distance how much Myrtle Beach was growing in the 1930s. (Courtesy Burroughs and Chapin Company, Inc.)

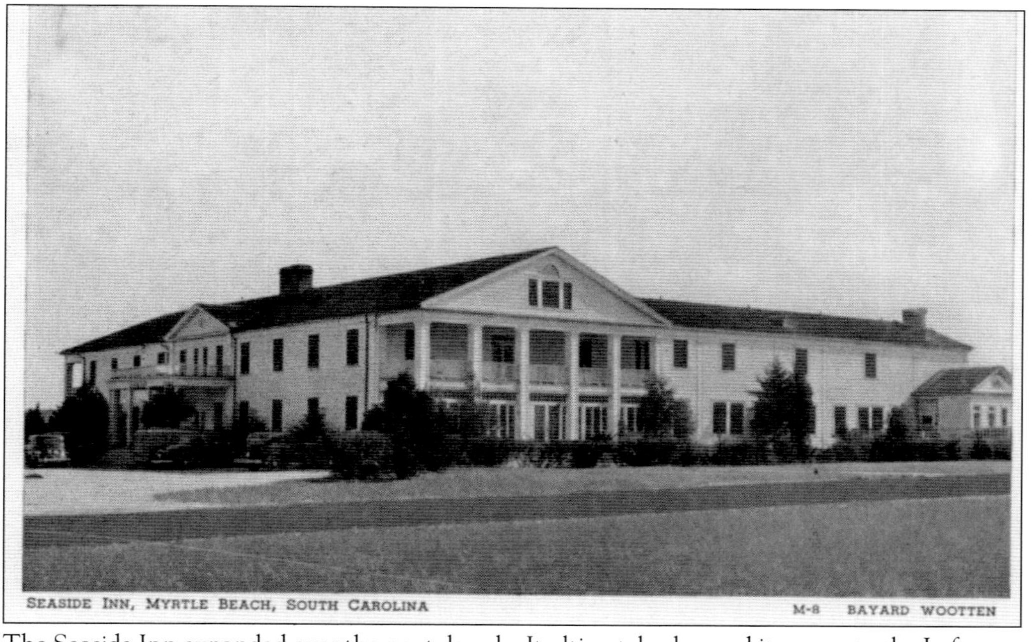

The Seaside Inn expanded over the next decade. It ultimately changed its name to the Lafayette Hotel in 1938. Less than 200 yards from the oceanfront, it was popular because of its convenience to the Pavilion and its amusements. The Lafayette stood at the center of what would become the Pavilion Amusement Park. It was razed around 1960.

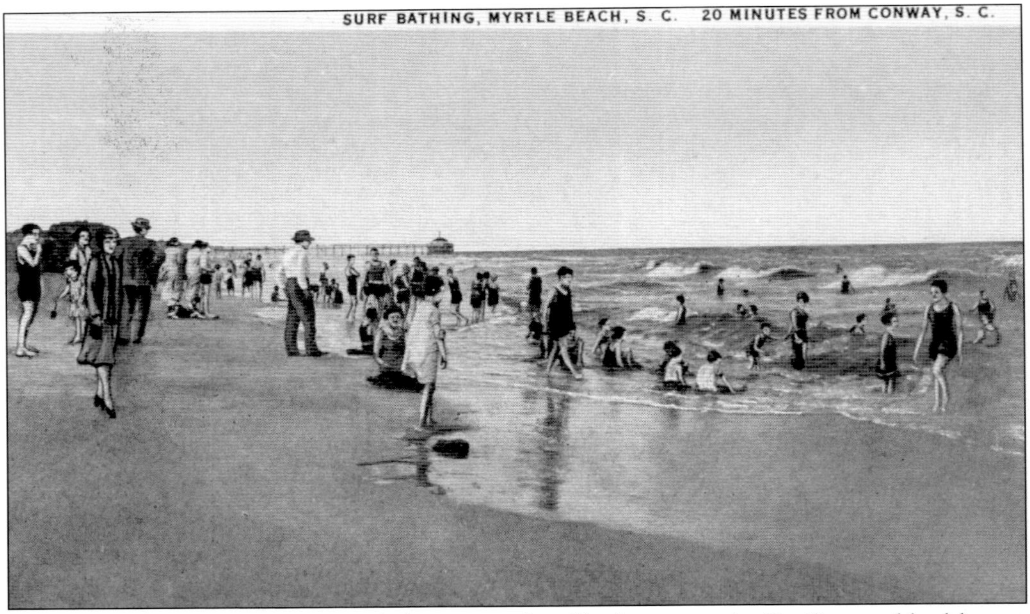

Warren C. Johnson again captured this scene of surf bathers near the Pavilion and bathhouse. Advertisements for the new development ran in both New York and Miami emphasizing the fact that Myrtle Beach stood halfway between the two cities. Brochures described Myrtle Beach as a "mainland seashore resort directly on the blue Atlantic." (Courtesy of Curt Teich Postcard Archives.)

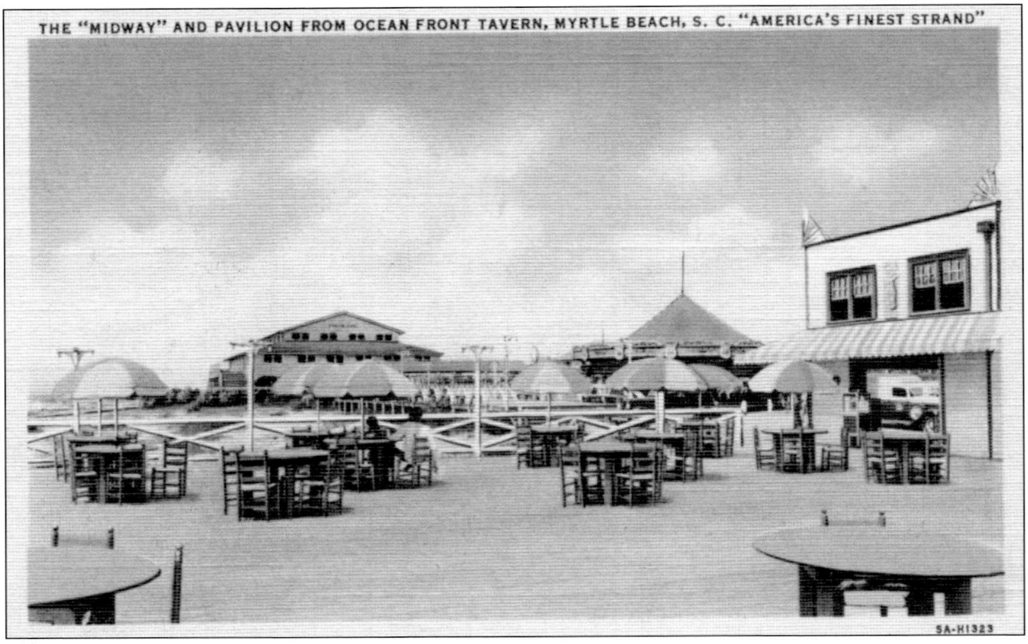

This postcard shows the Ocean Front Tavern, which was built just north of the Pavilion. By now, visitors were not only able to enjoy the amusements within the Pavilion, but an entire midway had been erected. In 1935, the publication *Myrtle Beach Today and Tomorrow* stated, "The greatest part of the activity of the beach centers around this particular location."

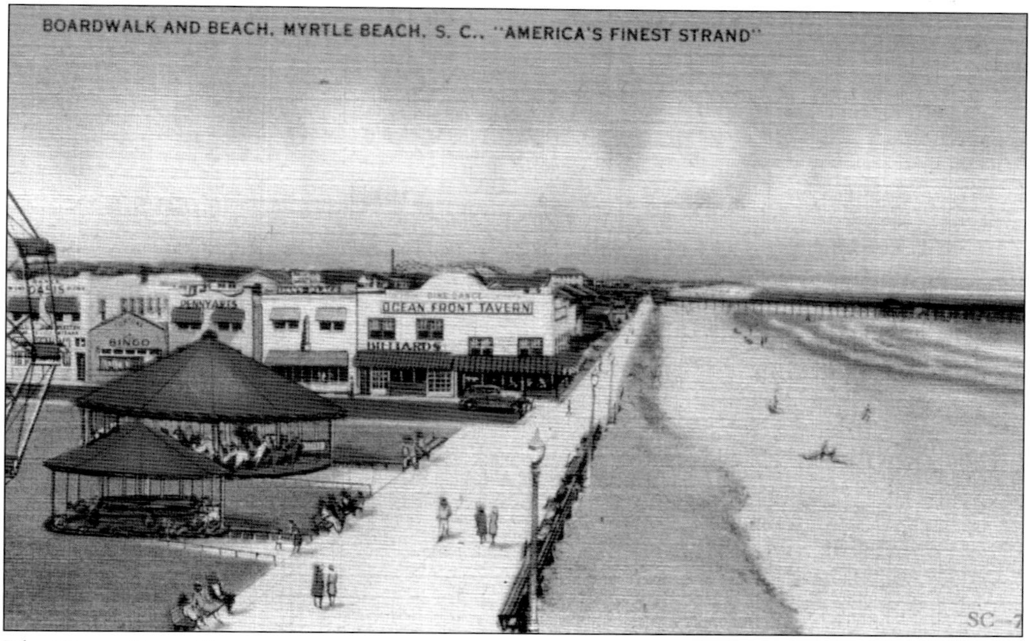

The Ocean Front Tavern eliminated its tables and outdoor seating to make way for parking for the increasingly popular attractions. Tourists could now enjoy Ferris wheels, a merry-go-round, hobbyhorses, and slides. Myrtle Beach was billing itself as "America's Finest Strand."

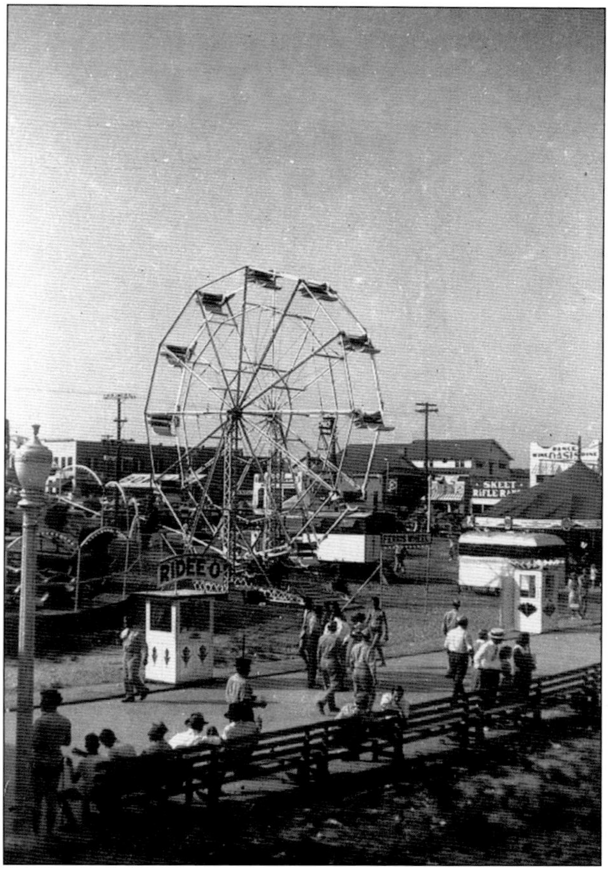

The year 1945 dawned with a midway, but no Pavilion. On December 28, 1944, the building went up in flames. It was not uncommon in winter for locals to hang out beneath the Pavilion's elevated structure and build fires to keep warm. Though never proven, it was speculated that it was this practice that ultimately caught the building on fire and burned it down. Nonetheless, the midway continued to attract visitors.

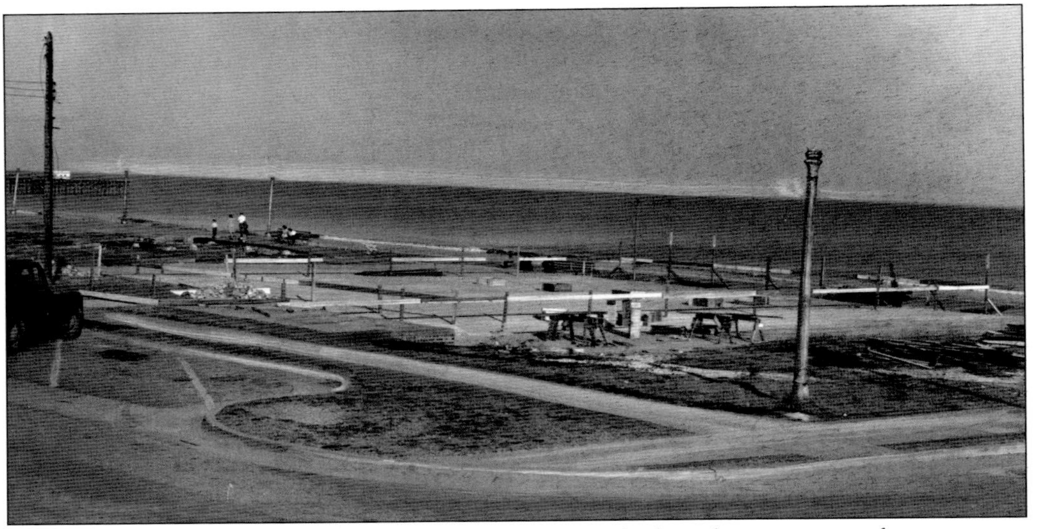

This rare photograph from 1946 shows the wooden forms laid out for a new oceanfront concrete bathhouse that was erected on the site where the previous Pavilion had been located at the end of Eighth Avenue North. A shortage of building materials during World War II had prohibited Myrtle Beach Farms from resurrecting the town's most popular attraction, but plans were under way to erect a new Pavilion.

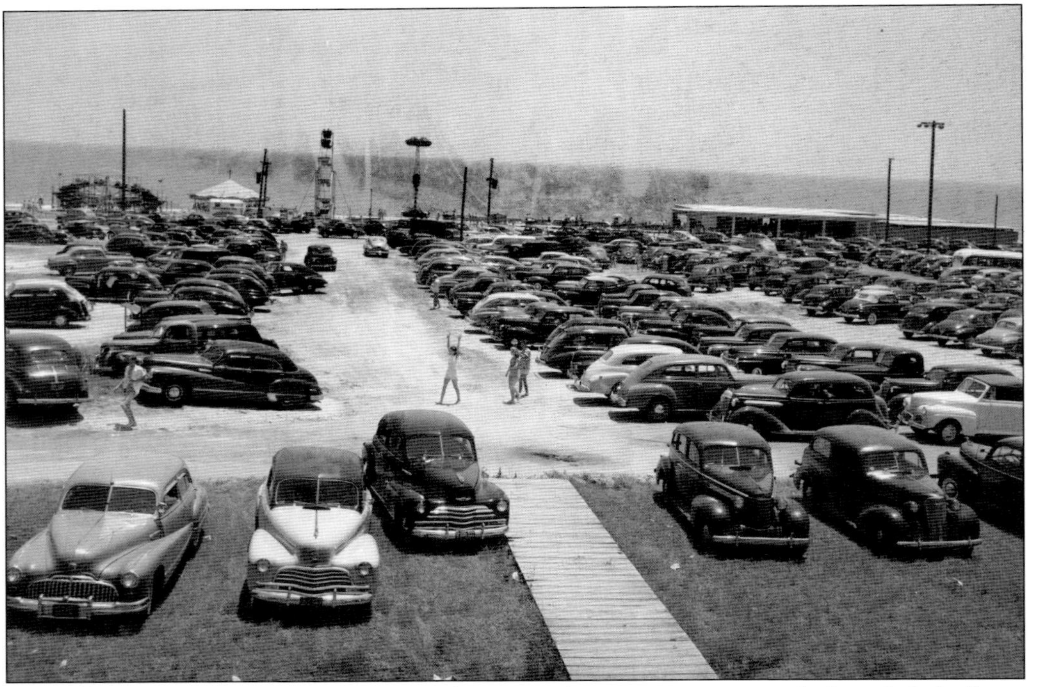

The new bathhouse was opened in 1947 adjacent to the amusement area, which included a Ferris wheel and merry-go-round. Plans for a new Pavilion called for it, too, to be constructed of concrete. It was also being designed to be much larger than the previous building to accommodate the growing number of visitors to the Strand. Myrtle Beach was officially a city now, having been incorporated in 1938.

Two

The Pavilion

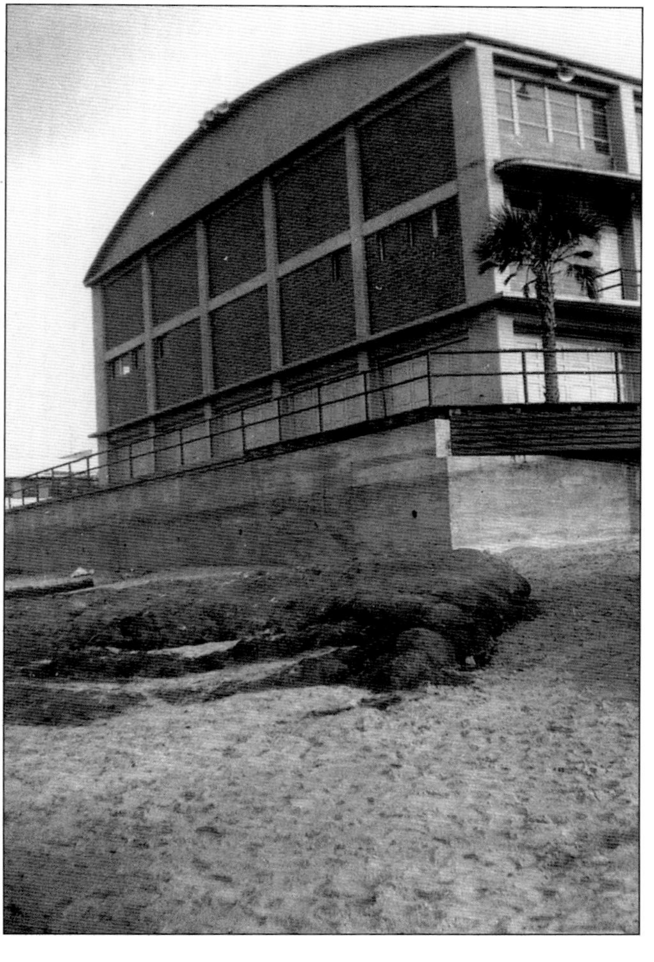

The Myrtle Beach Pavilion opened its doors in 1948. Designed by local architect James E. Cooney, it was built to last, and last it did, for almost 60 years. While predecessors had been constructed of wood and fell victim to fire, this Pavilion was made of concrete and could withstand winds up to 150 miles an hour. Its opening coincided with the opening of Highway 501 connecting Myrtle Beach and Conway. (Courtesy Horry County Museum.)

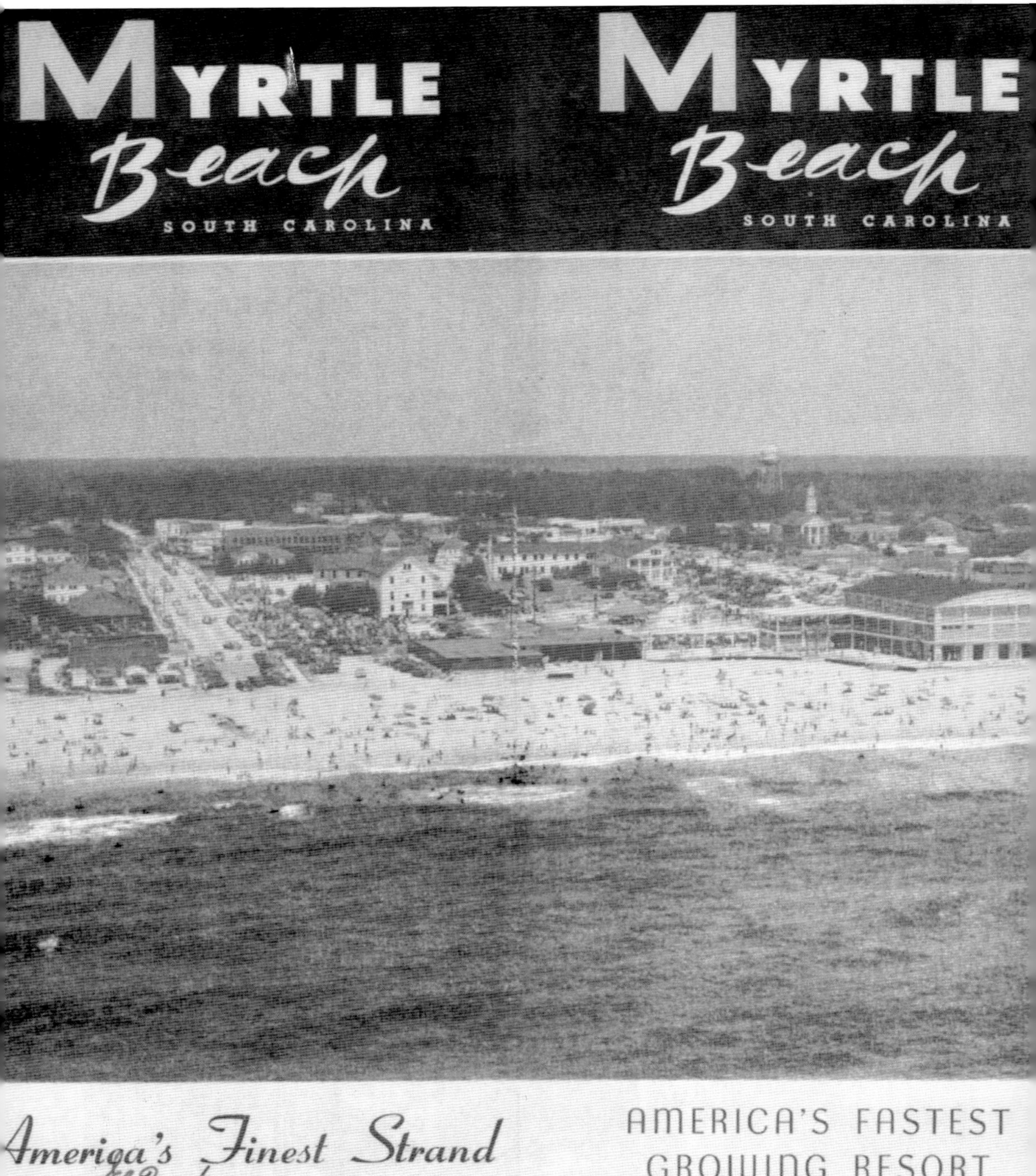

This brochure publicizing Myrtle Beach as America's fastest growing resort shows the new Pavilion in 1948 in its first year of operation. The old Seaside Inn is still across the street from the bathhouse area in this colorized photograph. The packed parking lot is testament that the Pavilion was already proving to be a hit. The inn was demolished in 1949, only a few months after the Pavilion opened. (Courtesy Sara Bryan.)

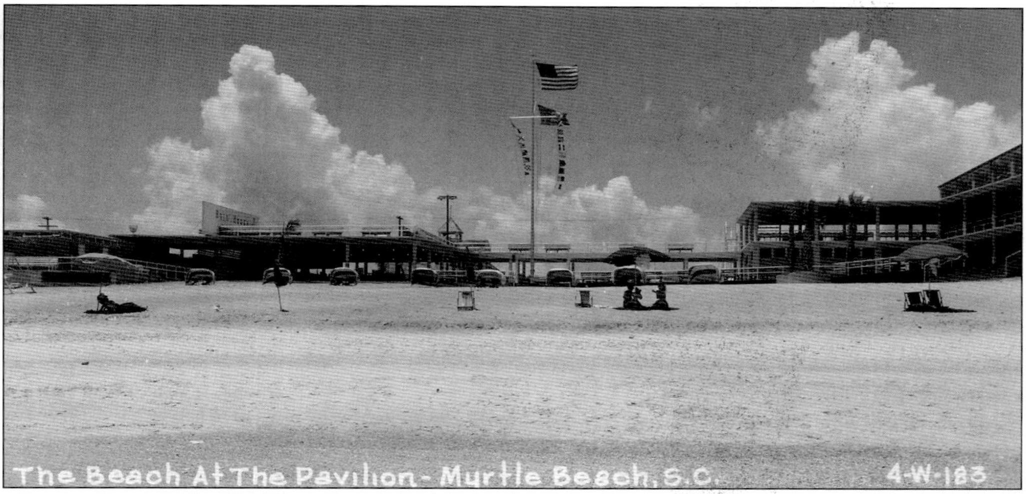

The Pavilion's official address was 812 North Ocean Boulevard. It had just opened for business when this beach scene was taken by Myrtle Beach Farms to be used in advertisements publicizing the new building. The large bathhouse sign visible in the upper left was painted red so that anyone walking down the beach could see it. The cabanas and umbrellas could be rented from lifeguards. (Courtesy Burroughs and Chapin Company, Inc..)

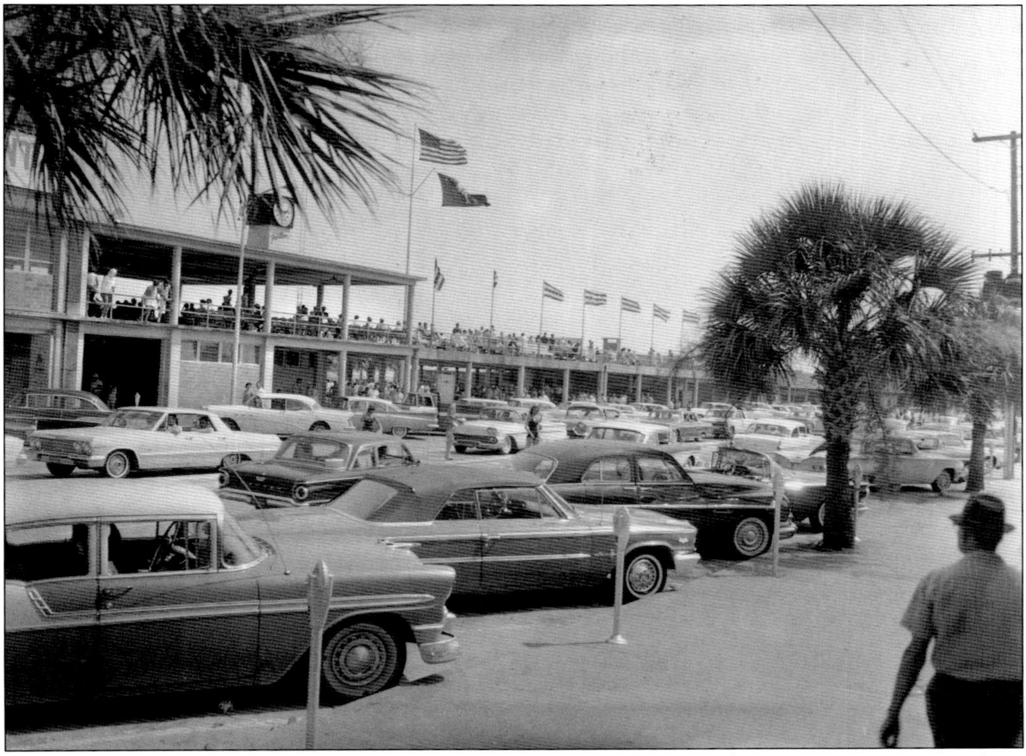

The best way to get to the Grand Strand in the 1950s was by car. There was no commercial air service into Myrtle Beach; the closest airport was in Wilmington, North Carolina. With interstates still years away, anyone driving to Myrtle Beach came along the coast via Highway 17 or west via the newly constructed Highway 501 from Conway. (Courtesy CML.)

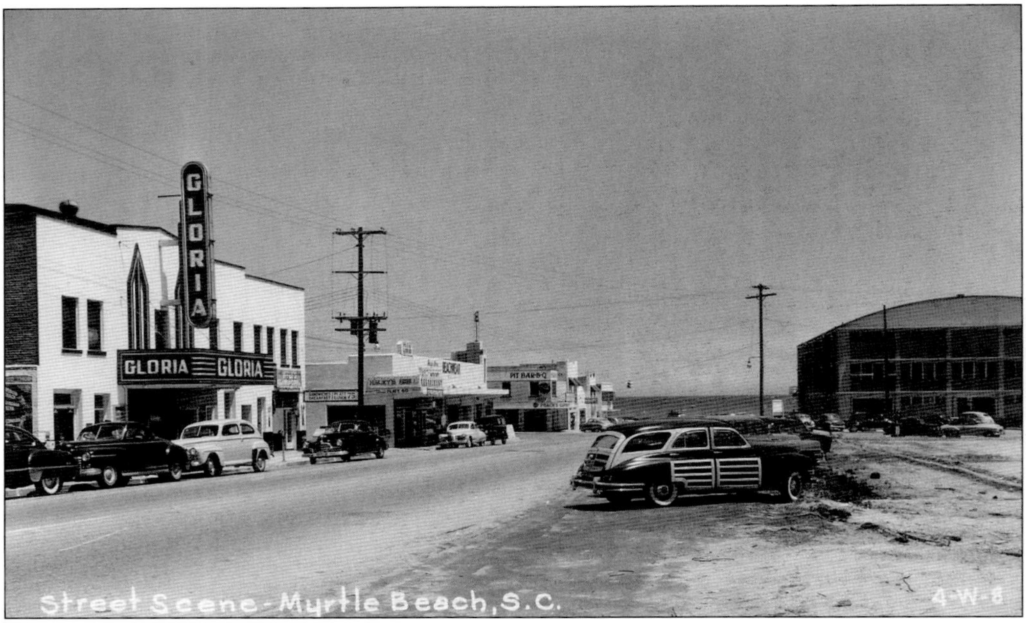

The Myrtle Beach Pavilion had only been open a year when this photograph was taken. Looking east towards the Pavilion along Ninth Avenue North, this image shows the Gloria Theater as well as the Peaches Corner snack bar in the distance. Peaches and the Gloria both began operation in 1937. (Courtesy Burroughs and Chapin Company, Inc..)

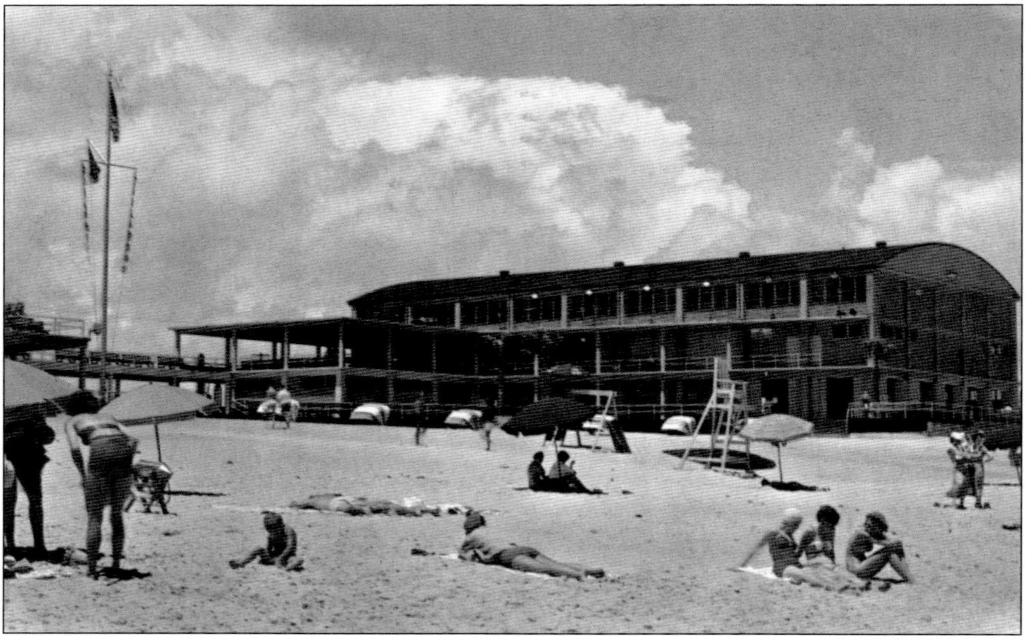

It did not take long for postcards celebrating the new building to start winging their way through the mail. A telltale signs that this particular postcard was from the Pavilion's first year is the fact that its iconic black and white clock has not yet been erected on its roof. The clock was added by 1951.

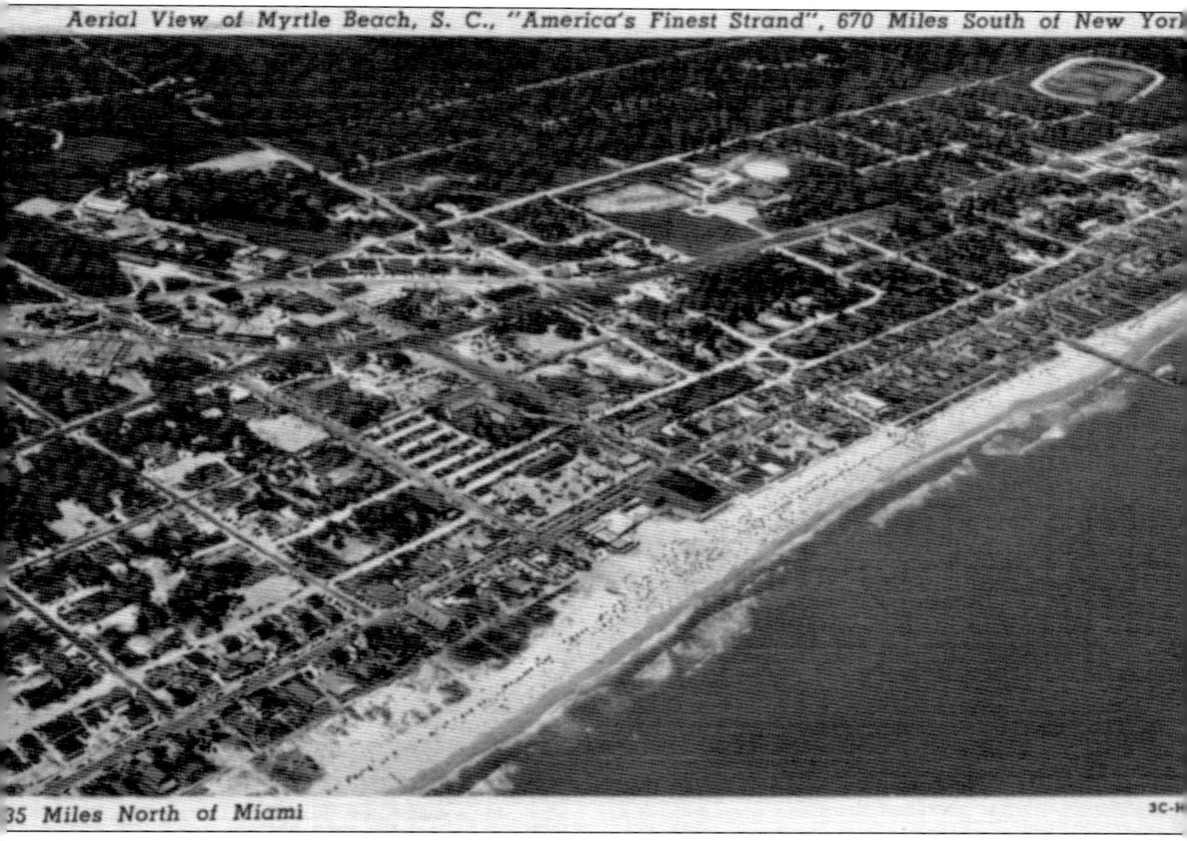

This 1950 aerial photograph postcard with the Pavilion at the center shows that both the Pavilion and Myrtle Beach were beginning to spread out in their development. The old Seaside Inn across the street was demolished in 1948, and more rides purchased from the Husted brothers had been moved in. Just north of the Pavilion is the Gay Dolphin Amusement Park, which operated until 1968. The oval shape in the top right of this picture was the Washington Park horse track. Located on the land that would one day be home to Myrtle Square Mall, the track operated from 1938 to 1947, closing two years before the new Pavilion opened. The track's entrance was about 300 feet from the corner of Oak Street and Twenty-first Avenue North.

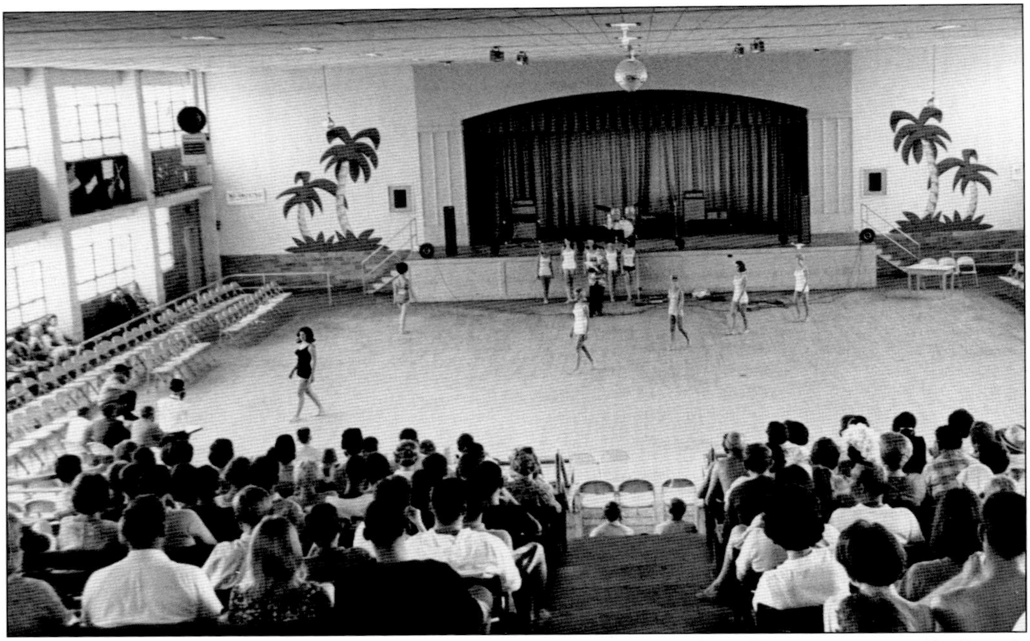

The Pavilion's association with pretty girls was not restricted to those hanging out on the beach or leaning over the rails on the Pavilion's deck. In 1950, the local Jaycees began a long running tradition of beauty pageants associated with the Pavilion by holding the Miss South Carolina Universe beauty pageant upstairs. The pageant was successful and continued to be held there until 1958. So intrigued were the locals by this new activity that many would attend the rehearsals. The dozens of windowpanes seen on either side of the building's upper floor were later darkened in an effort to keep the venue cooler during the summer. (Courtesy MBCC.)

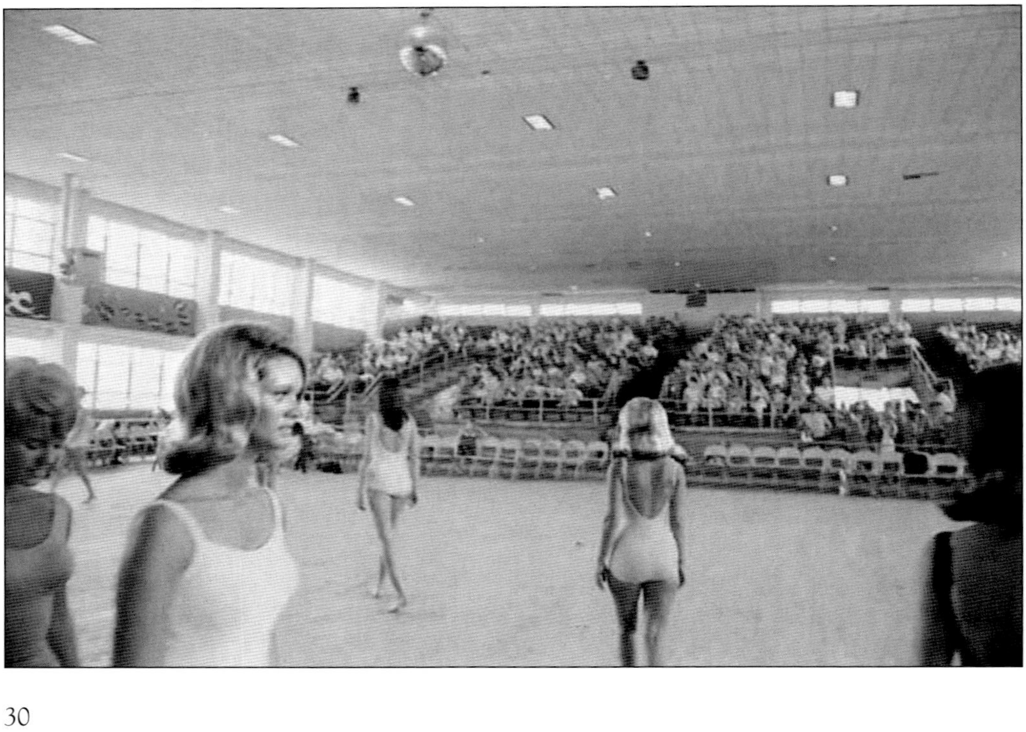

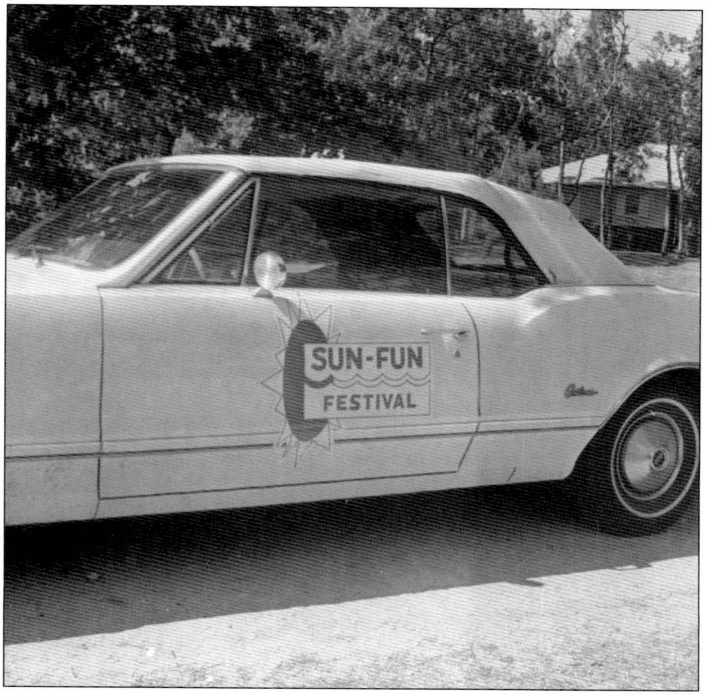

The Sun Fun Festival was held for the first time in 1951. Conceived by local businesses as a way to attract visitors at the end of the school year, it quickly became a symbol of the kick-off of the summer season. At the time, Myrtle Beach itself had a population of fewer than 5,000, so the entire community got involved. (Courtesy MBCC.)

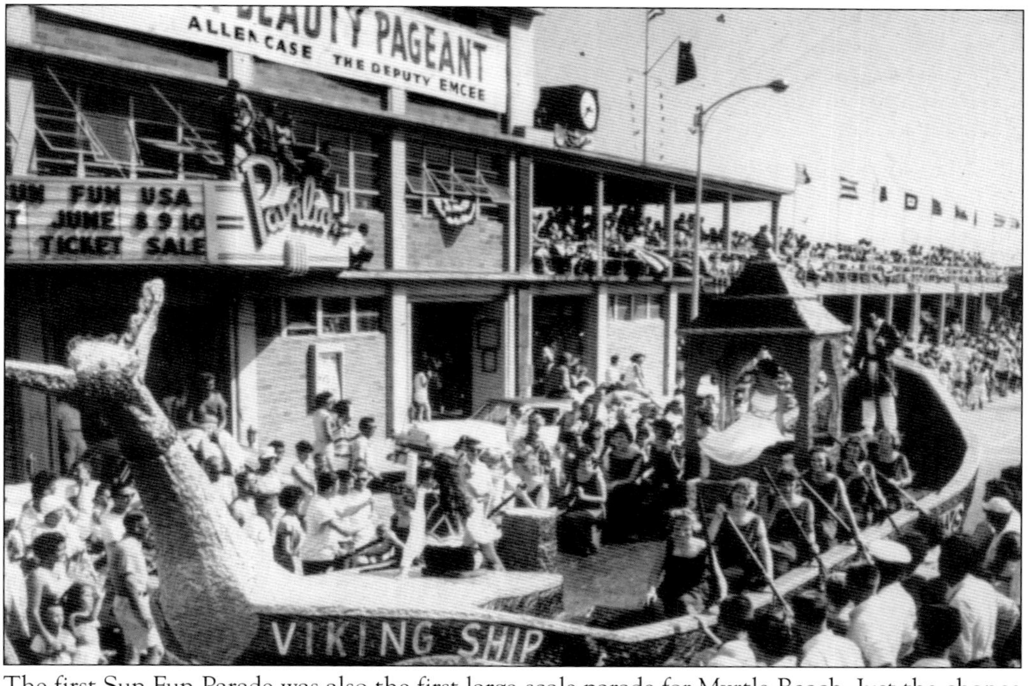

The first Sun Fun Parade was also the first large-scale parade for Myrtle Beach. Just the chance to see the elaborate floats, marching bands, and celebrities drew not just tourists, but spectators from surrounding counties as well. The Sun Fun Parade became so popular that for several years during the 1970s and 1980s, the parade was repeated in the afternoon in North Myrtle Beach. (Courtesy MBCC.)

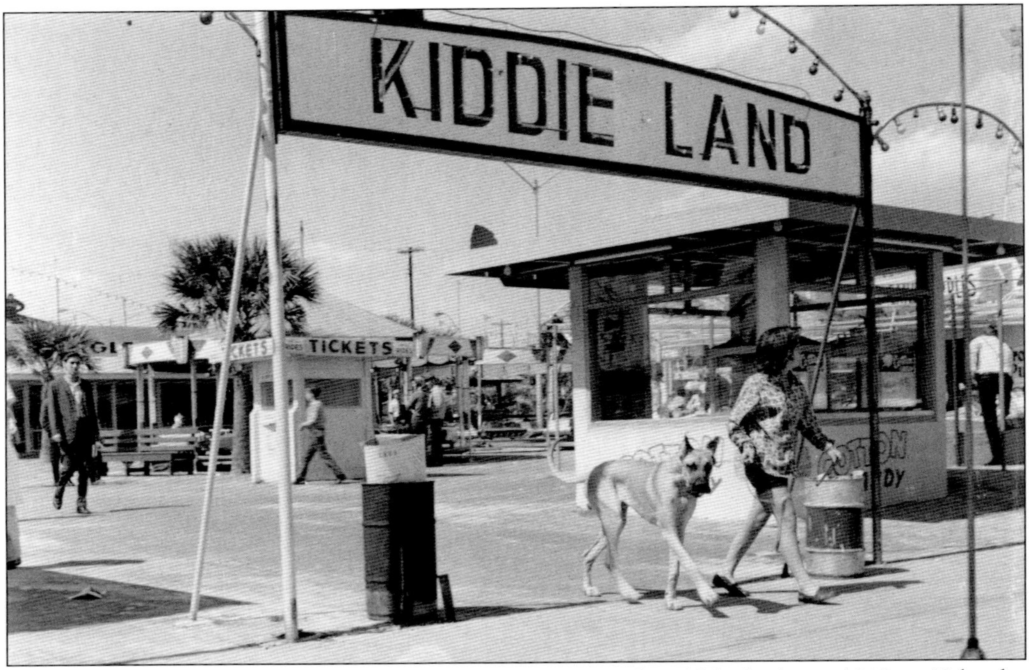

Called Kiddie Land by many, the amusements grew from a handful of rides in 1948 to 49 by the time the Pavilion closed in 2006. Details of the park and its rides are covered in the next chapter. In the 1980s, the Myrtle Beach Pavilion and its amusements were considered the number one tourist attraction in South Carolina and one of the finest parks in the entire United States. (Courtesy CML.)

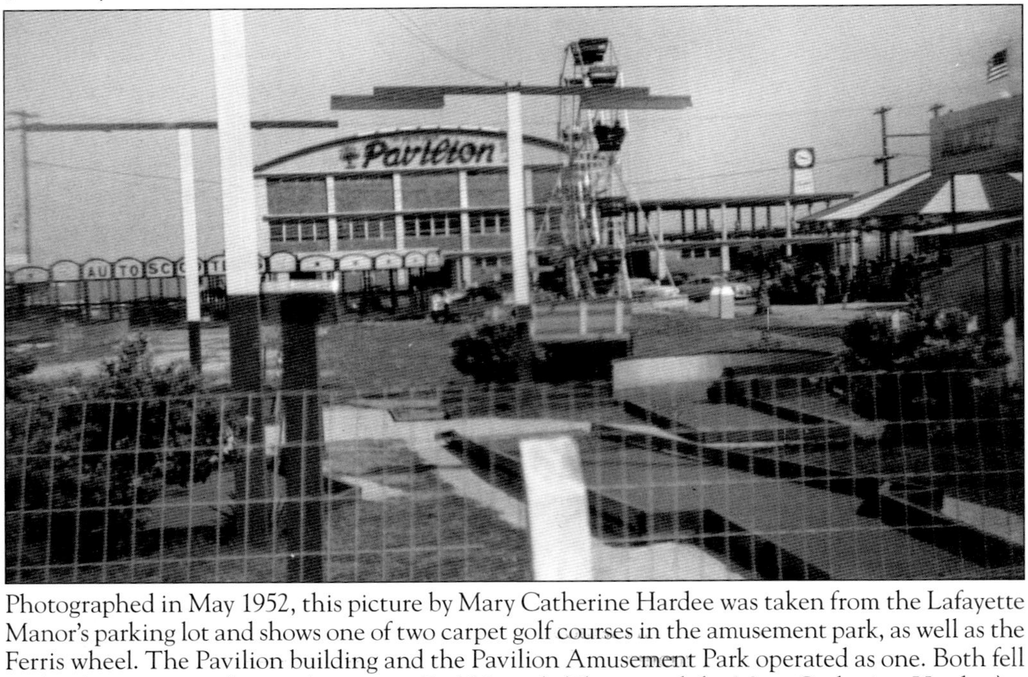

Photographed in May 1952, this picture by Mary Catherine Hardee was taken from the Lafayette Manor's parking lot and shows one of two carpet golf courses in the amusement park, as well as the Ferris wheel. The Pavilion building and the Pavilion Amusement Park operated as one. Both fell under the auspices of general manager Earl Husted. (Photograph by Mary Catherine Hardee.)

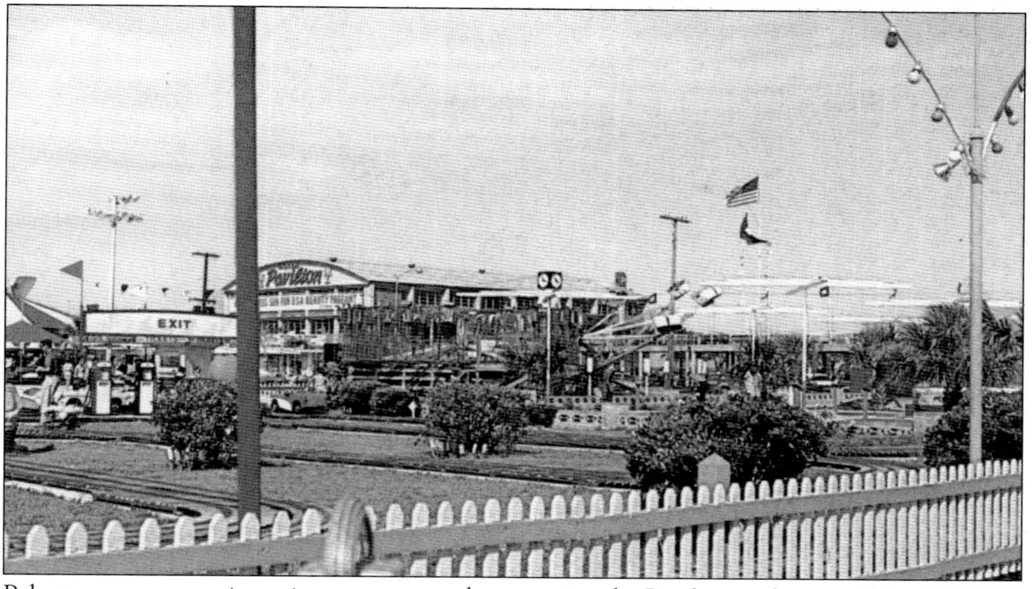

Palm trees were prominent in many postcards promoting the Pavilion and not just because South Carolina is known as the Palmetto State. They accentuated Myrtle Beach's longstanding claim that it was "the Riviera of the South." The motto was one that would continue to be used from the 1930s through the early 1970s. (Courtesy Burroughs and Chapin Company, Inc..)

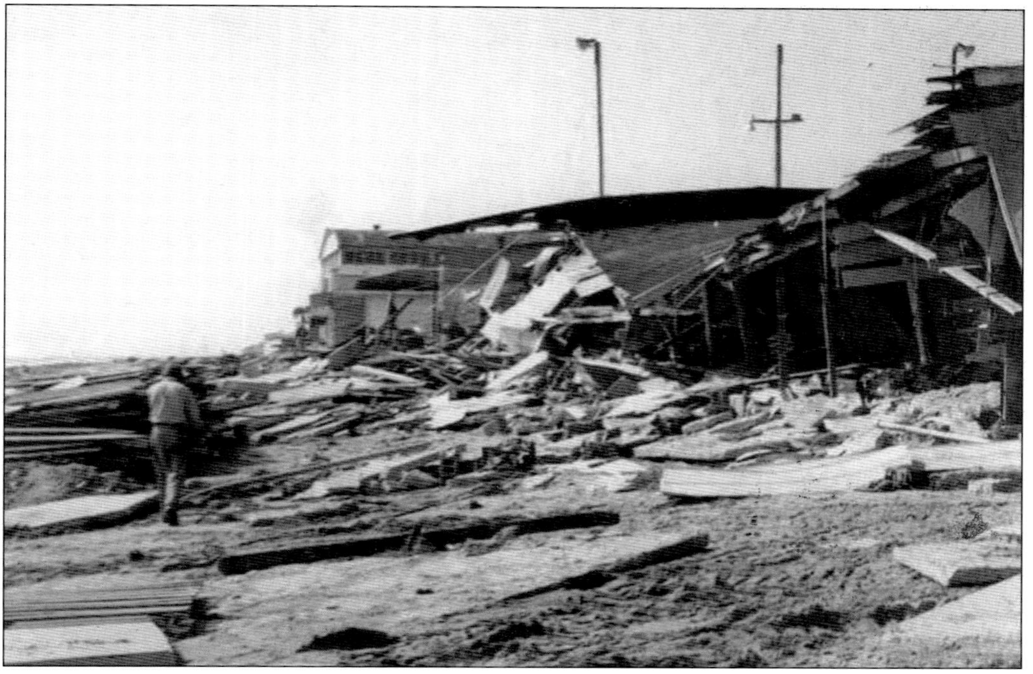

The Pavilion was built to withstand winds of up to 150 miles per hour, and on October 15, 1954, its strength was tested by Hurricane Hazel. The Category 4 storm blasted the Grand Strand with winds of up to 128 miles an hour. An estimated 80 percent of the oceanfront buildings in Myrtle Beach were damaged or destroyed. The Pavilion stood strong. The rebuilding after Hurricane Hazel transformed Myrtle Beach. (Photograph by Justin Plyler.)

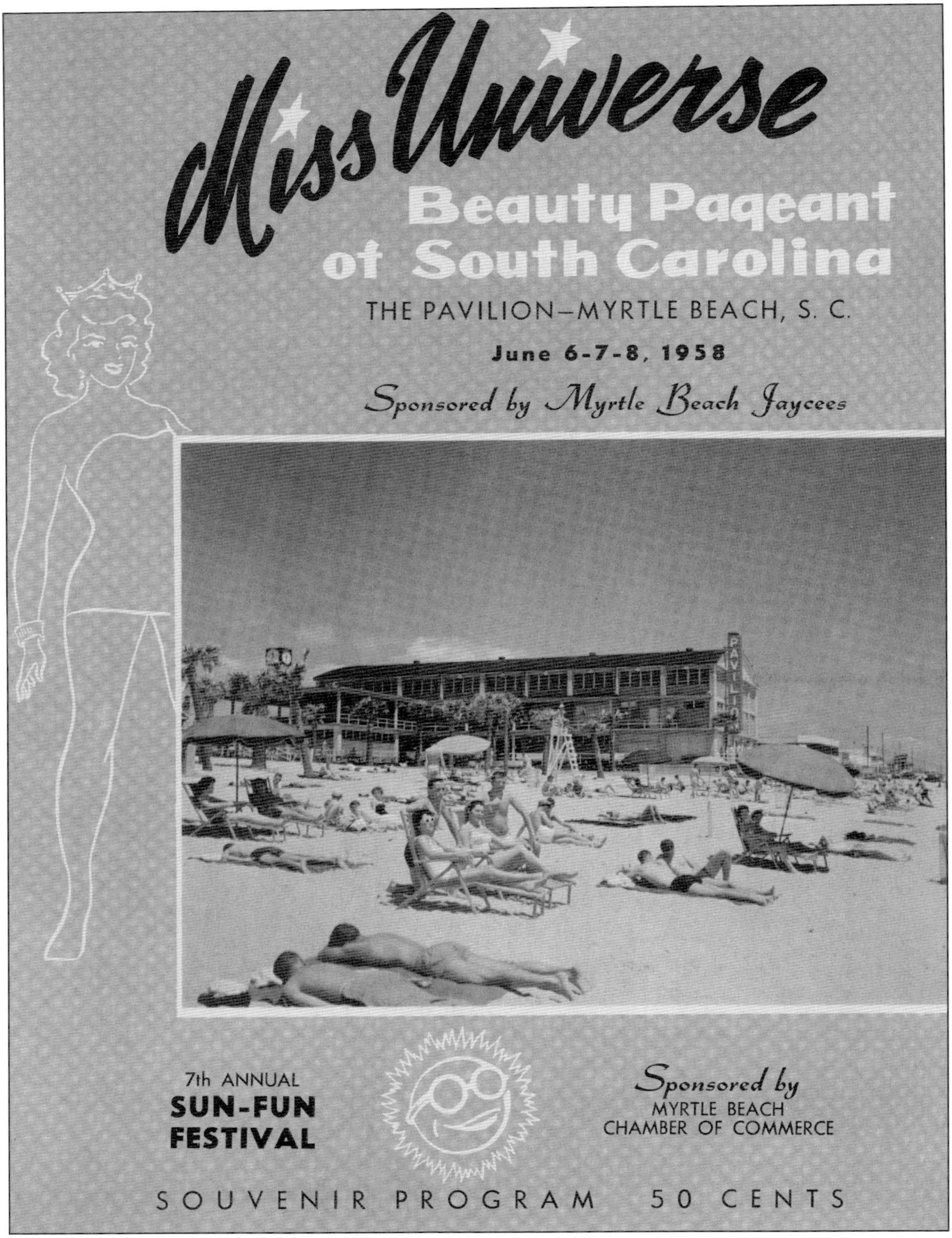

The programs on these two pages reflect just how important the Sun Fun Festival and its associated pageant had become to Myrtle Beach. The title is a bit misleading, however, because the pageant was a preliminary to the Miss Universe Pageant and not the Miss Universe Pageant itself. Still it carried quite a caché on its own and drew celebrity judges. Author Mickey Spillane came to Myrtle Beach in 1954 to judge the pageant and ended up making his home in nearby Murrells Inlet. (Courtesy CML.)

The Beautiful City of

MYRTLE BEACH

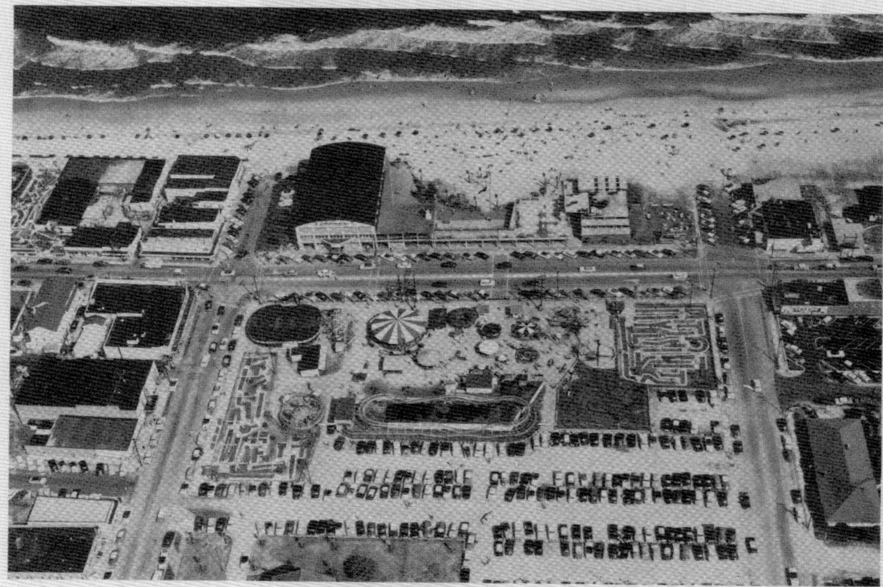

Welcomes you to the

Miss Universe Beauty Pageant
of South Carolina

— and —

The 7th ANNUAL

SUN-FUN FESTIVAL

3

The photograph on the cover of the program shows how the Pavilion and its amusement park continued to grow. Top community leaders were involved in the pageant's planning. In 1958, pageant program cochairs were Bill Herndon and Joe Thompson. Its committee consisted of Bobby Taylor, Lawrence LaBruce, Bob Thompson, Ted Murphy, Henderson Guerry, Johnny Singleton, John Campbell, Charlie Graham, J. D. Flowers, N. C. Huggins, Hazel Hatchell, Bob Prunty, Tommy Nance, and Clifton Hucks. The first Miss Sun Fun Festival took place the following year, in 1959. (Courtesy CML.)

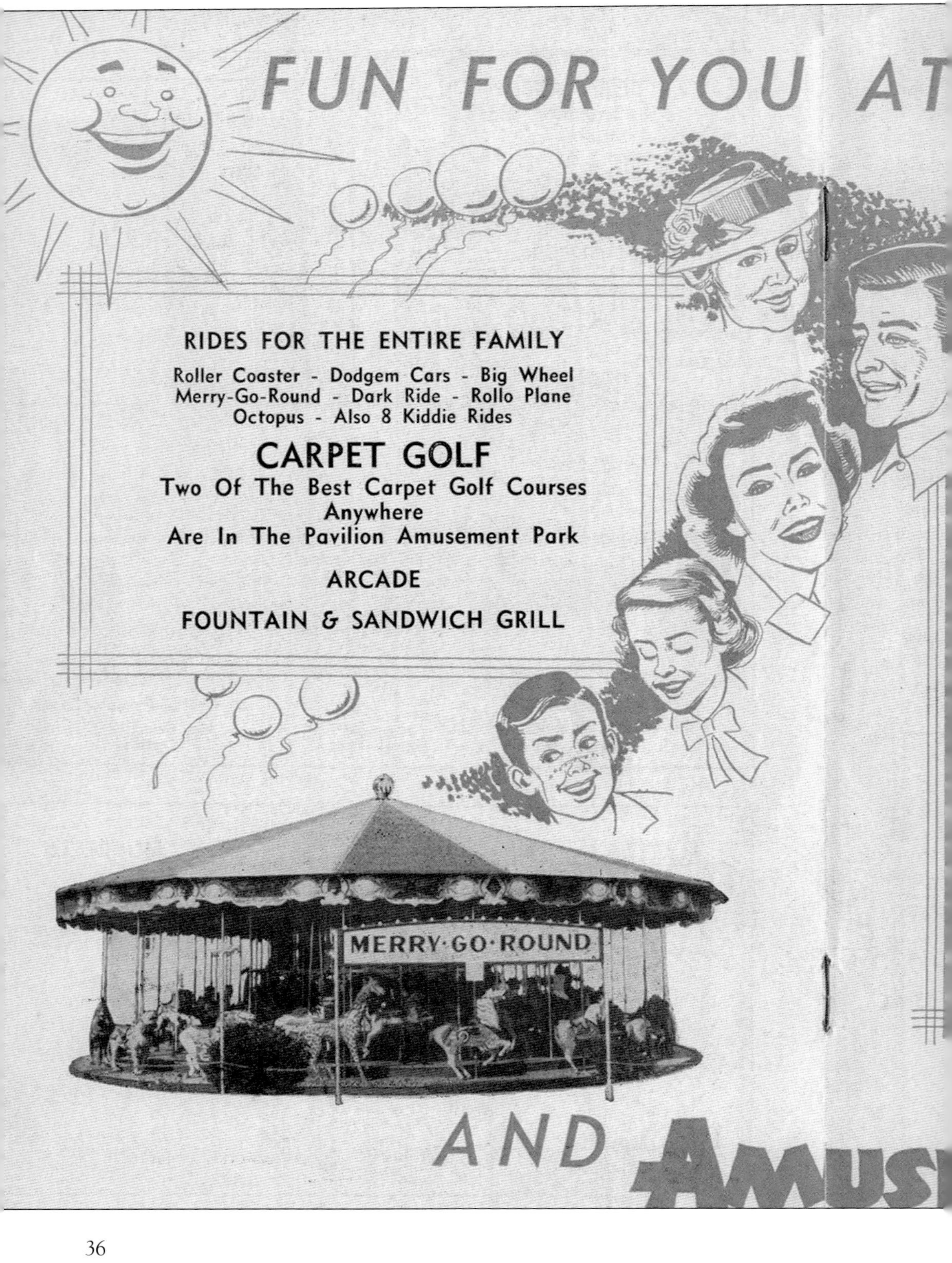
FUN FOR YOU AT
RIDES FOR THE ENTIRE FAMILY
Roller Coaster - Dodgem Cars - Big Wheel
Merry-Go-Round - Dark Ride - Rollo Plane
Octopus - Also 8 Kiddie Rides
CARPET GOLF
Two Of The Best Carpet Golf Courses
Anywhere
Are In The Pavilion Amusement Park
ARCADE
FOUNTAIN & SANDWICH GRILL
MERRY·GO·ROUND
AND AMUS

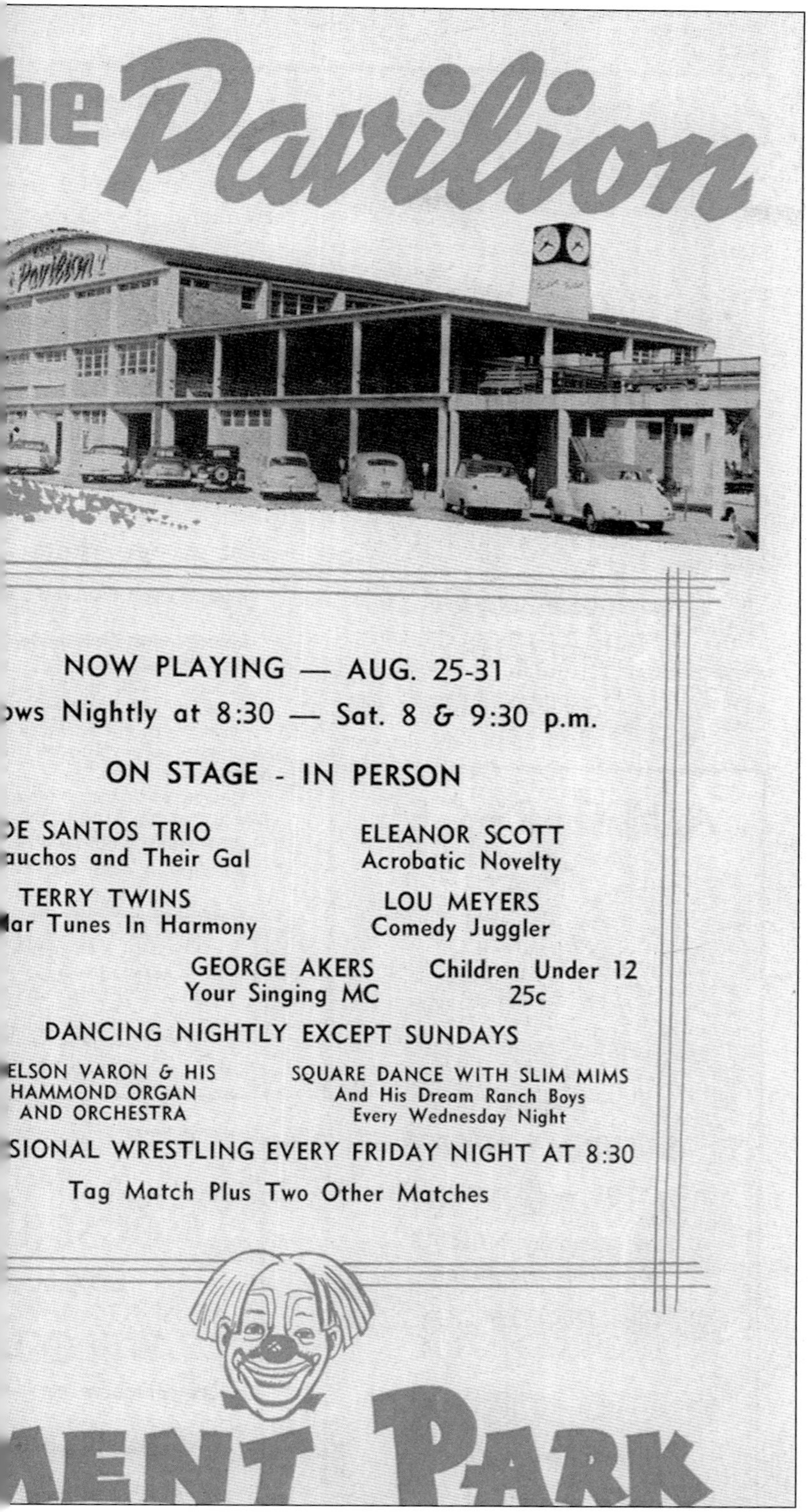

This 1955 advertisement for the Pavilion was published in the *Sun Fun Magazine*, a free publication produced especially to entice tourists. In addition to touting the rides, the advertisement also promoted the Pavilion's weekly lineup of activities. Headlining during August 15–31 was the De Santos Trio, billed as "Two Gauchos and Their Gal." Still, many of the acts who played were far better known. Roy Acuff was among the first big-name headliners. Each night had a theme. South Carolina native and Nashville star Slim Mims and his Dream Ranch Boys led square dancing each Wednesday. Professional wrestlers grappled every Friday. General manager Earl Husted had an ongoing array of performers and entertainers to keep the people coming back. High-wire acts could be viewed from the beach, and regular fireworks displays lit up the night. (Courtesy CML.)

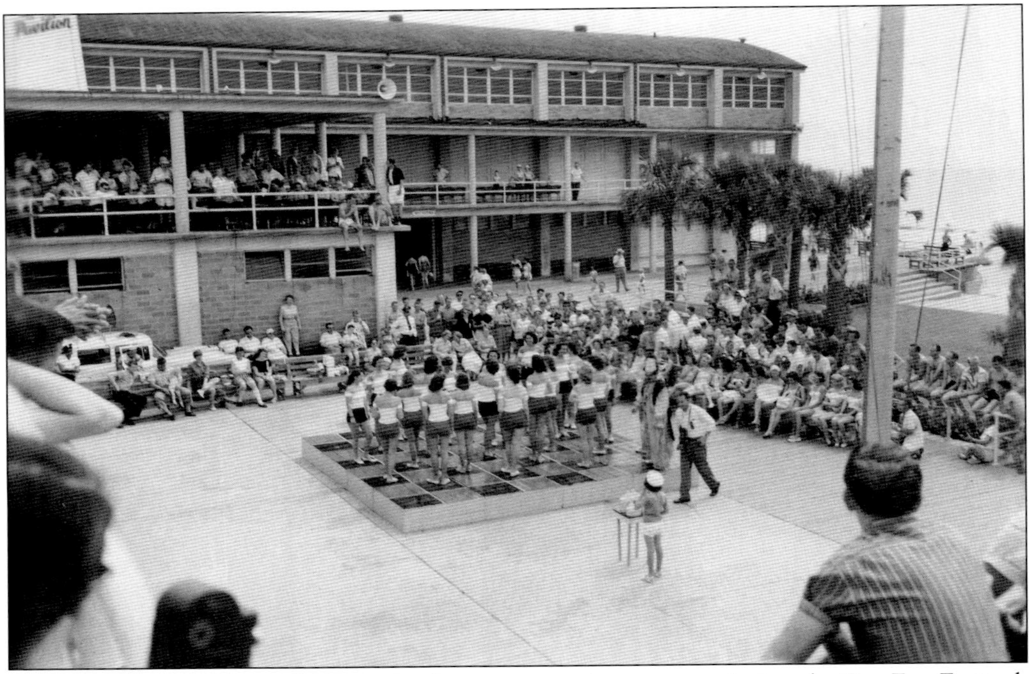

For over 50 years, games of human checkers were a mainstay event during the Sun Fun Festival. The first photograph is from 1951. Participants in the early games were generally local girls. In later years, players expanded to include beauty contestants or visiting festival queens on one side and local businessmen or some other group on the other. In the second photograph from the 1970s, members of the U.S. Air Force are among those joining in the fun. (Courtesy MBCC.)

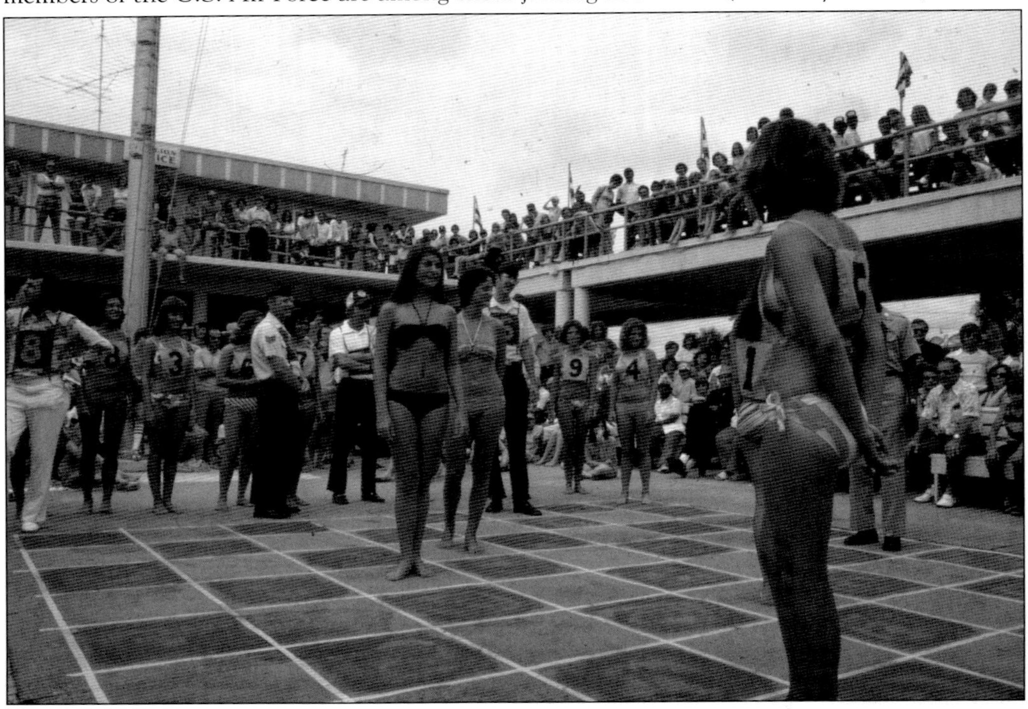

As fun-seekers entered the Pavilion from the boulevard, they came upon a two-minute photo booth area that was manned for many years by Jack Thompson. Thompson became a professional photographer and the Pavilion's de facto photographic historian. Tourists and locals alike would come to have their pictures taken using a variety of props and backgrounds. Area native Lynn Livesay (right) posed in the Miss Myrtle Beach half moon, which was a popular choice, second only to Mary Lou West's choice of the Myrtle Beach Jail (below, left). Ray and Larry Hobbs of Greensboro, North Carolina, took to the seas on their small boat (below, right). (Photographs courtesy Lynn Livesay, Patricia West Brocklesby, and Ray Hobbs.)

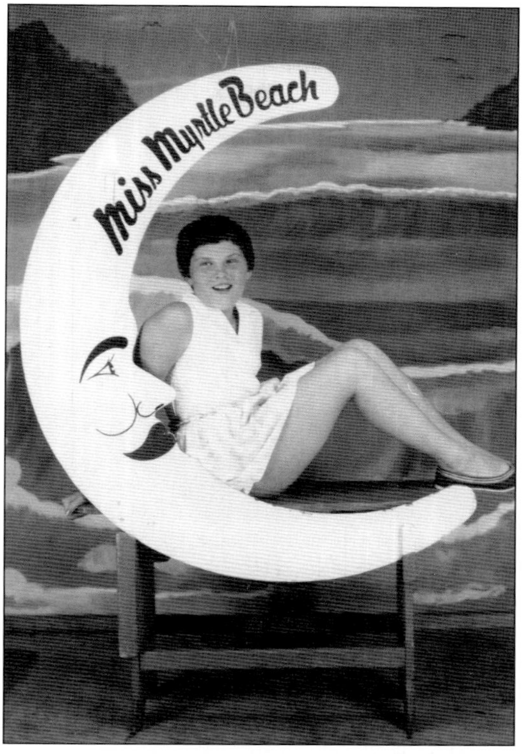

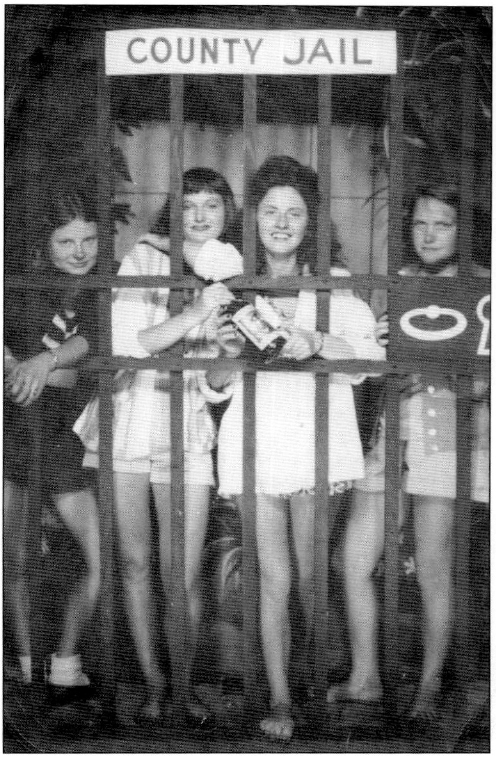

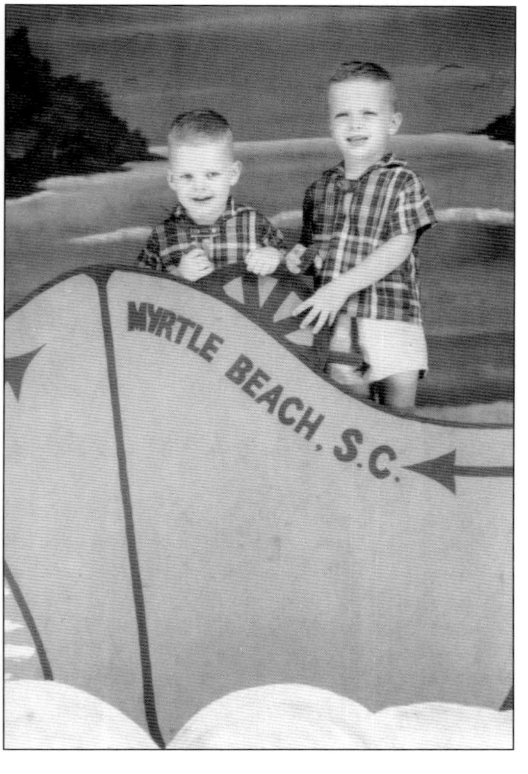

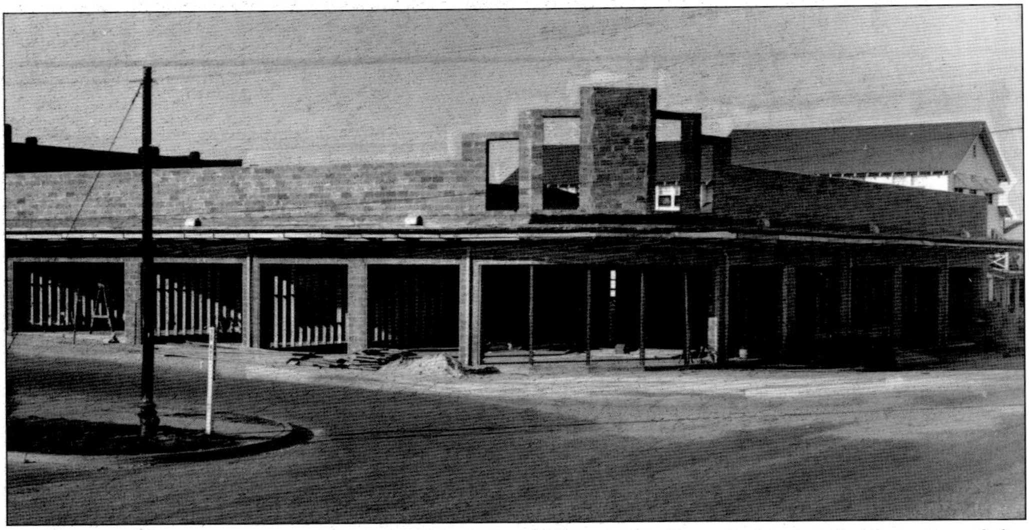

Built in 1950 on the corner of Ninth Avenue and Ocean Boulevard, diagonally opposite of the Pavilion, Sloppy Joes was a staple in Myrtle Beach for 25 years. It was known for its never-ending games of Bingo and food at any hour. Many people walking the strip on their way to or from the Pavilion would duck into Sloppy's for a quick few cards of Bingo and the chance to bring home a stuffed animal or gadget. Food ranged from complete breakfasts to a full lunch or dinner, consisting of a meat, vegetable, and drink (for 35¢). For the same price, one could get Joe's self-proclaimed world's largest foot-long hot dog, golden fries, and a coke. Sloppy Joe's was open 24 hours a day, 365 days of the year. Their motto was, "We may doze, but never close." Sadly, that was not the case. They moved locations in 1975 and later closed. (Courtesy CML.)

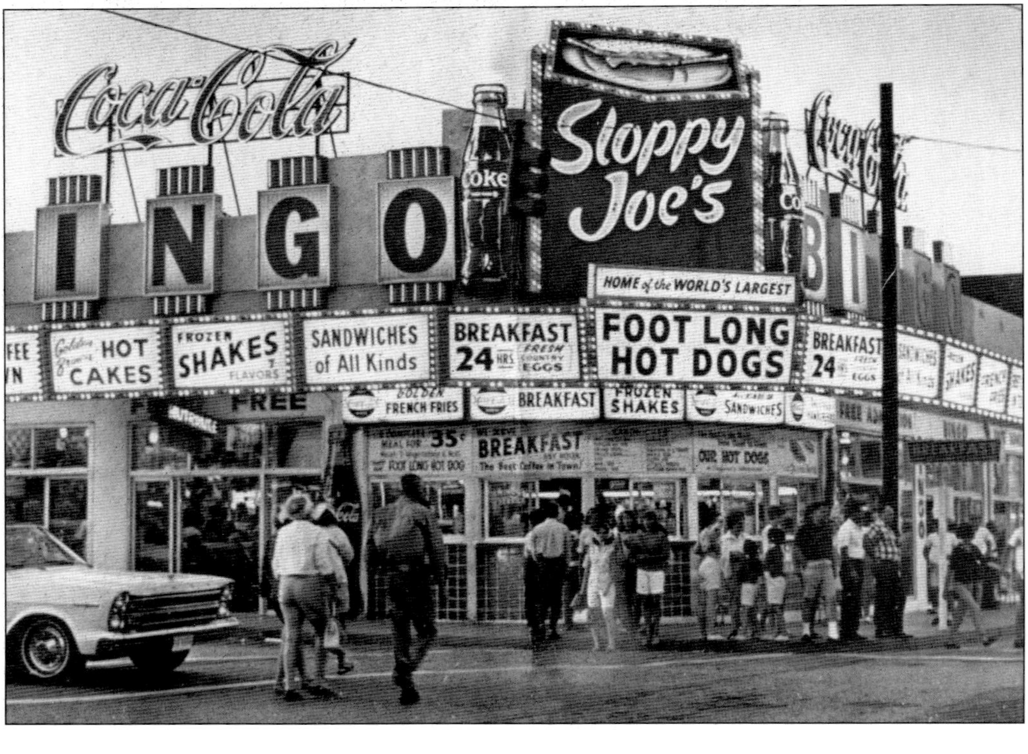

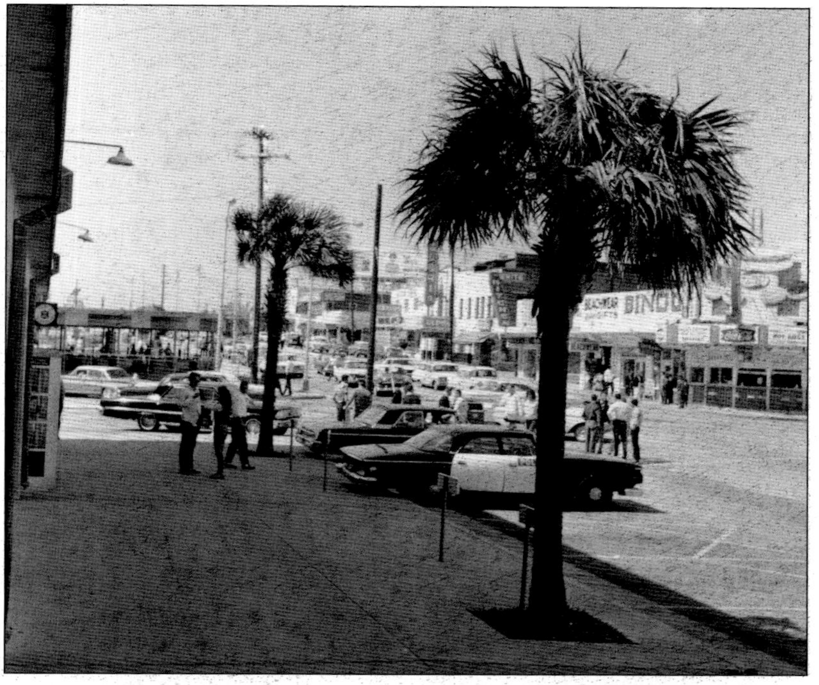

Looking west up the Ninth Avenue North side of the Pavilion towards Sloppy Joe's gives a sense of just how popular the area had become in the 1950s. Next door to Sloppy Joe's is the Gloria Theater. The Gloria was Myrtle Beach's second theater, having opened in 1937. The first theater was Ben's Broadway, which opened in 1936. (Courtesy CML.)

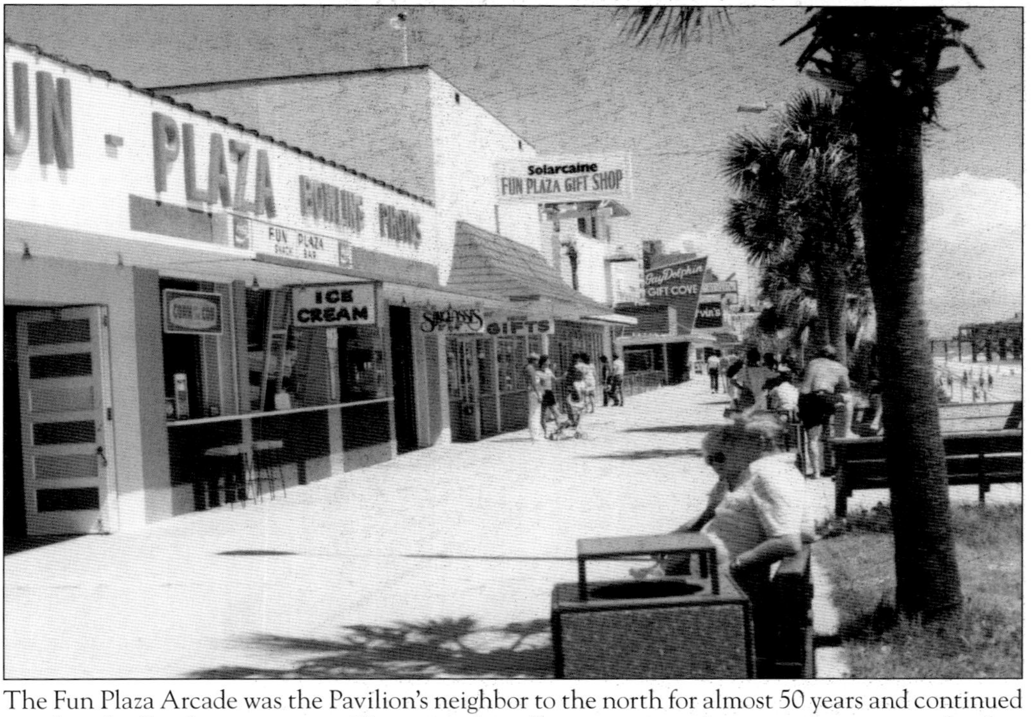

The Fun Plaza Arcade was the Pavilion's neighbor to the north for almost 50 years and continued on after the Pavilion was gone. There was friendly competition between the two arcades, but Fun Plaza owner Red Waldorf was an admirer of Pavilion executives Edgar Burroughs and Earl Husted. He felt confident that if the Pavilion was doing well, Fun Plaza would also do well. (Courtesy MBCC.)

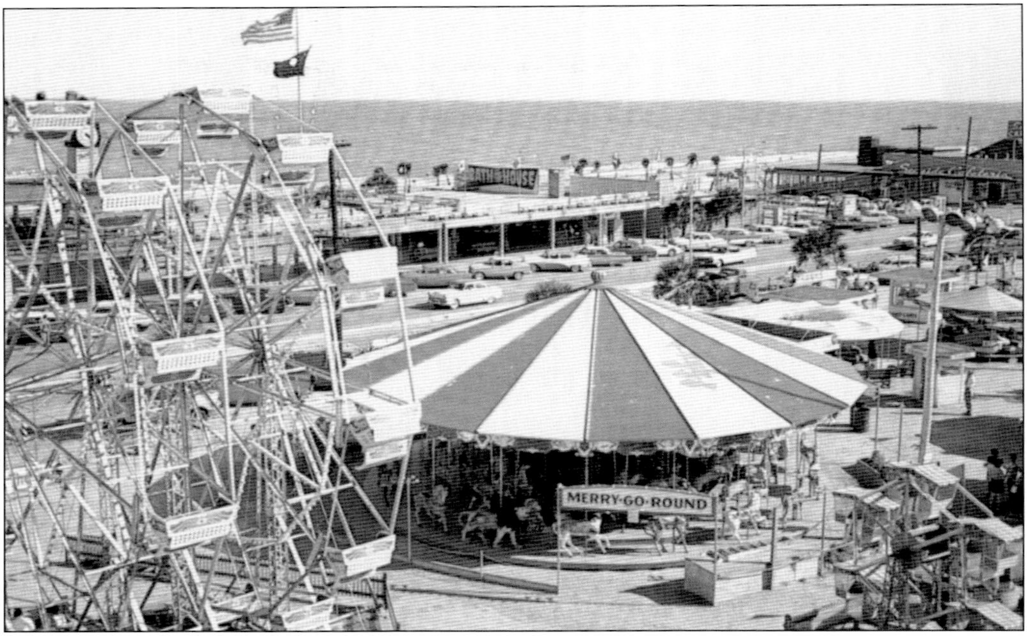

This postcard photograph taken from the top of one of the Pavilion Amusement Park's concession stands shows the park's twin "Big Eli" Ferris wheels. To the right is the miniature Ferris wheel that operated as one of the park's kiddie rides. The sign for the bathhouse is on the building's roof. (Courtesy Burroughs and Chapin Company, Inc..)

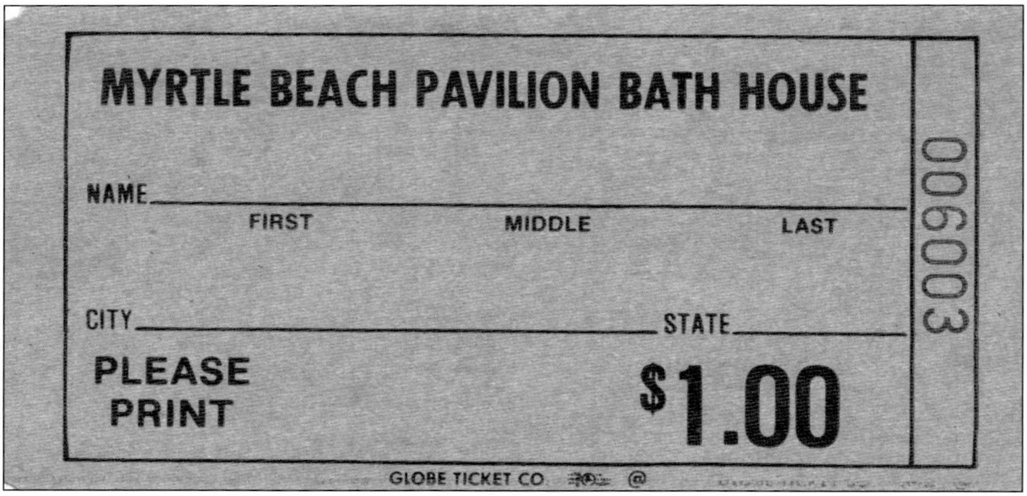

MYRTLE BEACH PAVILION BATH HOUSE

NAME ______________________________
FIRST MIDDLE LAST

CITY ______________________ STATE __________

PLEASE PRINT

$1.00

0060003

GLOBE TICKET CO.

The Pavilion bathhouse, built in 1947 on the corner of Eighth Avenue North and Ocean Boulevard, continued to operate until 1986. In the beginning, Robert "Bud" Montgomery remembers having to fill the water tanks for the showers by hand. He said he learned early to fill them only partially to keep people from lingering. A $1 ticket bought locker rental and showers for the full day. (Courtesy Jimmy Lathan.)

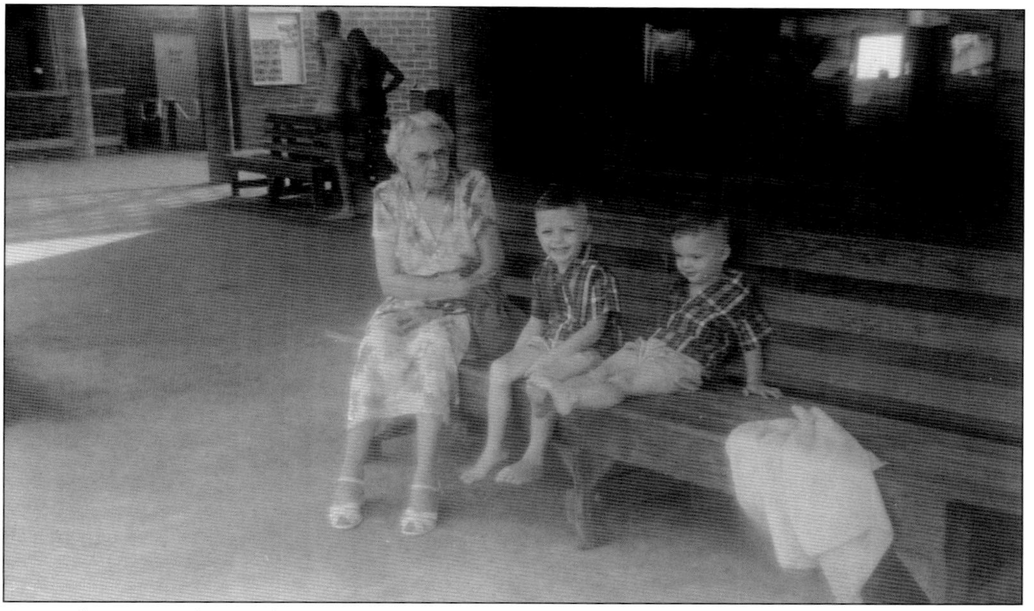

Greensboro, North Carolina, native Ray Hobbs recalls waiting outside the bathhouse with his brother Larry and his grandmother Mary Rountree Hobbs of Roanoke, Virginia. The boys had spent the day at the beach with their parents and were waiting for them to shower and change in the bathhouse. (Courtesy Ray Hobbs.)

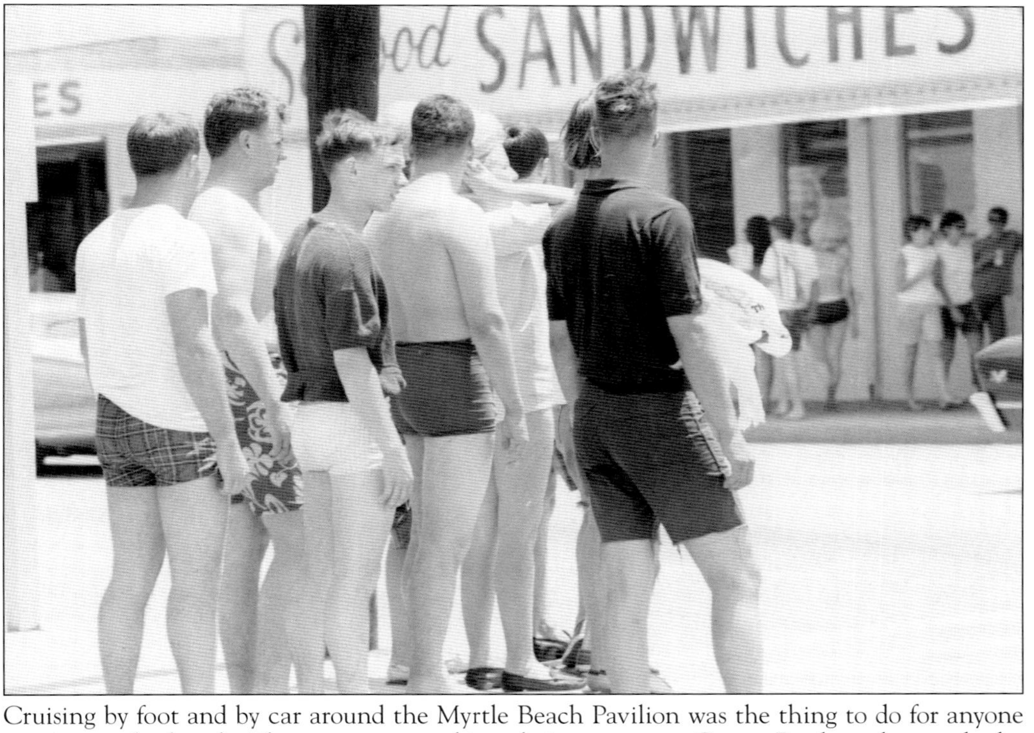

Cruising by foot and by car around the Myrtle Beach Pavilion was the thing to do for anyone coming to the beach. These men are making their way across Ocean Boulevard towards the Pavilion from Ninth Avenue North. Peach's Corner is in the distance. (Courtesy MBCC.)

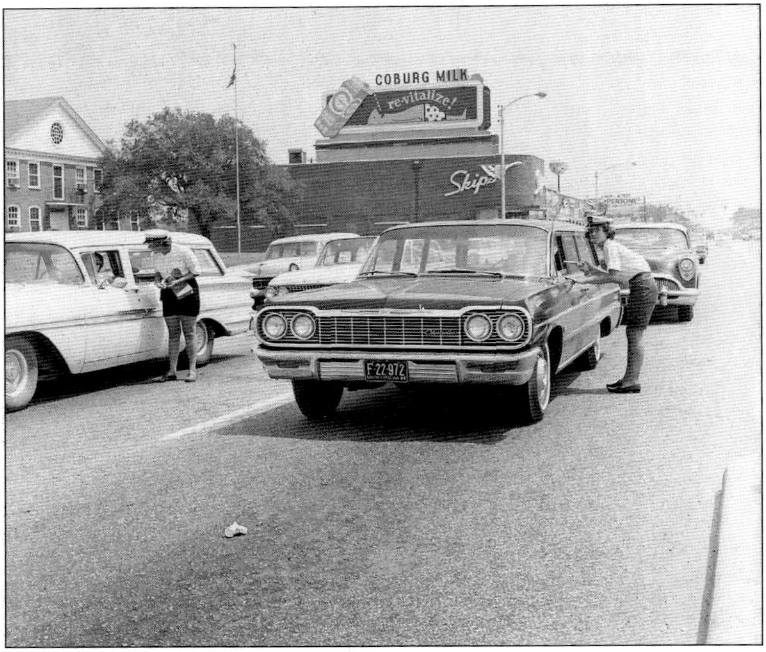

It was hard to escape getting involved in the early Sun Fun Festival. Local girls were recruited as Sun Fun Police who would stop cars along Kings Highway and write tickets for anyone who was found not wearing shorts or a bathing suit. The good-natured fines were used to raise money first for the Ocean View Memorial Hospital and later for projects like new band uniforms for the high school. (Courtesy CML.)

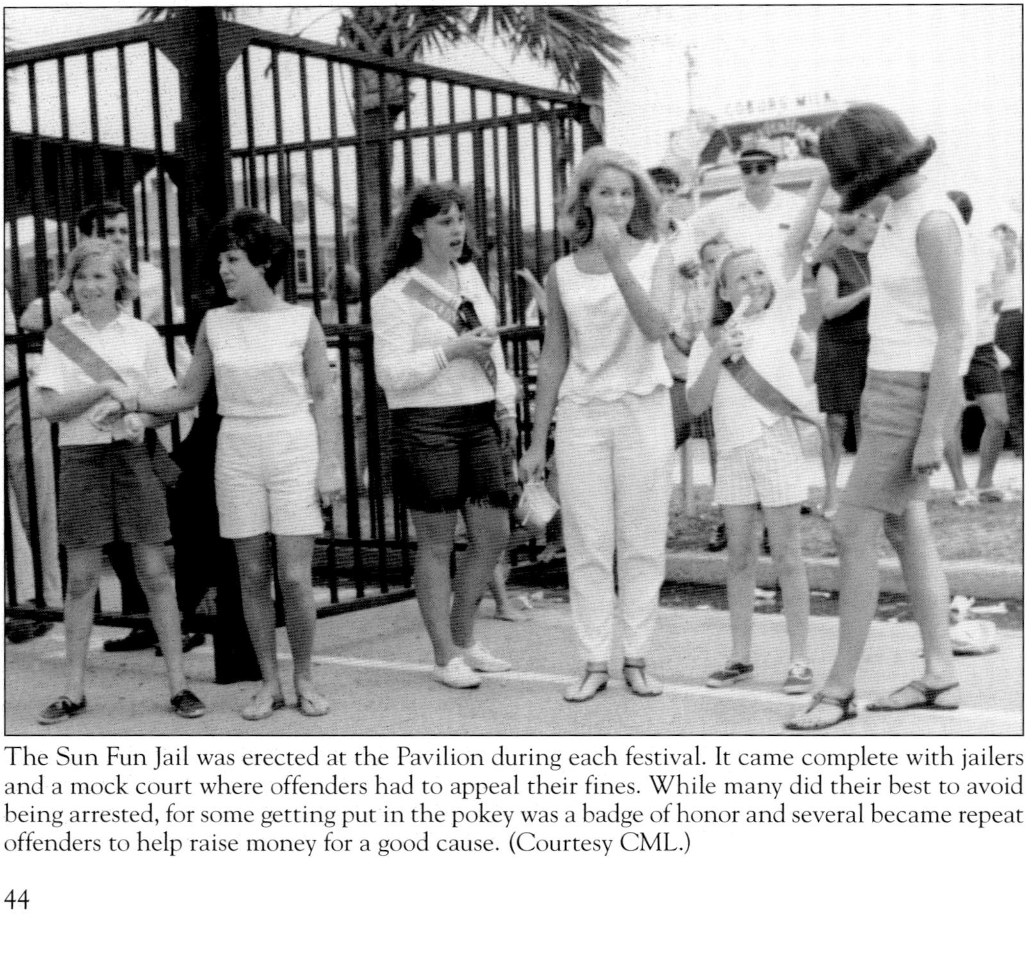

The Sun Fun Jail was erected at the Pavilion during each festival. It came complete with jailers and a mock court where offenders had to appeal their fines. While many did their best to avoid being arrested, for some getting put in the pokey was a badge of honor and several became repeat offenders to help raise money for a good cause. (Courtesy CML.)

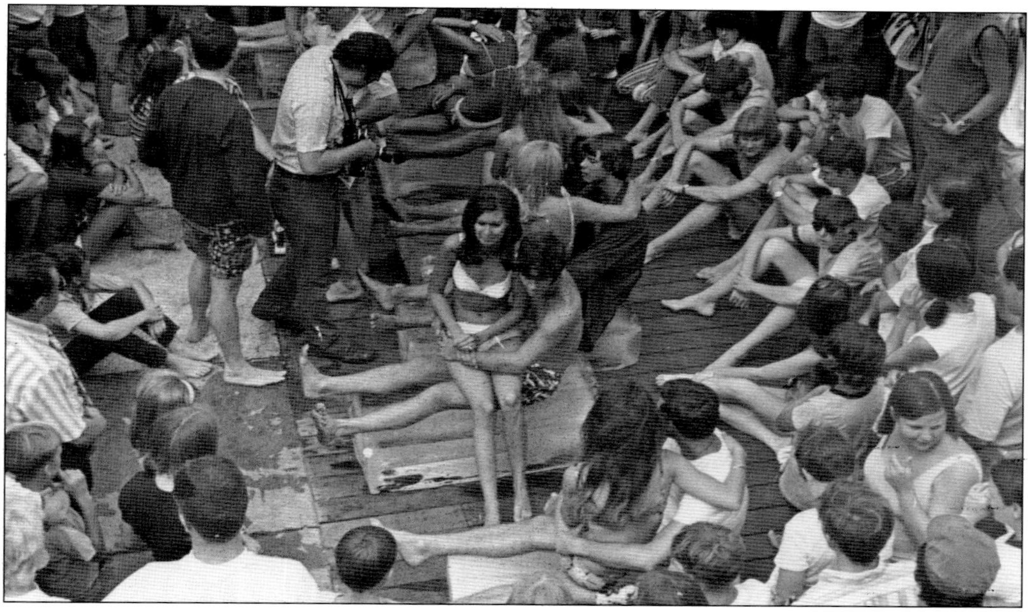

Ice-sitting contests were among the wilder spectator stunts that were held throughout the Sun Fun Festival. Huge blocks of ice were brought in from the ice house on Oak Street and men would sit on the blocks with girls in their laps while the ice melted and the crowd shouted encouragement. The objective was to see who could hold on the longest before the cold got to them. (Courtesy MBCC.)

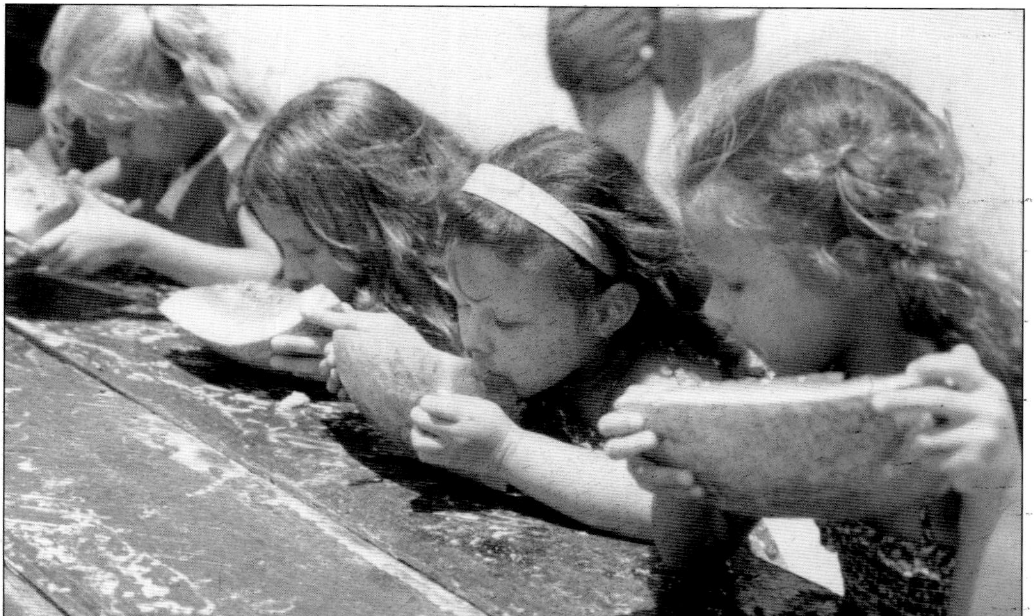

The boardwalk at the Pavilion would have to be hosed down after the annual watermelon-eating contest. While it was originally created for kids, contestants of all ages could participate. Watermelon eating was only rivaled in its popularity by the bubble gum–blowing contest; both competitions would be resurrected each year during Sun Fun. (Courtesy MBCC.)

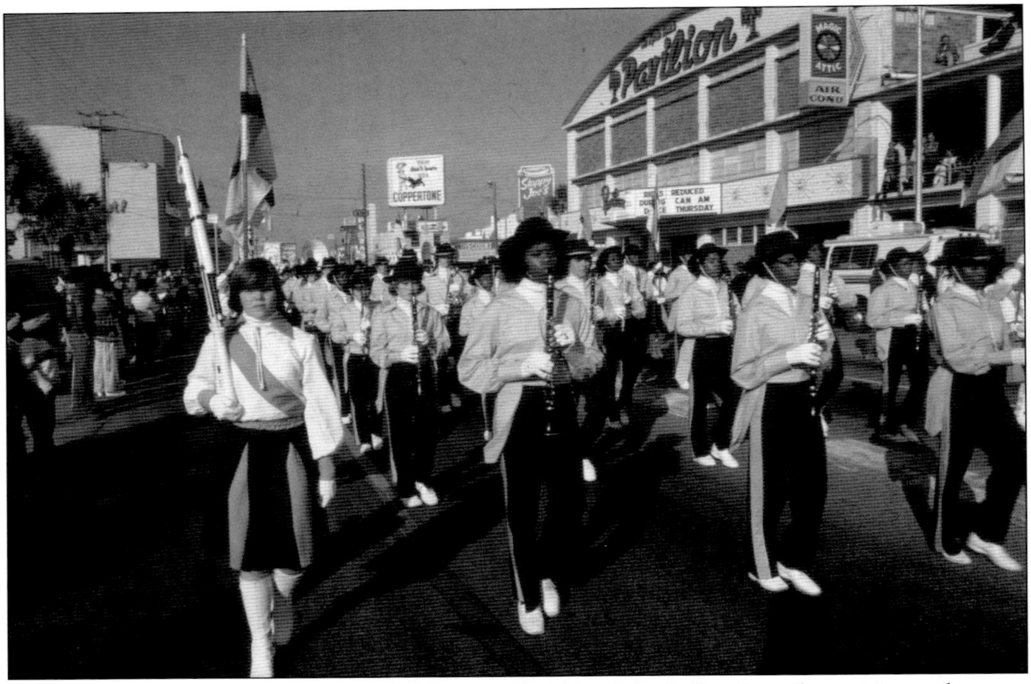

The first Can-Am Days Festival was held in April 1961 in Myrtle Beach to draw visitors who were taking spring break from Canada. The annual Can-Am Days Parade, like the Sun Fun Festival, used the Pavilion as a favorite viewing area. The festival later shifted to be held each March. Festivities drew an average of 75,000 visitors from the U.S.'s neighbor to the north. (Courtesy MBCC.)

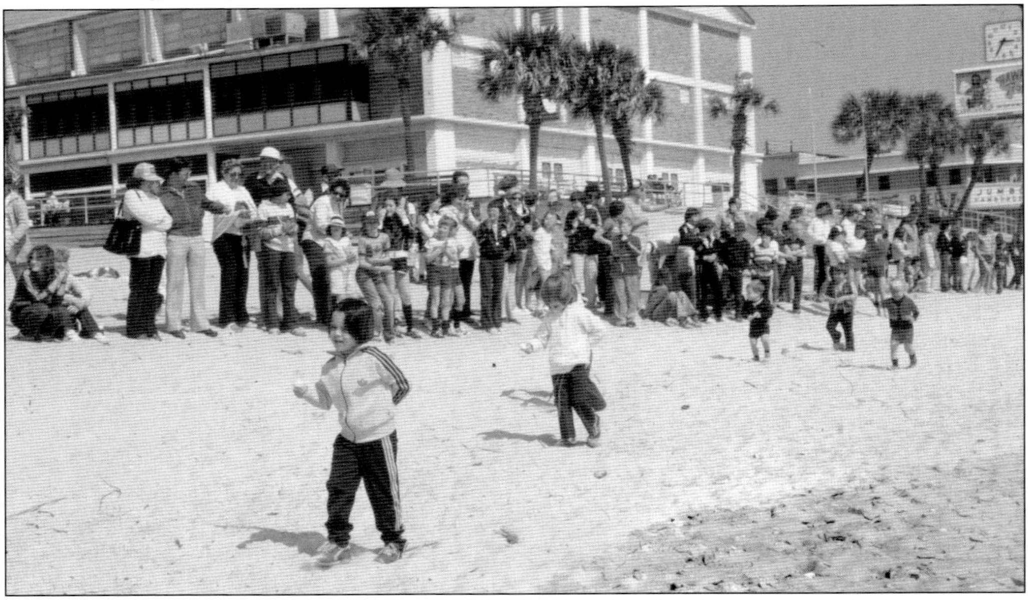

Just as with the Sun Fun Festival, the emphasis on the Can-Am Days festivities was fun. This footrace for youngsters along the beach was just one of the activities planned to involve kids of all ages. While the March weather may have seemed a bit chilly for locals, the often snow-weary Canadians found the temperatures, which averaged in the high 50s, welcoming. (Courtesy MBCC.)

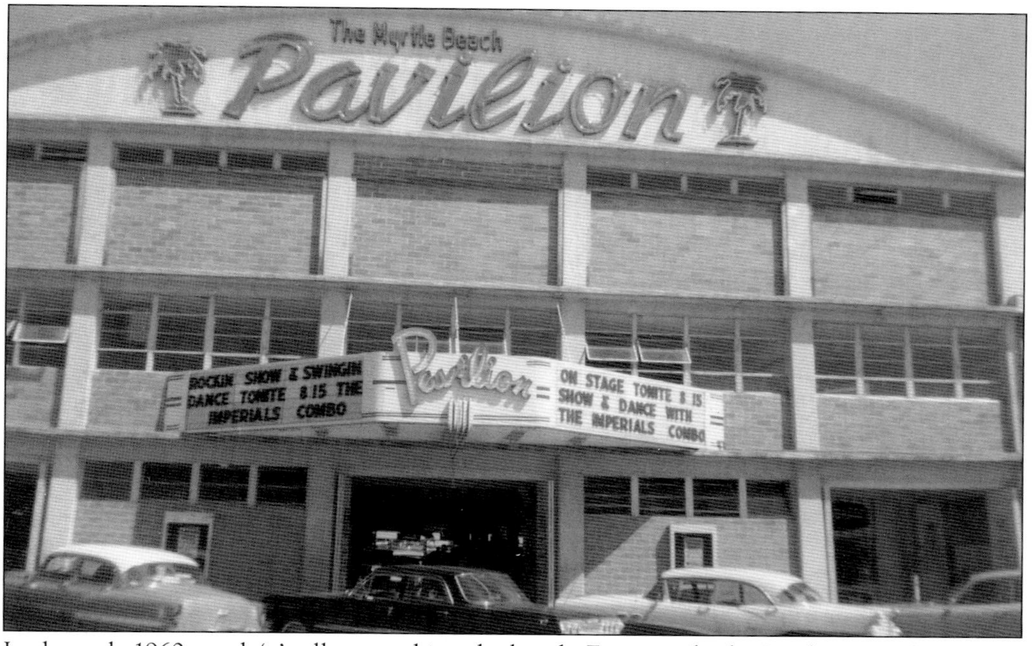

In the early 1960s, rock 'n' roll was rocking the beach. Every week, the Pavilion was showcasing new bands. This week in 1964, the band was the Imperials Rock and Roll Combo from Danville, Virginia, which played beach music and rock and roll. Lead singer Melvin "Mickey" Brafford fell in love with Myrtle Beach and would come back time and time again with his family and his children. (Courtesy Mickey Brafford.)

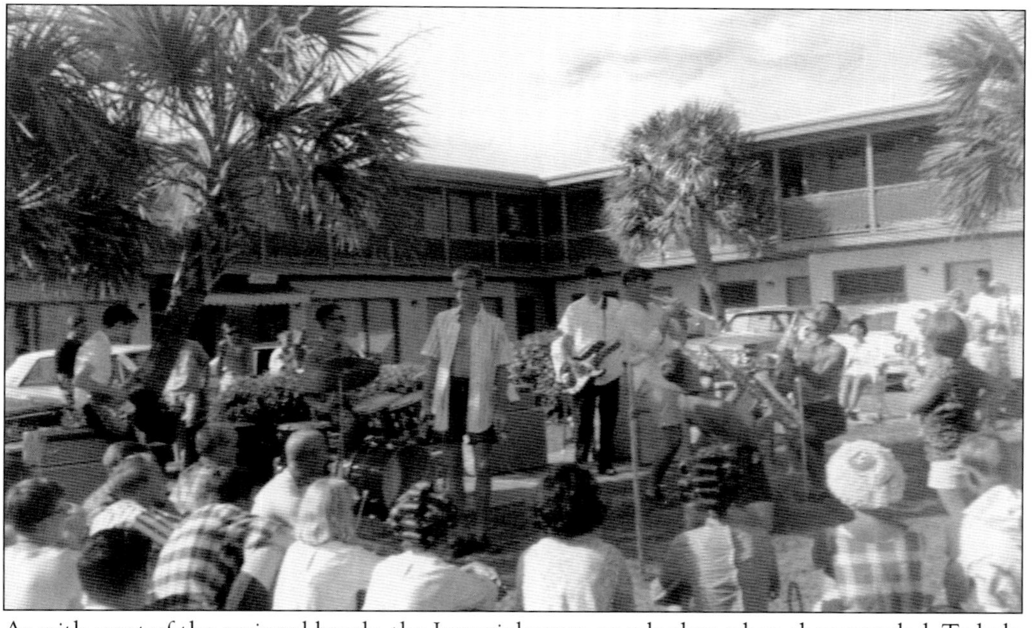

As with most of the regional bands, the Imperials were on a budget when they traveled. To help supplement their stay in Myrtle Beach, they also performed at a few pool parties in the afternoon at the Sahara Hotel on Twenty-ninth Avenue North, where they were staying. They drew such a crowd that the police came and shut the party down. (Courtesy Mickey Brafford.)

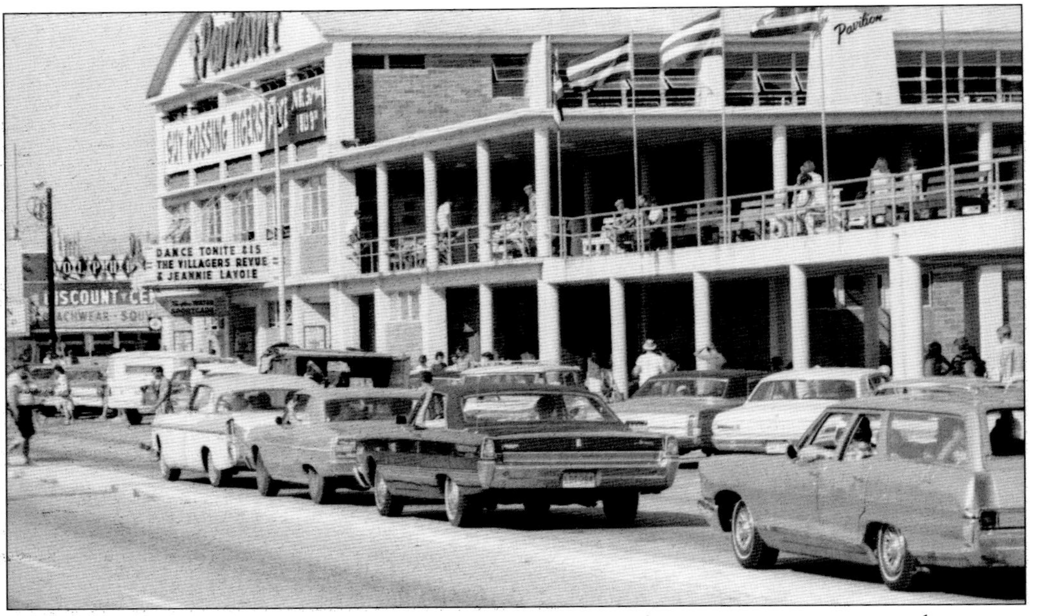

In the summer of 1966, the headliners were the Villagers, whose summer experiences later were recounted in a musical. Many of the bands playing the Pavilion had national and international acclaim. Performers like Jerry Lee Lewis, The Drifters, and Martha Reeves and the Vandellas played there. Carolina beach music and rock and roll reigned supreme. Despite packed houses, there was a rule: no alcohol would be served during public performances. (Courtesy MBCC.)

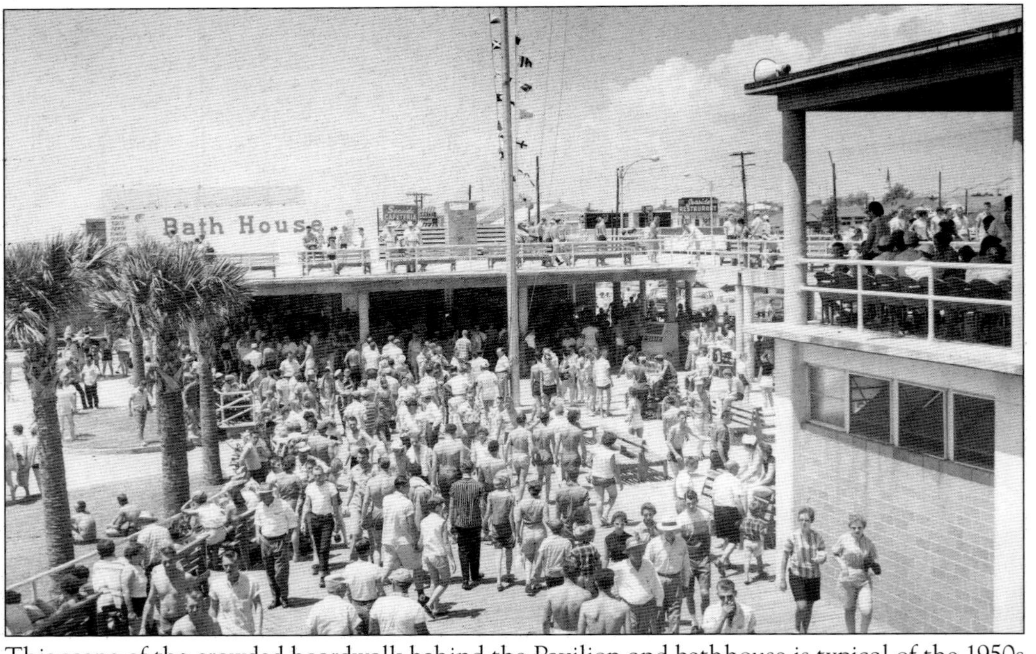

This scene of the crowded boardwalk behind the Pavilion and bathhouse is typical of the 1950s and 1960s. For many vacationers to Myrtle Beach, it was customary to make the Pavilion their first stop, even before the checked into their hotel. It was a tradition that would continue for many until the Pavilion's closure. (Courtesy MBCC.)

The boardwalk that stretched behind the Pavilion had at one point been 4 miles long, connecting cottages on either side. By the 1960s, the boardwalk consisted of the section that was behind the Pavilion and a section north, still connecting it to its neighbor, the Ocean Front Tavern, which had opened its doors in the mid-1930s. (Courtesy MBCC.)

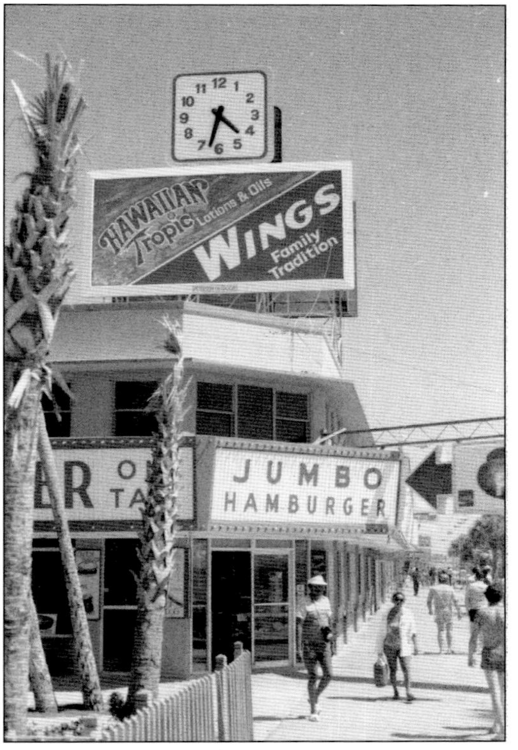

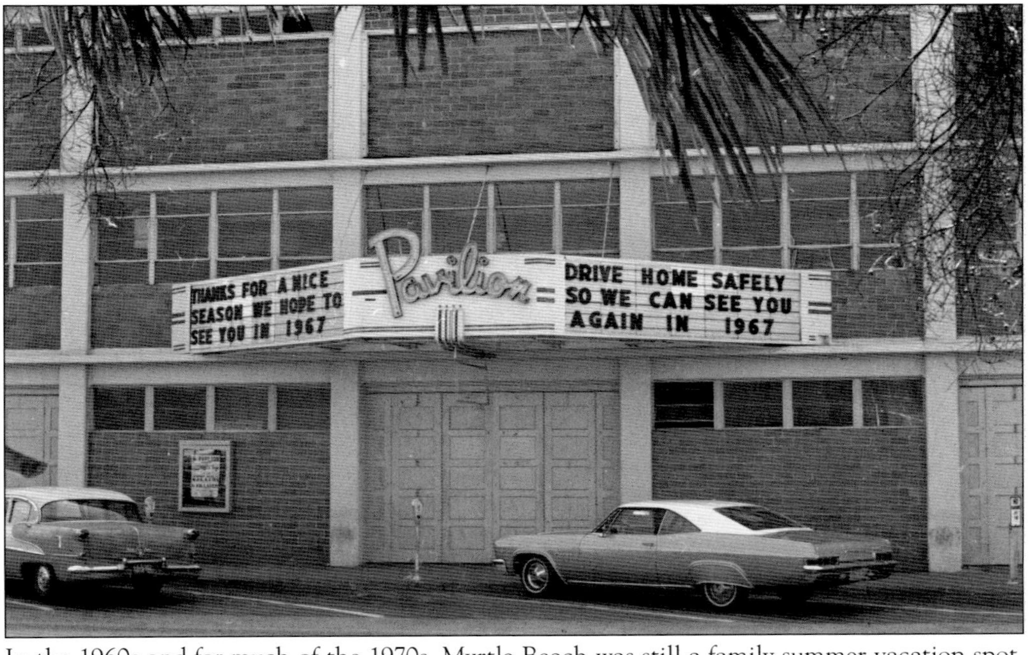

In the 1960s and for much of the 1970s, Myrtle Beach was still a family summer vacation spot. While spring break would bring in the crowds of teenagers, most tourists vacationed between the first of June and Labor Day, when schools were out. As more golf courses were added to the area, the tourist season began to expand. (Courtesy MBCC.)

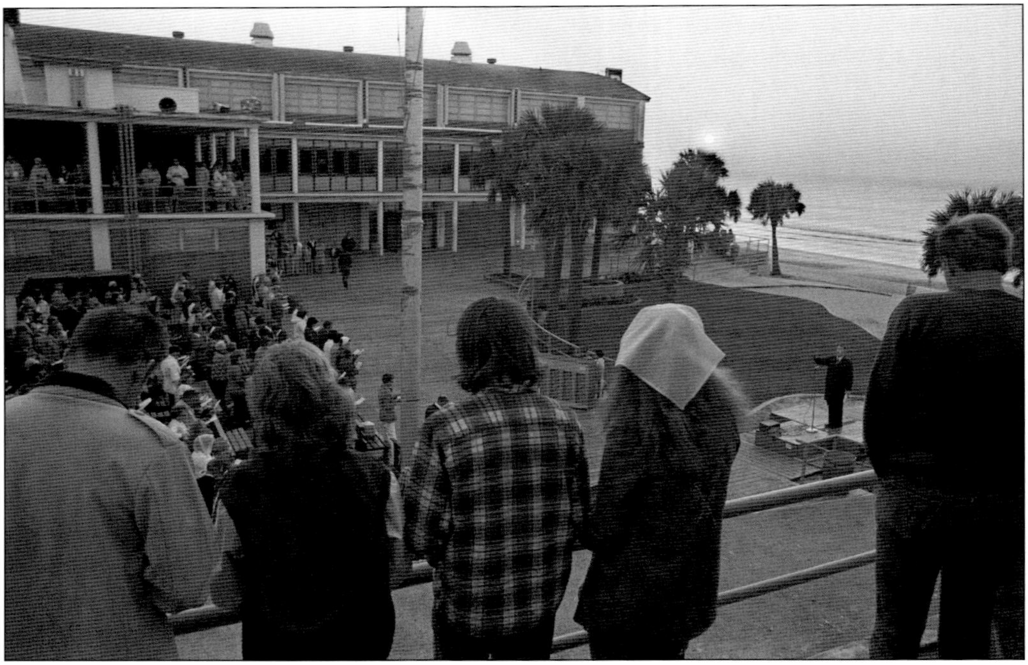

Easter sunrise services were traditionally held on the boardwalk overlooking the ocean at the Pavilion. Hundreds would gather in the pre-dawn light on Easter Sunday and celebrate with singing, scripture reading, and a homily. The service was designed to include pastors from each of the Christian denominations. Duties would rotate from year to year. (Photograph by Tim Ribar.)

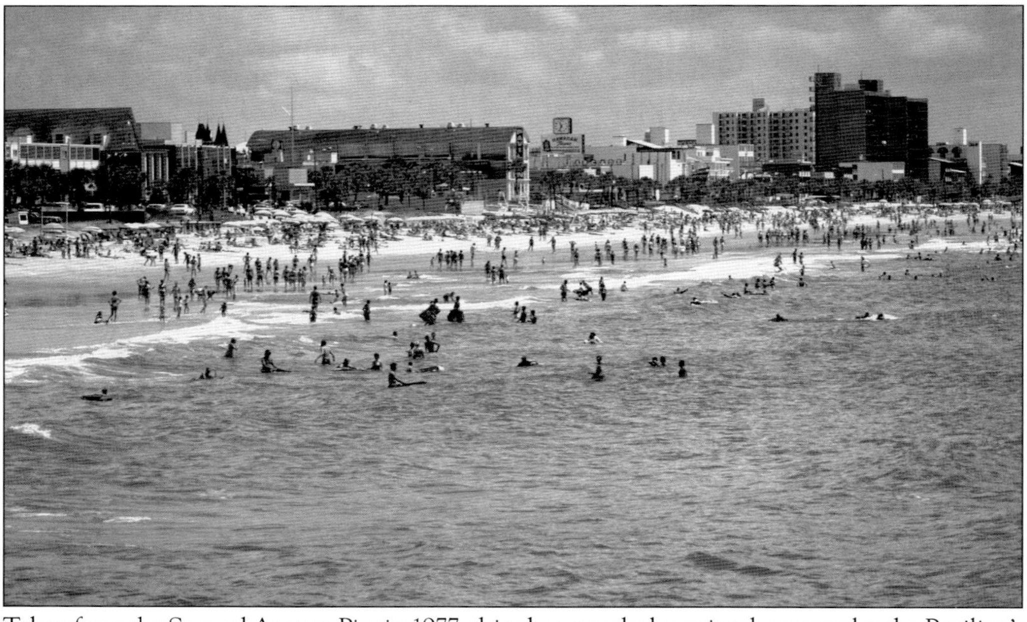

Taken from the Second Avenue Pier in 1977, this photograph shows just how popular the Pavilion's beach would be at the height of summer. To the left behind the Pavilion's roofline are the spires from Castle Dracula. The wax museum burned later that year and was replaced by an expanded Ripley's Believe It or Not! Museum. (Photograph by Tim Ribar.)

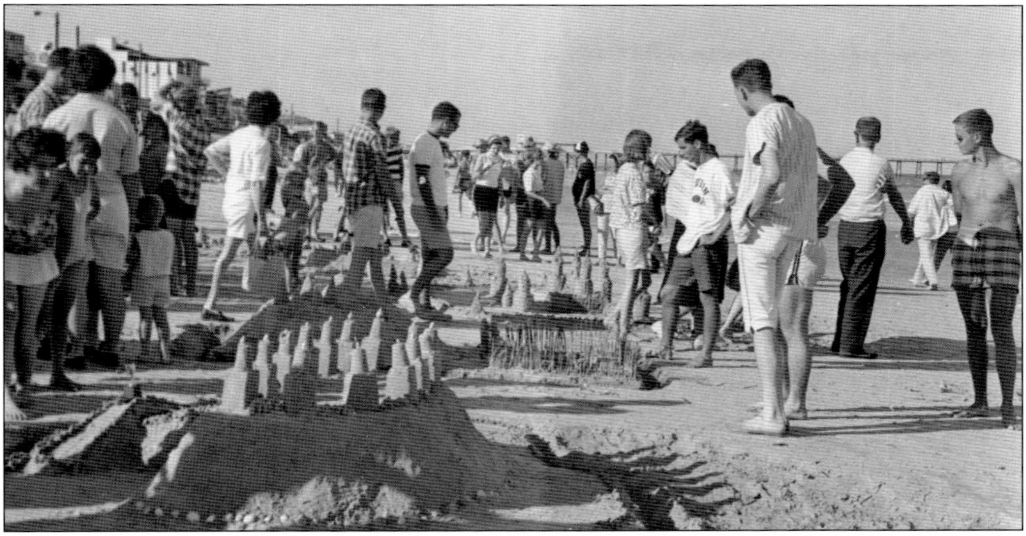

On any given day, the beach area in back of the Pavilion could be seen dotted with sandcastles and the remnants of sandcastles. In these photographs, one from the 1950s and the other from the 1970s, visitors are competing in sandcastle-building contests. Such contests were generally held around the Sun Fun Festival and even sometimes during the chilly Can-Am Days Festival. Contestants would compete individually or as teams. Awards were given by age groups. These structures were built using buckets and some forms. In later years, competing in the sandcastle building would become a profession for some. In 1991, castle-builders at Myrtle Beach set a world's record for the longest sandcastle, constructing one that measured 10.5 miles long. In 2007, builders erected a sandcastle measuring 49.55 feet high, which claimed honors as the world's tallest. (Courtesy MBCC.)

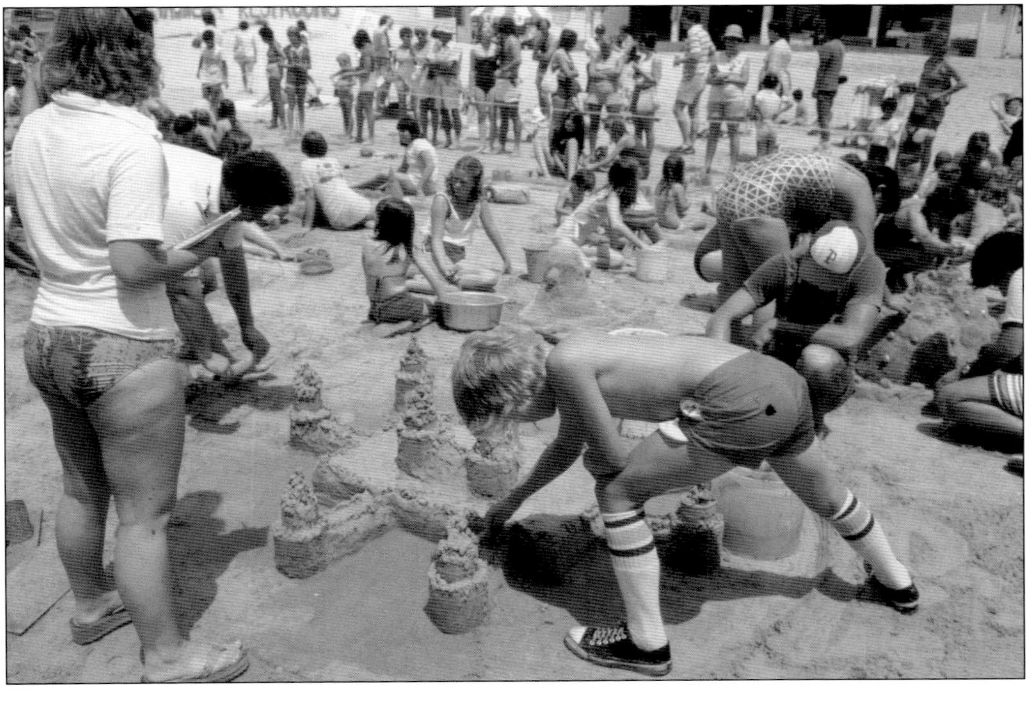

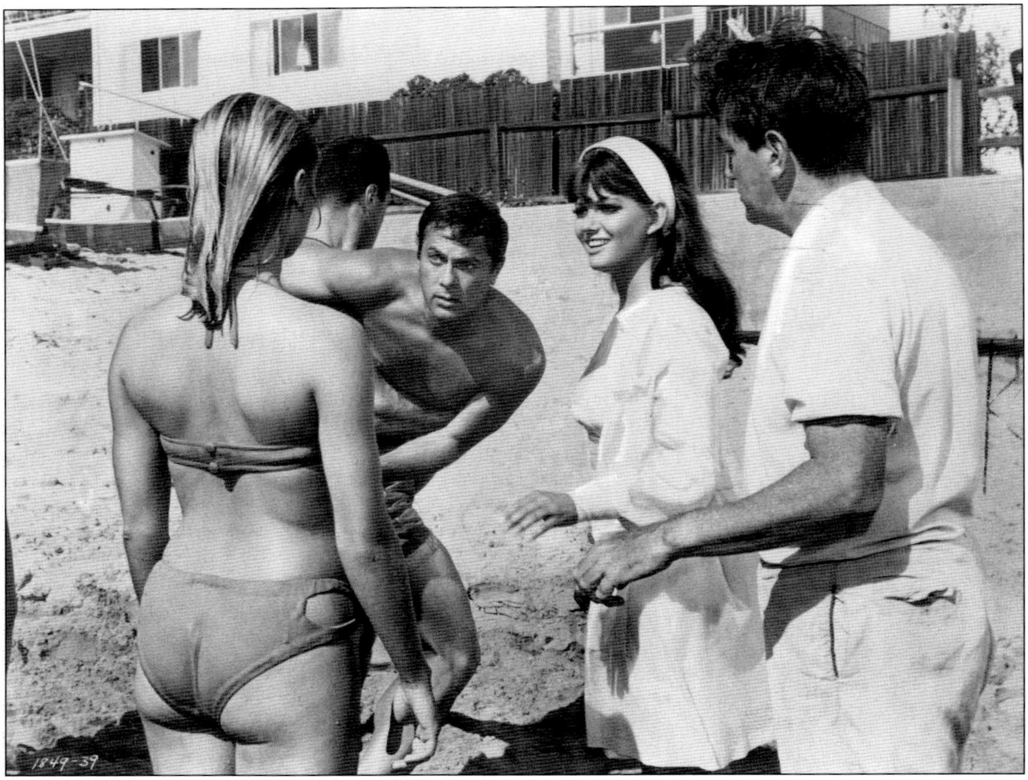

Acclaimed actors Tony Curtis and Claudia Cardinale were among the Hollywood stars who spent time at the Pavilion when they came to Myrtle Beach in 1966 to star in the movie *Don't Make Waves*. The Grand Strand doubled as a California beach in the film. Curtis played a New Yorker who falls asleep on the West Coast beach, only to wake up amid all sorts of wild events. (Courtesy MBCC.)

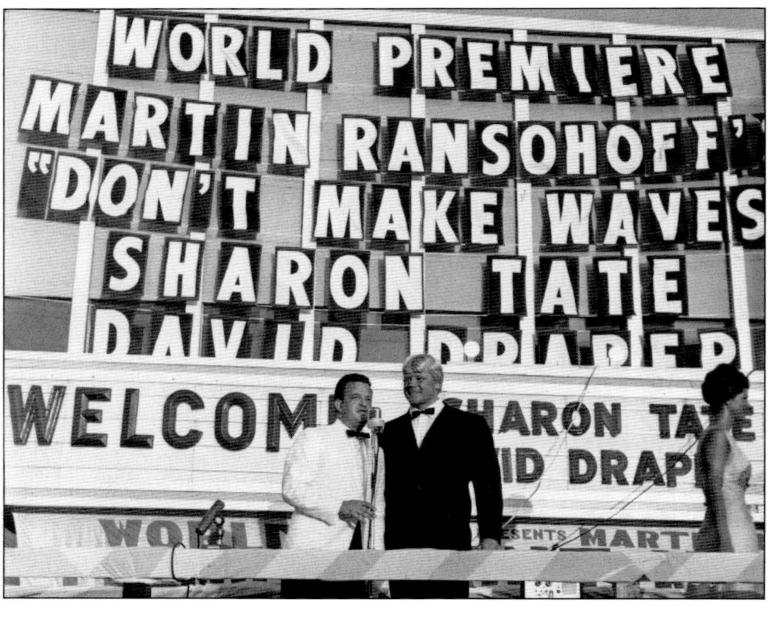

The 1967 world premiere of *Don't Make Waves* took place at Rivoli Theater just three blocks from the Pavilion. Attending the gala event were actress Sharon Tate and costar David Draper. Tate played a skydiver who resuscitates Tony Curtis after he is hit by a surfboard. Draper, a well-known bodybuilder, played a muscleman on the beach. (Courtesy MBCC.)

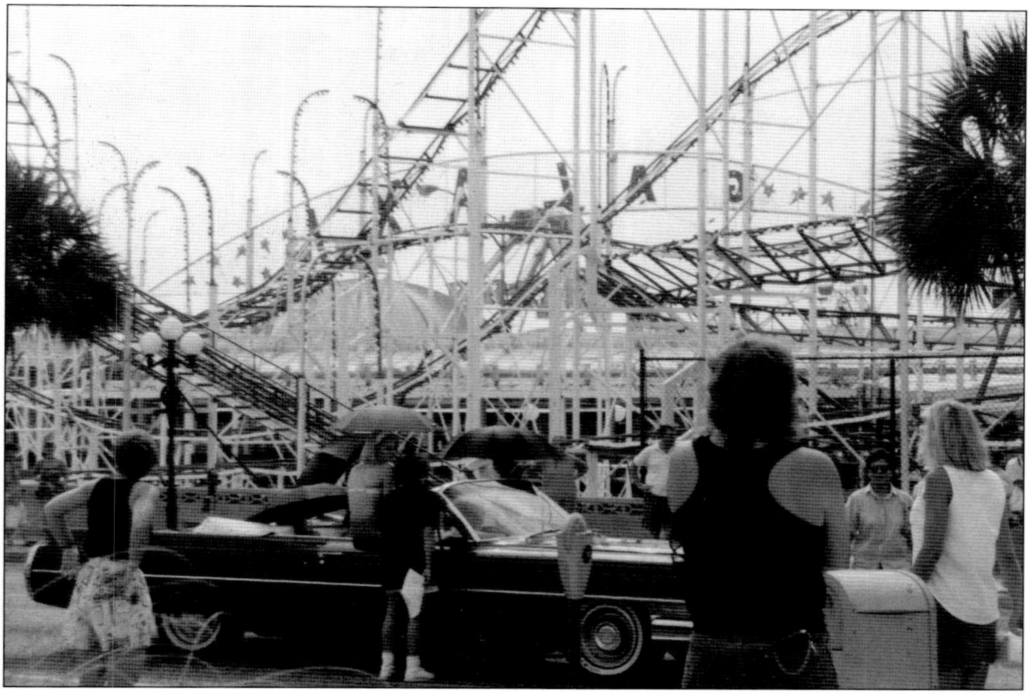

The Pavilion starred in a few movies and commercials over the years. In 1987, the movie *Shag* starring Phoebe Cates and Bridget Fonda filmed some scenes around the Pavilion, although most of the shooting took place in North Myrtle Beach. The Disney film *Wild Hearts Can't Be Broken* caused quite a stir in 1990 when it filmed on the Pavilion's boardwalk. The movie told the story of 1930s entertainer Sonora Carver, who would jump horses from platforms into pools. The jumps never took place during the movie, but just the hint that they might brought protests from animal rights groups. Other movies filmed in Myrtle Beach included *Chasers* in 1994, and *Swimming* in 1996. (Courtesy MBCC.)

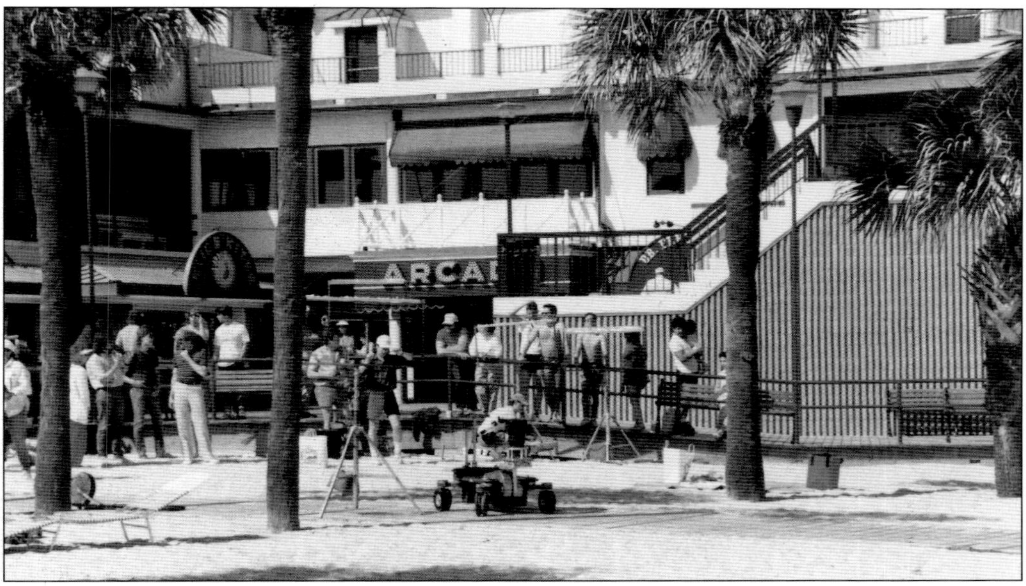

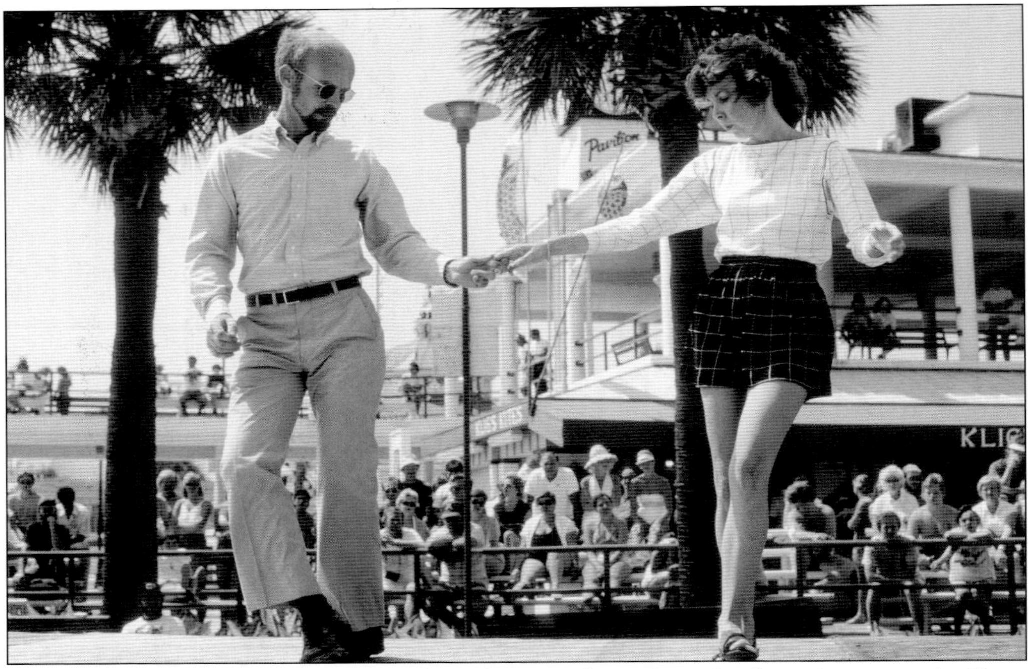

No mention of the Pavilion can be made without speaking about the dance known as the Shag, demonstrated here by National Shag Hall of Famer Barry Thigpen and his wife, Pat. Alternately referred to as a variation of the jitterbug or the swing, shaggers consider the dance in a class of its own. Its origins were in the 1920s and some say the early Pavilion itself. The Shag became South Carolina's official state dance in 1984. (Courtesy Tim Ribar.)

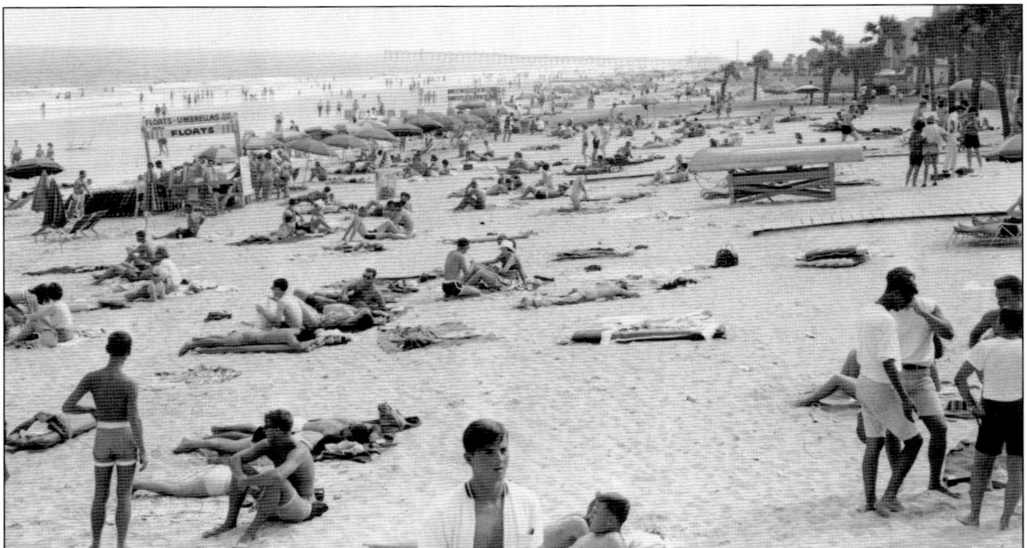

Without a doubt, the favorite place for any beachgoer to lay their towel was in front of the Myrtle Beach Pavilion. As a place for tanning and people watching, this spot had it all. When the sun and surf became too much, the Pavilion and its bathhouse provided a place to clean off and get a cool drink or bite to eat. (Courtesy CML.)

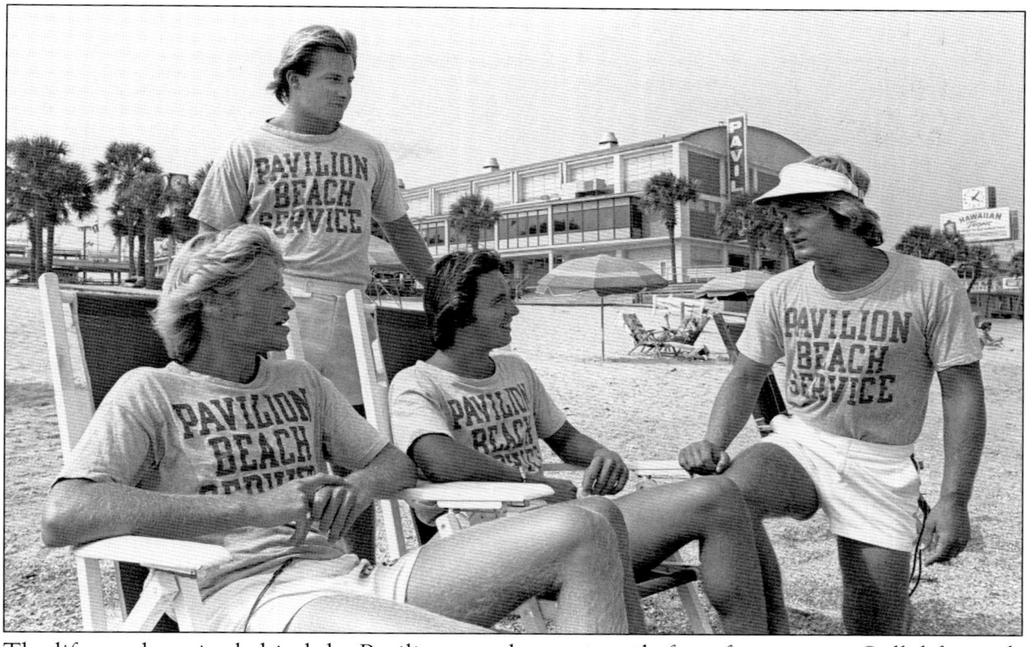

The lifeguard service behind the Pavilion was there primarily for safety reasons. Still, lifeguards also rented floats, chairs, umbrellas, and cabanas for those in need. Floats were rented by the hour or the day. Chairs, umbrellas, and cabanas were available by the day or week. (Courtesy Tim Ribar.)

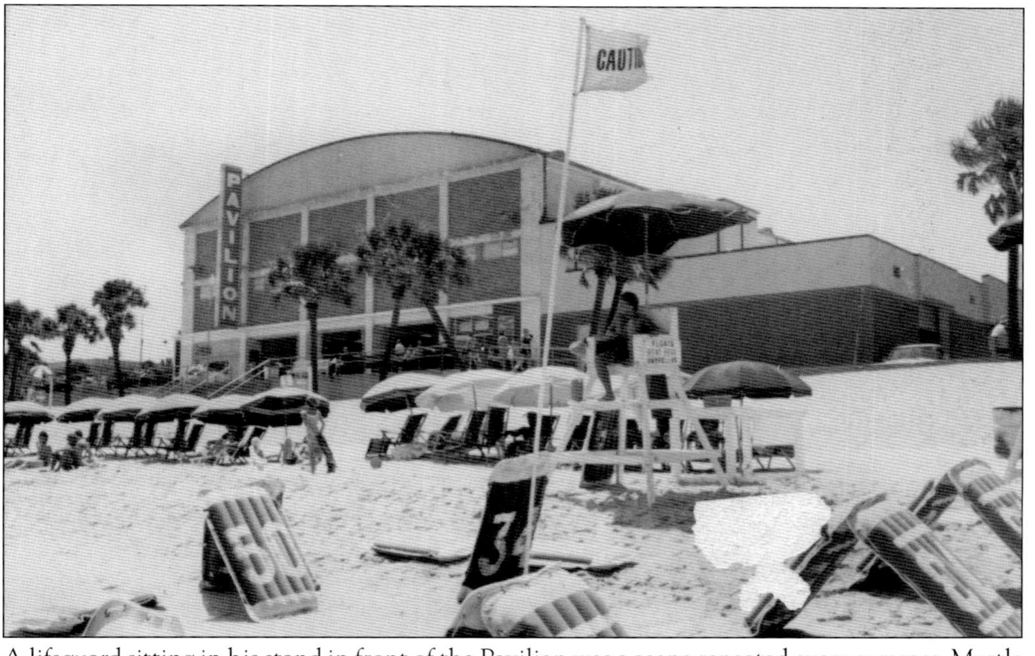

A lifeguard sitting in his stand in front of the Pavilion was a scene repeated every summer. Myrtle Beach's first recorded drowning was Ruth Burroughs in 1902. She was the daughter of one of the town's founders, Franklin Burroughs, and the family made a long-standing commitment to keep surf bathers safe. (Courtesy Jimmy Lathan.)

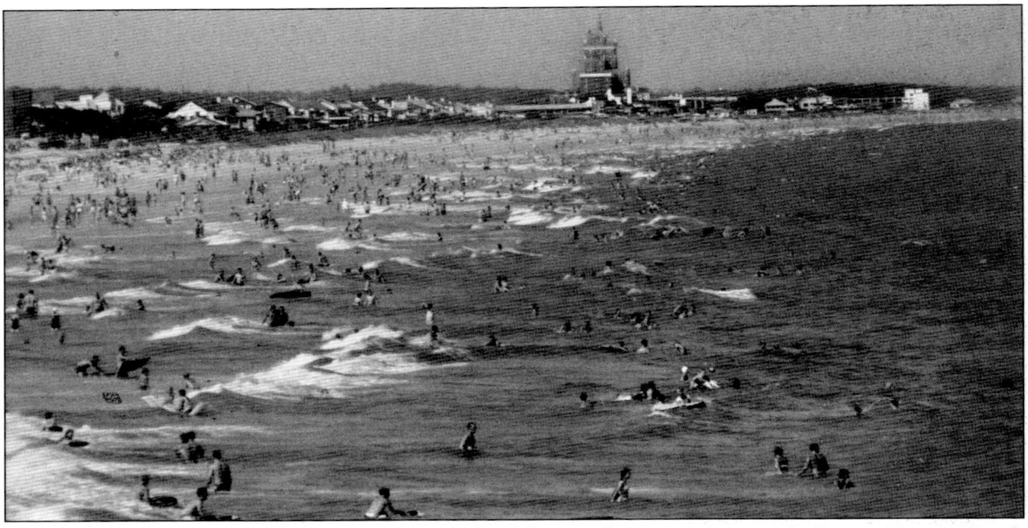

This castle-like structure visible 2 miles north of the Pavilion was the stately Ocean Forest Hotel. The Ocean Forest opened its doors February 21, 1930, and was the first hotel located outside of Myrtle Beach Pavilion area. A whole development was planned around it and included Myrtle Beach's first golf course. That course is now Pine Lakes Country Club. The Ocean Forest was imploded in 1974. (Courtesy MBCC.)

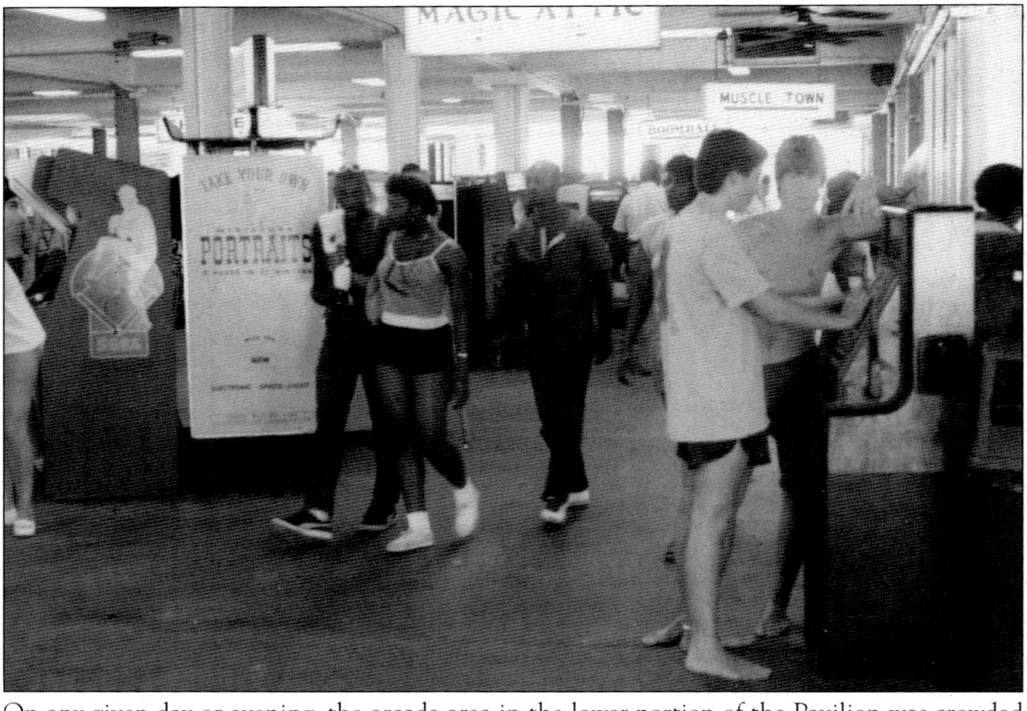

On any given day or evening, the arcade area in the lower portion of the Pavilion was crowded with people coming to play games or have their pictures taken in the photo booth. Because it was so crowded, former Magic Attic manager Jimmy Lathan says that during the 1970s a local motorcycle gang made it a rite of initiation to ride their bikes through the Pavilion and not get caught. (Courtesy MBCC.)

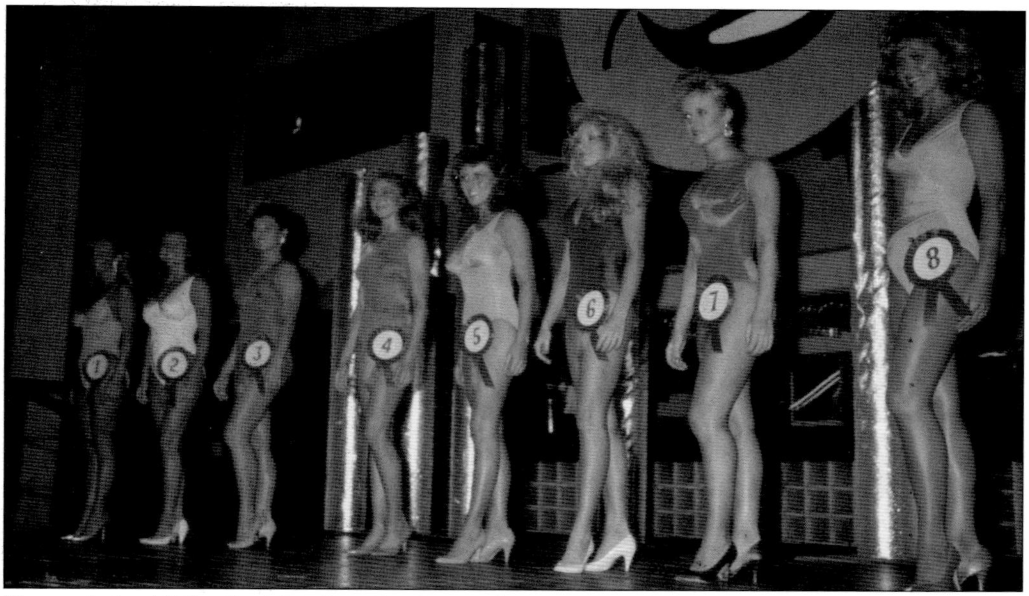

Up until the 1970s, the Miss Sun Fun Festival pageant was held at the Myrtle Beach Pavilion. After the Myrtle Beach Convention Center opened, the event was moved there. The winner would represent Myrtle Beach for an entire year, visiting other festivals and towns to promote tourism in the Grand Strand. She would even travel to Canada each winner to promote Can-Am Days. (Courtesy MBCC.)

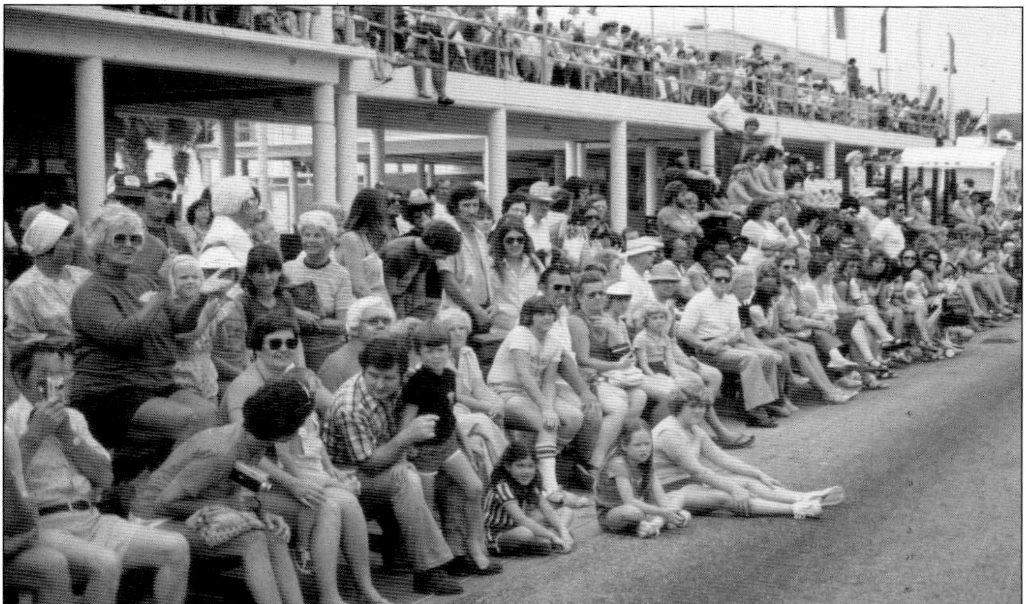

There was no better place to watch a parade than from the Pavilion. For many years, reviewing stands were erected to accommodate both VIPs and the huge crowds. Early parades would be staged at the Myrtle Beach High School parking lot on Sixteenth Avenue North and make the circle along Kings Highway, over to Ocean Boulevard, and then in front of the Pavilion. (Courtesy MBCC.)

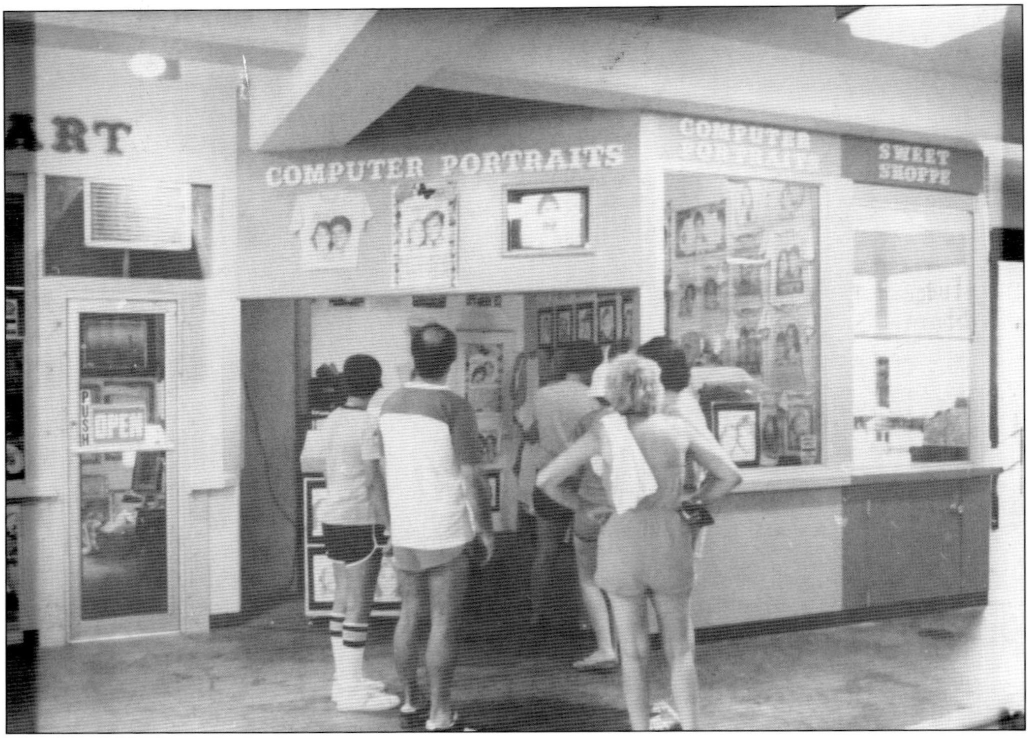

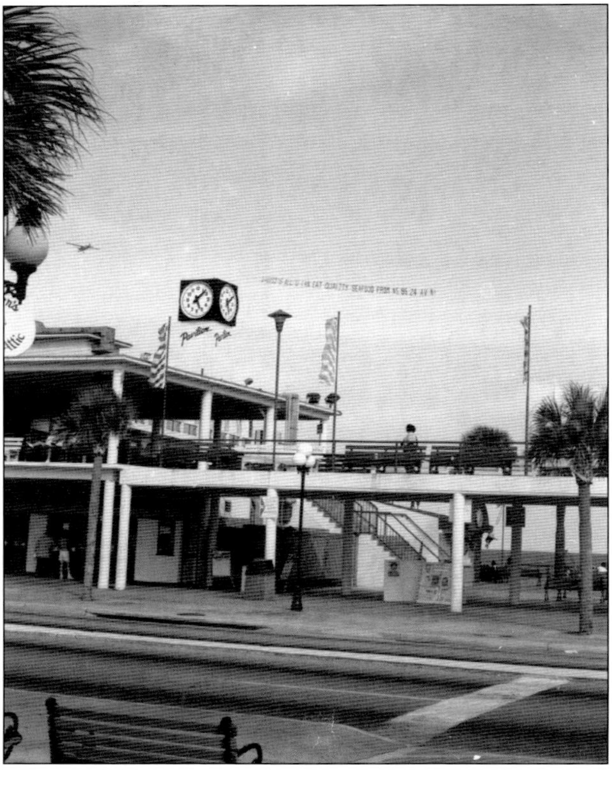

Photo booths have been present at the Pavilion almost since the days its doors opened in 1948. While early pictures would have the subject sitting around patiently for two minutes while they developed, the installation of a computer photo booth in the 1980s cut down on the time considerably. (Courtesy Jimmy Lathan.)

Planes flying banners advertising everything from tanning lotion to upcoming events can be seen flying along the coastline of Myrtle Beach. The planes, for the most part, take off from the Grand Strand Airport, based in North Myrtle Beach. The airport was the original site for commercial flights into the Myrtle Beach area before service was switched to the former Myrtle Beach Air Force Base on the south end. (Courtesy MBCC.)

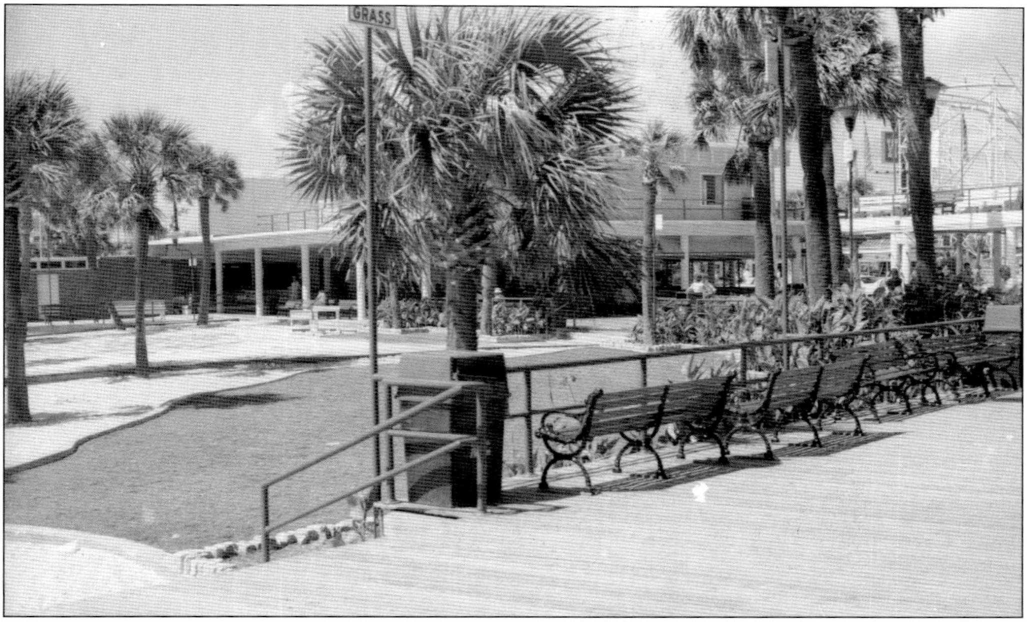

While the Pavilion itself changed little over its nearly six decades, the landscaping was an ever-evolving process. This photograph from the late 1970s shows a partial lawn and palmetto trees. Keeping a lawn here was sometimes a futile exercise because of the sand; many years, there was no lawn at all. (Courtesy MBCC.)

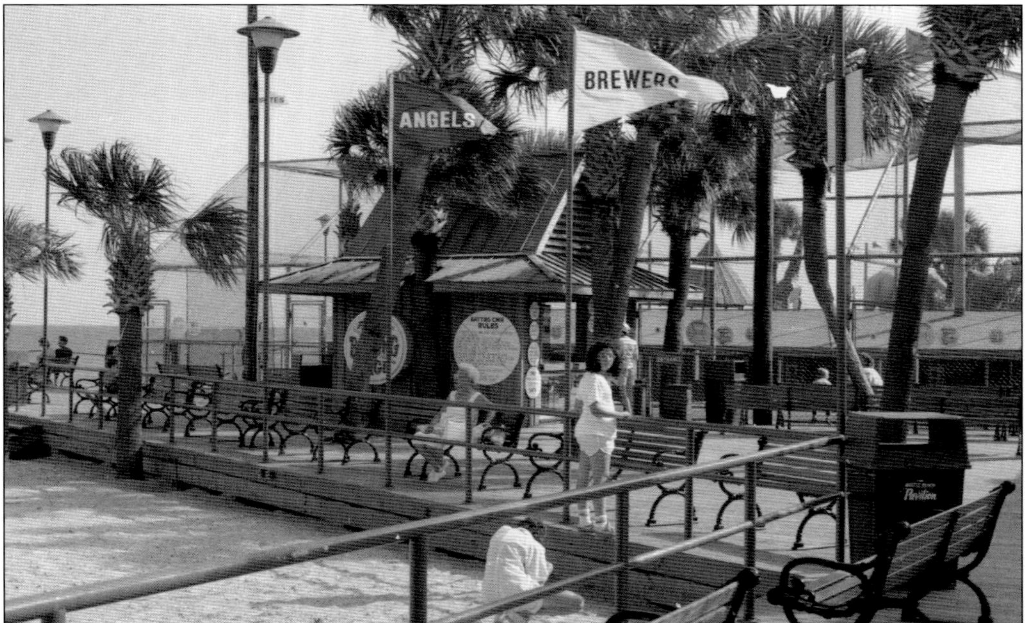

This batting cage was erected in 1985 on the site of the old Pavilion bathhouse. The concrete bathhouse had been built in 1947. Once the structure was demolished, the Pavilion no longer provided lockers or showers for beachgoers, ending a practice that had been associated with the Pavilion since the Myrtle Beach bathhouses of the early 1900s. (Courtesy MBCC.)

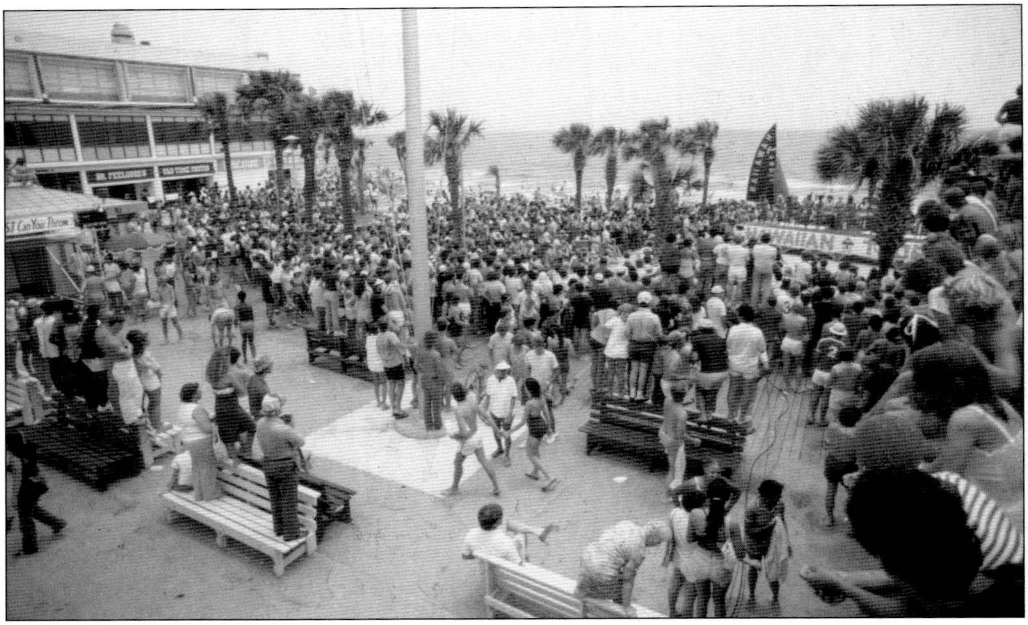

The Miss Bikini Wahine Pageant was a tradition that began in 1971 and was an immediate hit along the beach. Sponsored by Hawaiian Tropic tanning lotion, the event was free to anyone who happened to be at the Pavilion or on the beach at the time. The pageant took place on a stage to generally standing-room-only crowds behind the Pavilion just off the beach. Miss Bikini Wahine joined Miss Sun Fun in helping promote Myrtle Beach and the Grand Strand and in later days would compete in the Miss Hawaiian Tropic International contest in Hawaii. Wahine means woman in the Hawaiian language. (Above, courtesy MBCC.)

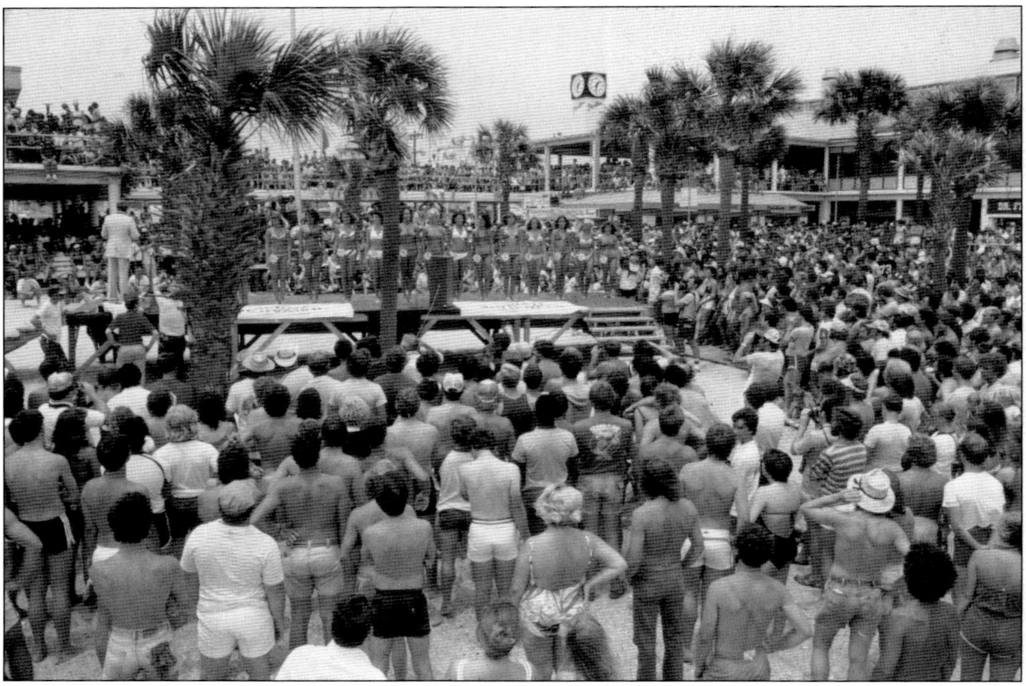

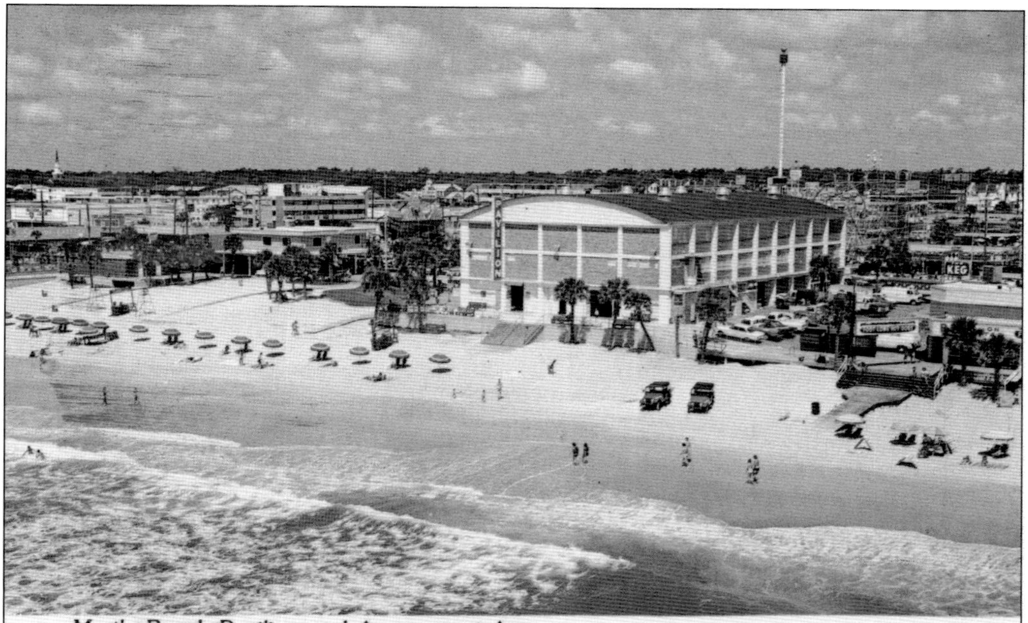

Myrtle Beach Pavilion and Amusement Area

This aerial view from the mid-1970s shows the Pavilion before it was expanded and given its stucco face-lift in 1985. The Astro Needle is visible in the background. The 200-foot-tall tower took people up for views of the Grand Strand between 1970 and 1981.

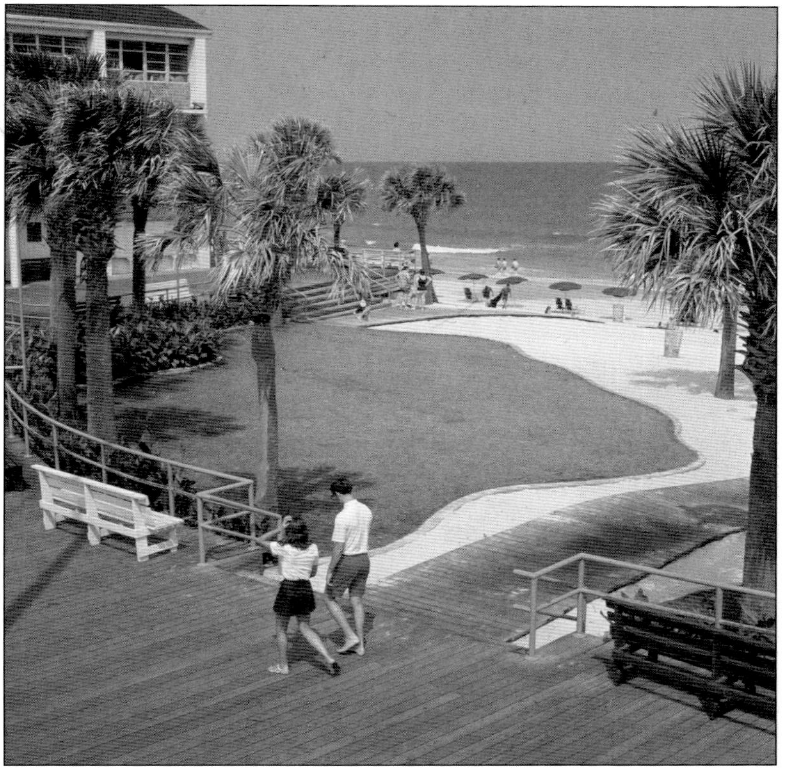

Taken from the upper deck of the Pavilion, this photograph shows the boardwalk area in spring, before the tourist season opened up and the crowds began to arrive. Even when there was no special event taking place, the Pavilion's boardwalk was a place to take a stroll and enjoy the ocean. (Courtesy MBCC.)

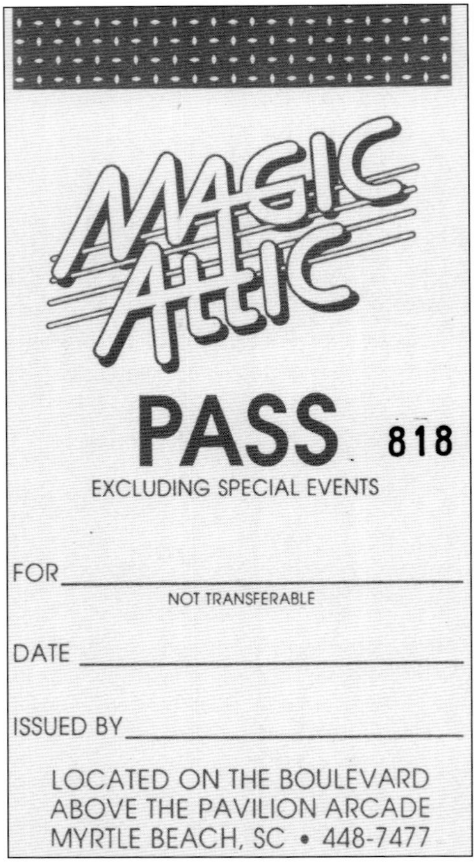

A pass to the Pavilion's Magic Attic was a coveted item. Just about every beach band imaginable played the night club at one time or another. In 1978, even the Rolling Stones surprised guests by taking to the stage after a concert earlier at the Myrtle Beach Convention Center. Former Magic Attic manager Jimmy Lathan says the band Stratus was playing when the Stones appeared, played "Jumping Jack Flash," and then disappeared again. (Courtesy Jimmy Lathan.)

For almost a decade beginning in 1980, the band Sugar Creek played the Pavilion to packed crowds. The marquee in the rare 1980s photograph below touts one of the band's earliest appearances at the beginning of the season. It also announces the arrival of the new ride known as the Scrambler. The Scrambler was a classic carnival ride and was built by the same company that built the "Big Eli" Ferris wheels. (Photograph by Mickey Brafford.)

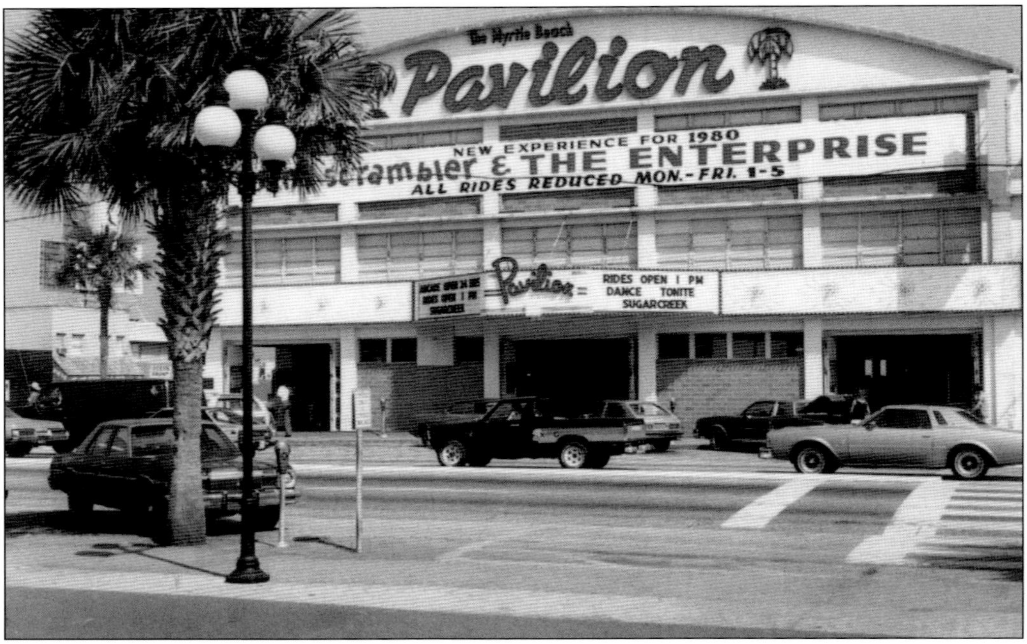

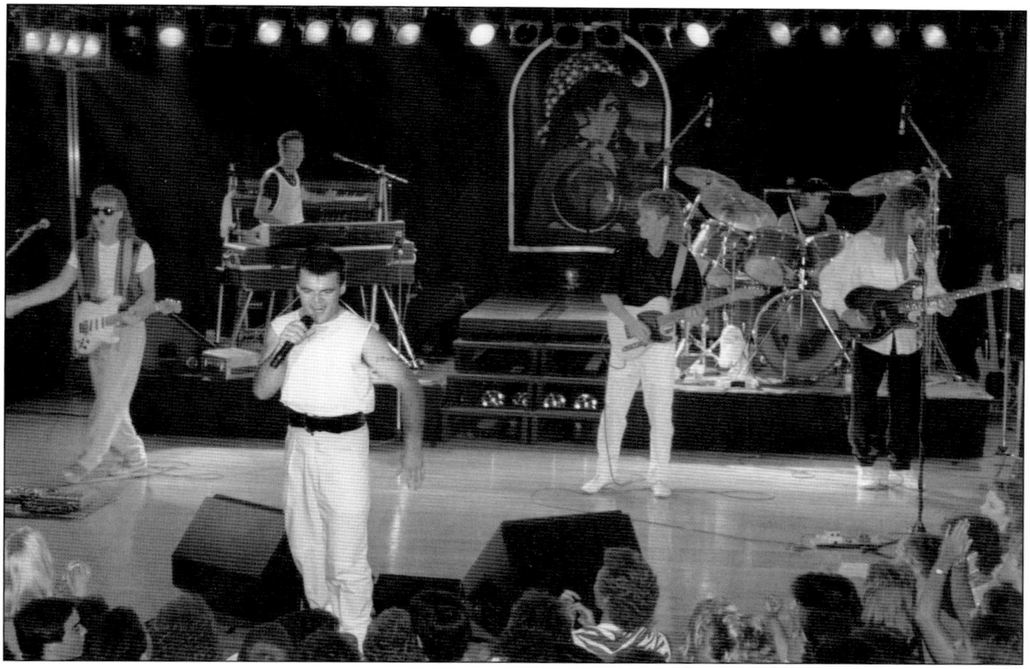

The band Sugar Creek was the Pavilion's house band in the 1980s, playing an average 40 times a summer for seven straight years. They held a record 276 straight sell-out dates as a capacity crowd of 2,000 "Creak Freaks" would pack the Magic Attic time and time again. Local fire codes limited the Attic to 2,000 guests, but the managers often opened the doors to the decks to allow more to be able to enjoy the music. The largest crowd recorded, according to former Magic Attic manager Jimmy Lathan, was 3,528 for an Eastern Seaboard concert in the mid-1970s. Sugar Creek was among the bands who staged a reunion for the Pavilion's farewell season. (Photographs courtesy Jimmy Lathan.)

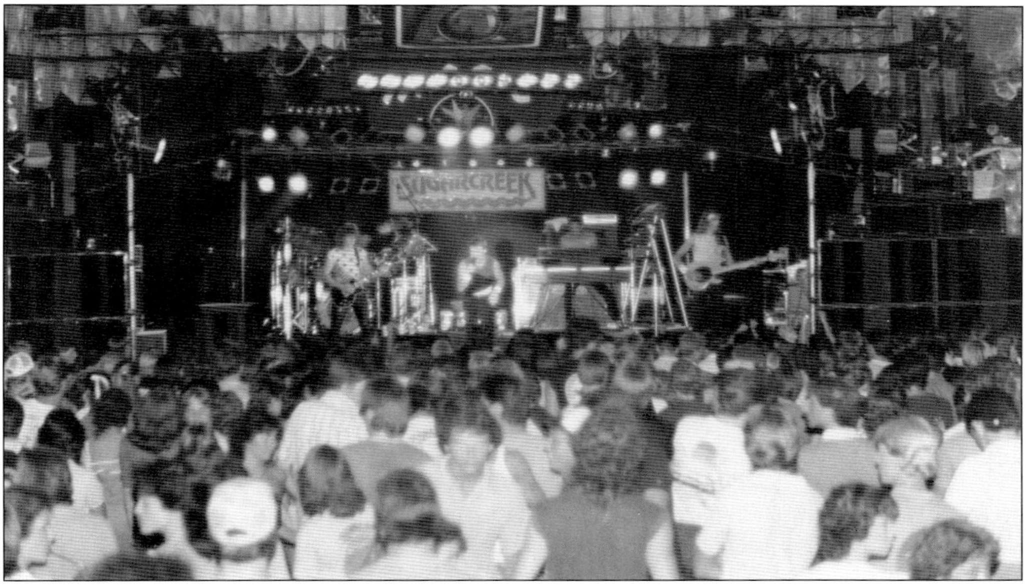

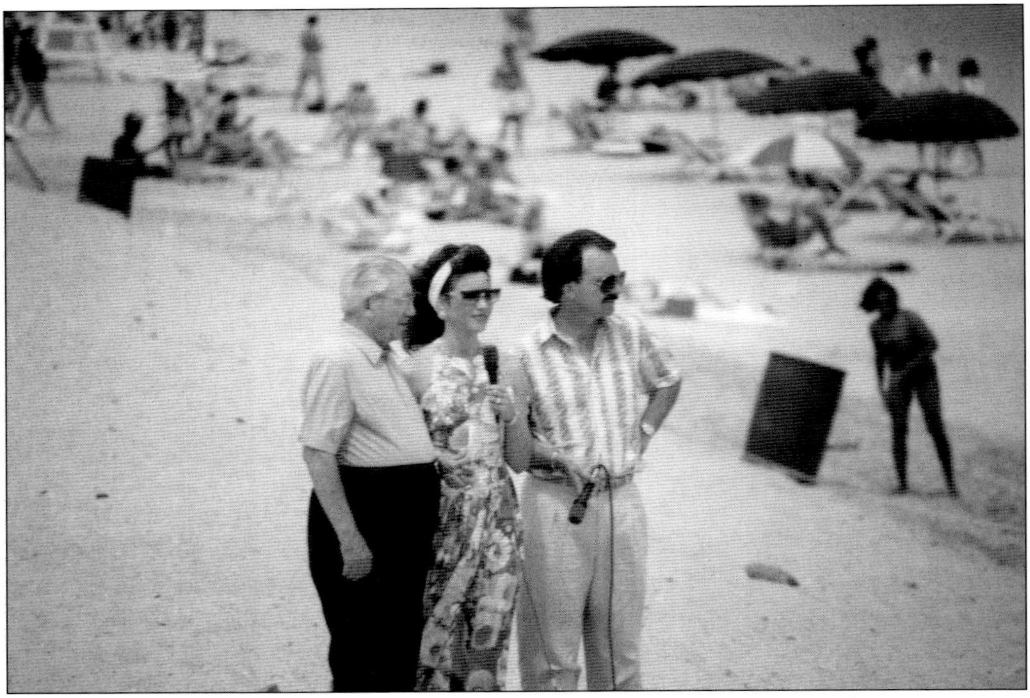

Pavilion general manager and Burroughs Chapin vice president Earl Husted joins Lorianne Crook and Charlie Chase on the beach in back of the Pavilion in 1989. The pair were hosts of the popular country music news television and radio show called *Crook and Chase*. This was Husted's final year as general manager, having worked at the Pavilion more than 50 years. (Courtesy Jimmy Lathan.)

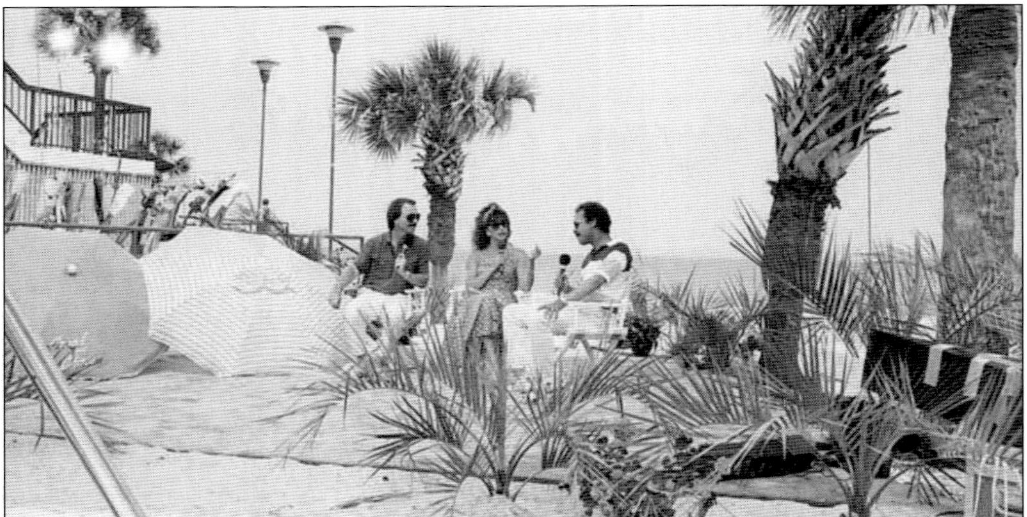

The *Crook and Chase* show originated their program during the Sun Fun Festival from a set built on the back side of the Pavilion. ABC's Spencer Christian appears with them in this photograph. In 1989, the couple was inducted into the South Carolina Boardwalk Hall of Fame, which was located in front of the Pavilion. (Courtesy MBCC.)

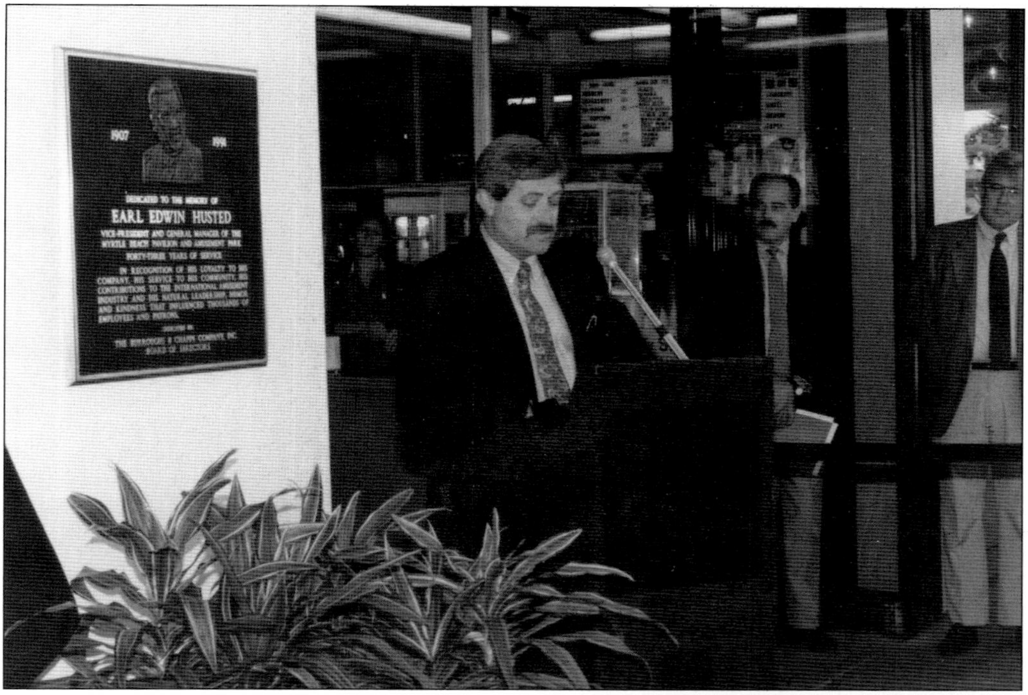

Longtime Pavilion general manager Earl Husted died in 1991. In 1993, general manager Rick Zeckman dedicated a plaque in honor of Husted as Burroughs and Chapin CEO Edgerton Burroughs and vice president of development Bill Pritchard helped mark the occasion. Earl Husted was first hired in 1948 to oversee the Pavilion's concessions and entertainment. He retired as a vice president. (Courtesy Jimmy Lathan.)

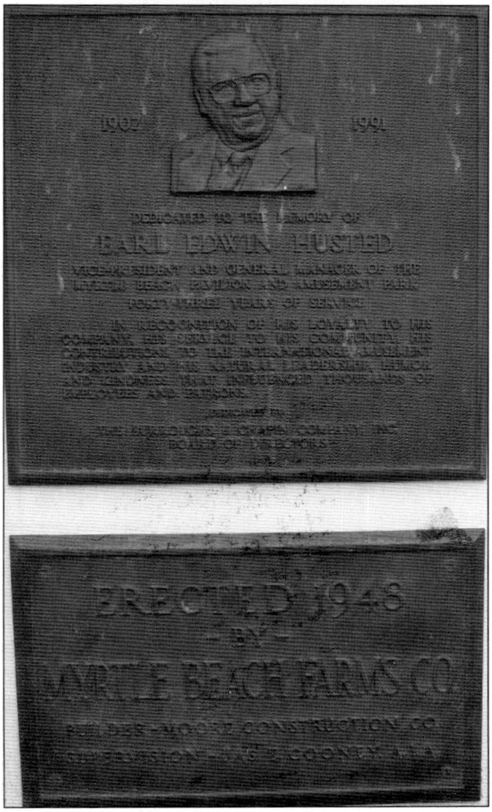

Earl Husted oversaw the growth and development of the Pavilion for over 40 years. He and his brother Sherwin had met Edgar Burroughs in 1949 at the Tobacco Festival in Conway, where their traveling carnival was helping entertain. Burroughs hired Husted and contracted the carnival to entertain at the newly opened Pavilion in 1949. Under Husted, the Pavilion became one of the U.S.'s top amusement parks.

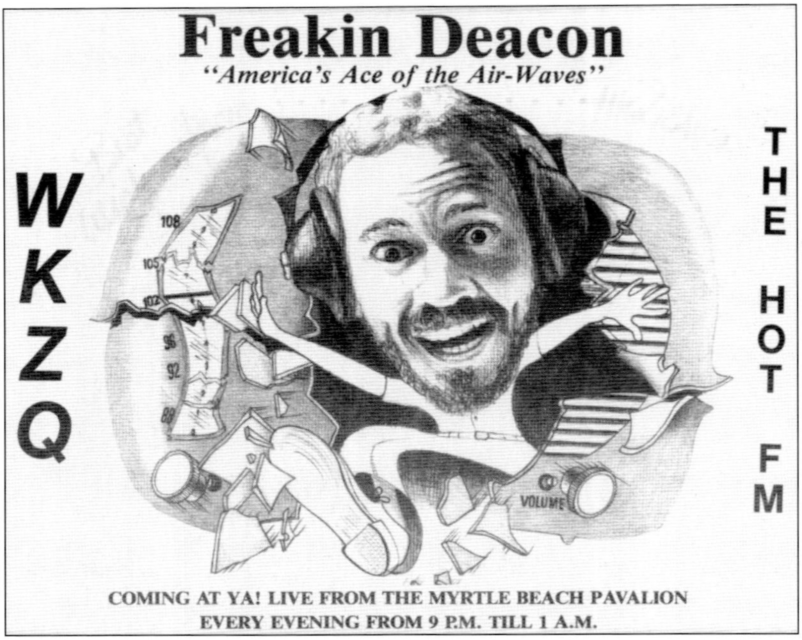

This flier is one of many handed out to Pavilion-goers, inviting people to come by and listen to WKZQ radio's Freakin' Deacon. The Q-Crew and Gary "Deacon" Dawson broadcast live from the Pavilion on a regular basis. Dawson was named *Billboard*'s Radio Personality of the Year in 1983. (Courtesy Gary Dawson.)

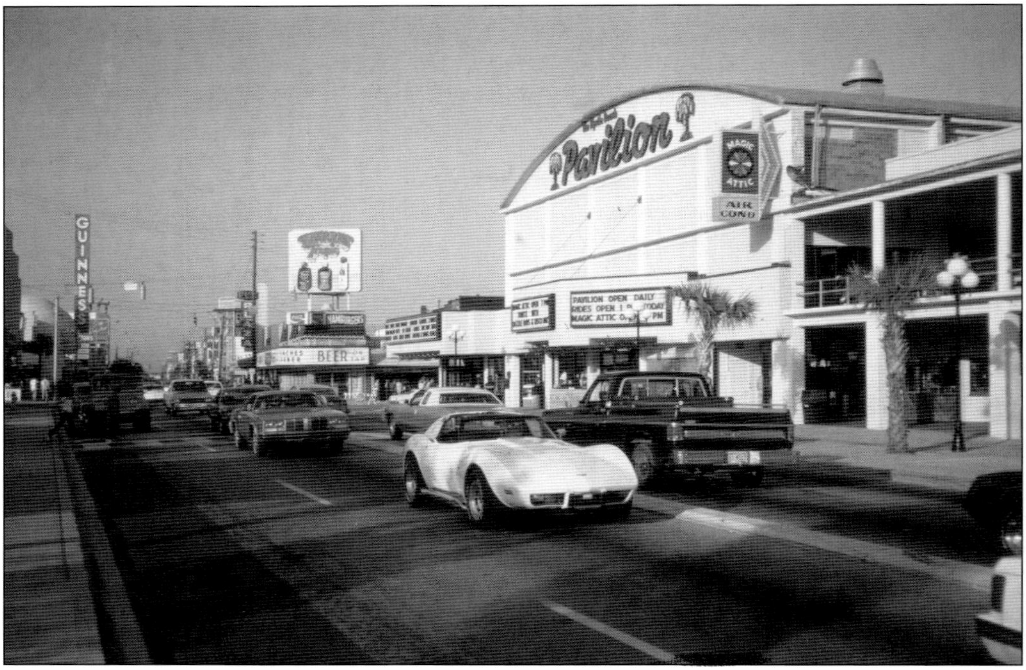

This late-afternoon photograph shows the cars beginning to build up in front of the Pavilion. This strip of road in front of the Pavilion's address of 812 North Ocean Boulevard was known for its cruising. By the time the sun would set, bumper-to-bumper traffic would be creeping along between Eighth and Ninth Avenues North, sometimes taking up to 15 minutes to travel the distance. (Courtesy MBCC.)

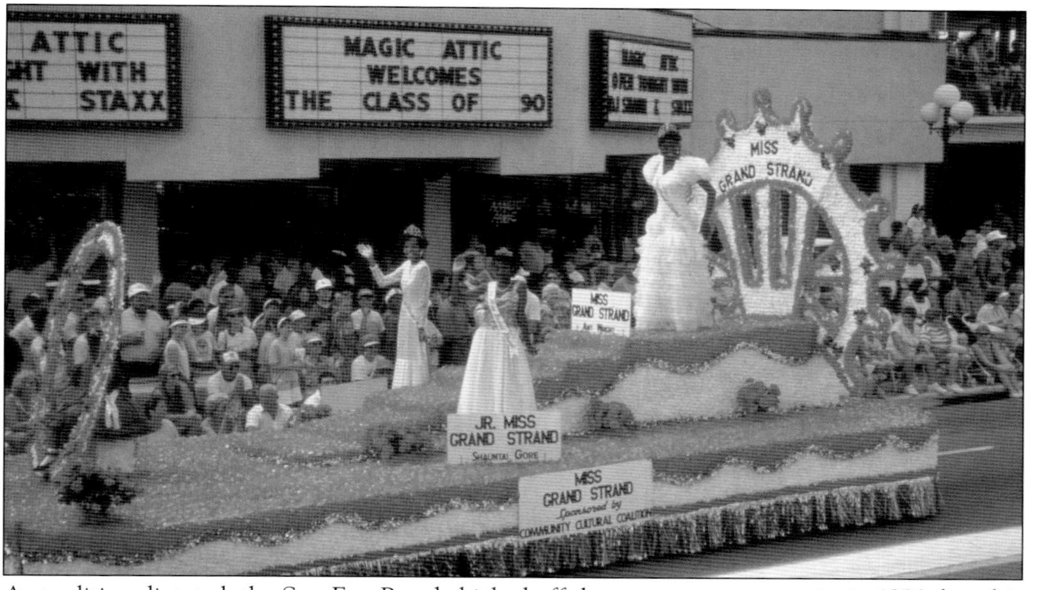

As tradition dictated, the Sun Fun Parade kicked off the summer season again in 1990, but this would be a decade of change for the Pavilion. Owners Burroughs and Chapin were trying to keep up with the times. The Pavilion had gotten a face-lift in the 1980s, and its golden brick had been resurfaced with stucco, but the company felt that far more was needed. (Courtesy MBCC.)

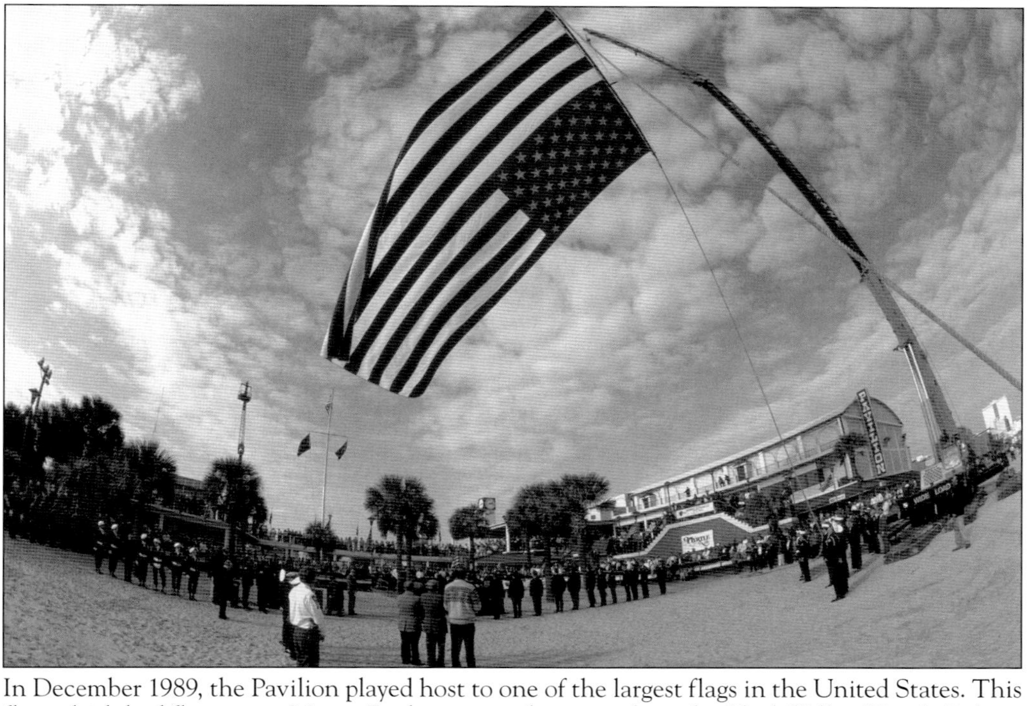

In December 1989, the Pavilion played host to one of the largest flags in the United States. This flag, which had flown atop Mount Rushmore, made its way from the Black Hills of South Dakota to the beaches of South Carolina, where it had to be hoisted via construction crane as veterans and members of the armed forces took part in a ceremony honoring Old Glory. (Photograph by Tim Ribar.)

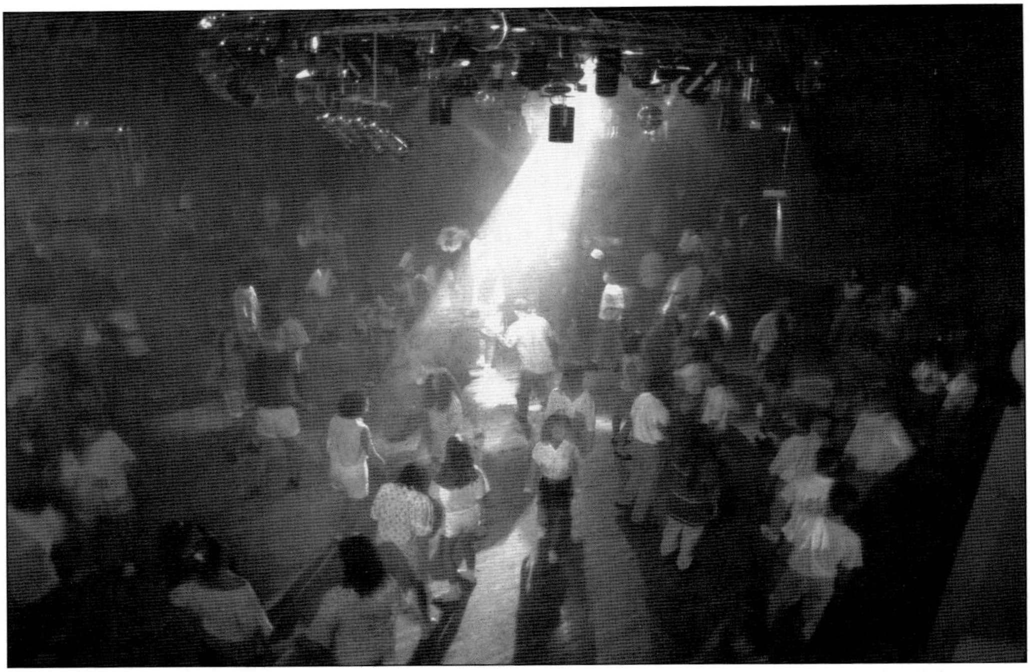

The Magic Attic's name was always one up for debate for employees of the Pavilion. After years of people simply performing at "the Pavilion," the entertainment area was renamed the Magic Attic in reference to its upstairs location. While some employees did not like the term "attic," the name stuck in one form or another until the end. (Courtesy Tim Ribar.)

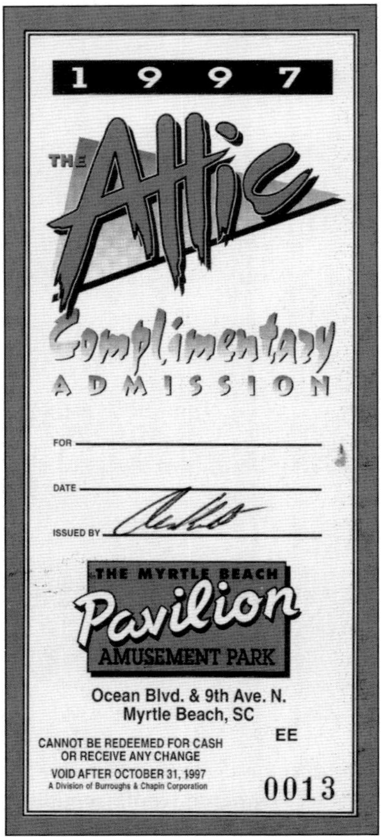

The name Magic Attic was shortened to simply "the Attic" by the early 1990s and was still one of the prime concert venues on the Grand Strand, due largely in part to its location. It was also a place where parents felt safe allowing their kids to attend because there was no alcohol allowed. The no alcohol policy was implemented for the venue when it opened in 1949 and remained. Alcohol was only served during private events. (Courtesy Jimmy Lathan.)

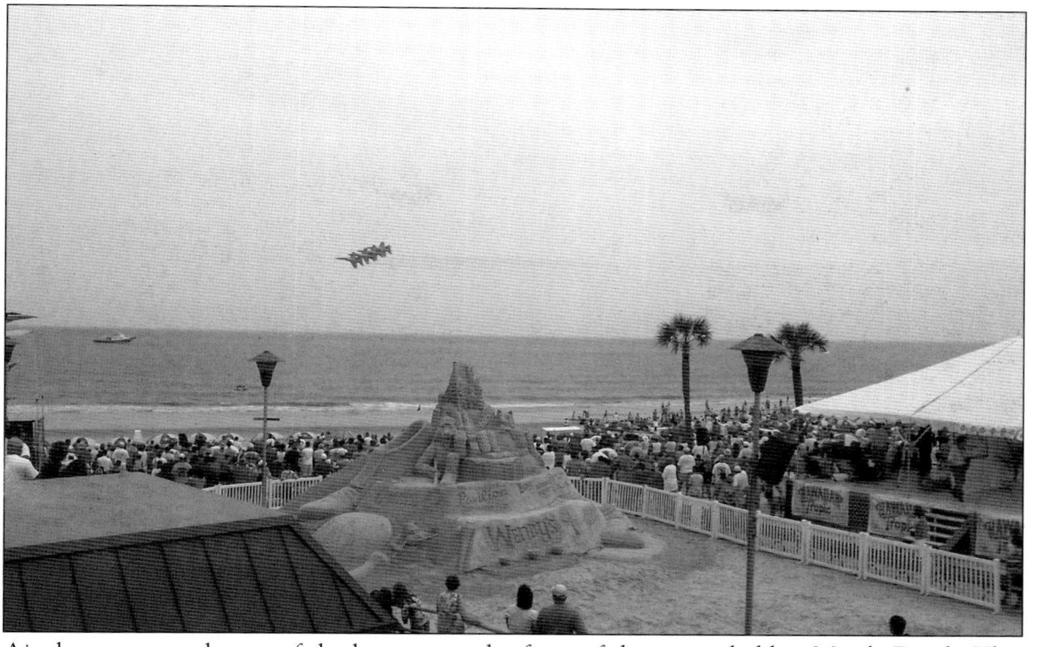

Air shows garnered some of the largest crowds of any of the events held in Myrtle Beach. This 2004 photograph shows the U.S. Navy's Blue Angels precision flying team performing maneuvers over the ocean in back of the Pavilion during the Sun Fun Festival. Over the years, there were also shows conducted by the U.S. Air Force's Thunderbirds and the U.S. Army's Golden Knights parachute team.

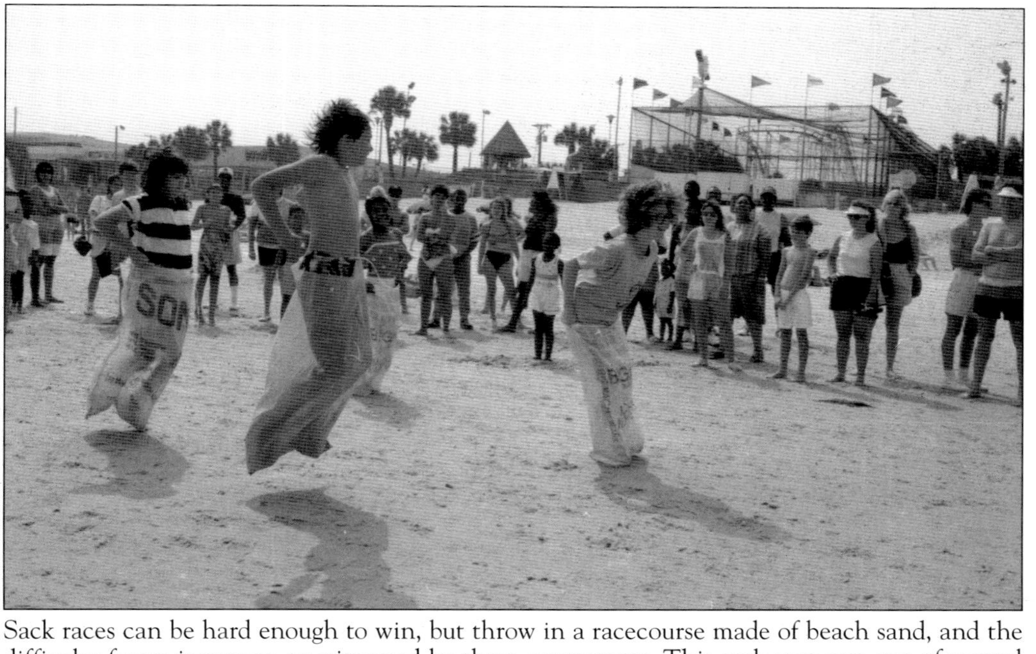

Sack races can be hard enough to win, but throw in a racecourse made of beach sand, and the difficulty factor increases, as witnessed by these contestants. This sack race was one of several family friendly competitions that the Myrtle Beach Chamber of Commerce would regularly sponsor during their festivals. (Courtesy MBCC.)

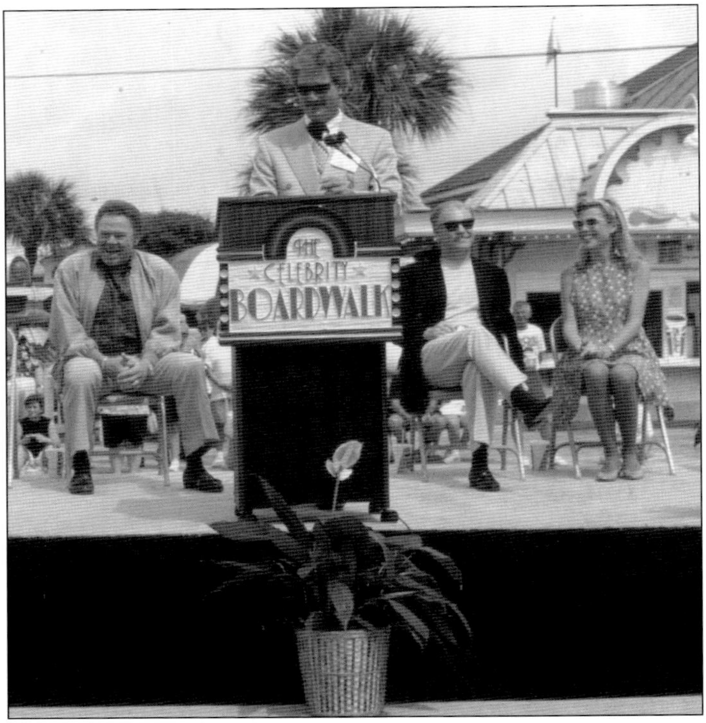

Myrtle Beach Chamber of Commerce official Carson Benton presided as television personality Vanna White, Carolina Opry founder Calvin Gilmore, and country music star Roy Clark were inducted into the Walk of Fame at the Pavilion in 1986. White is a native of North Myrtle Beach, and Clark played concerts at the beach countless times. (Courtesy CML.)

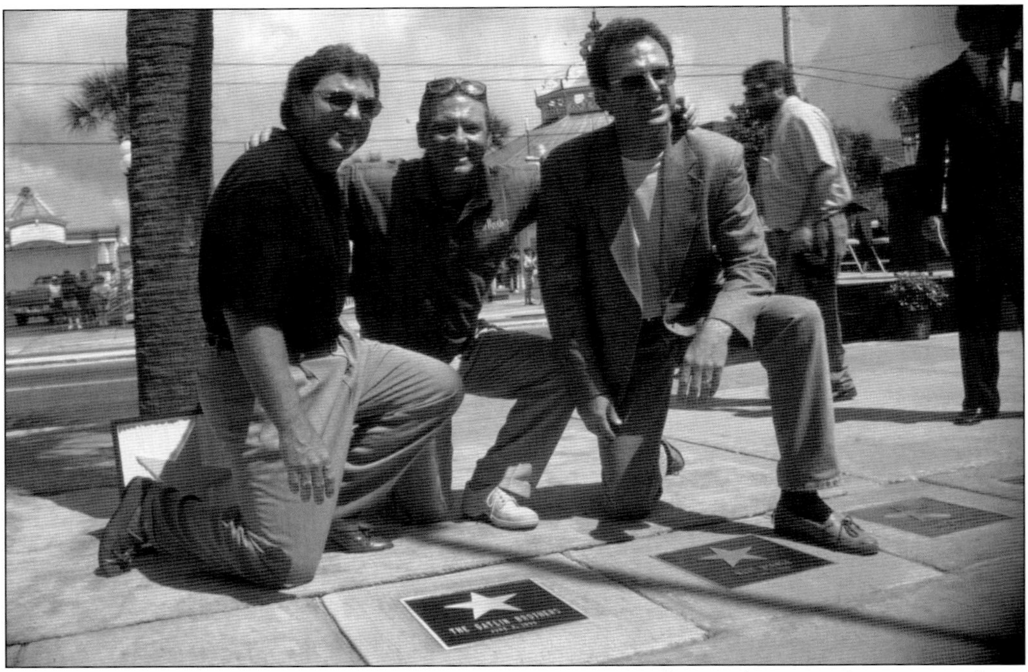

The Gatlin Brothers, who for a time had a theater in Myrtle Beach, were also among those honored by the Walk of Fame. Styled after the Hollywood Walk of Fame, inductees received a plaque in the sidewalk along Ocean Boulevard in front of the Pavilion. When the Pavilion was torn down, the plaques were removed. (Courtesy MBCC.)

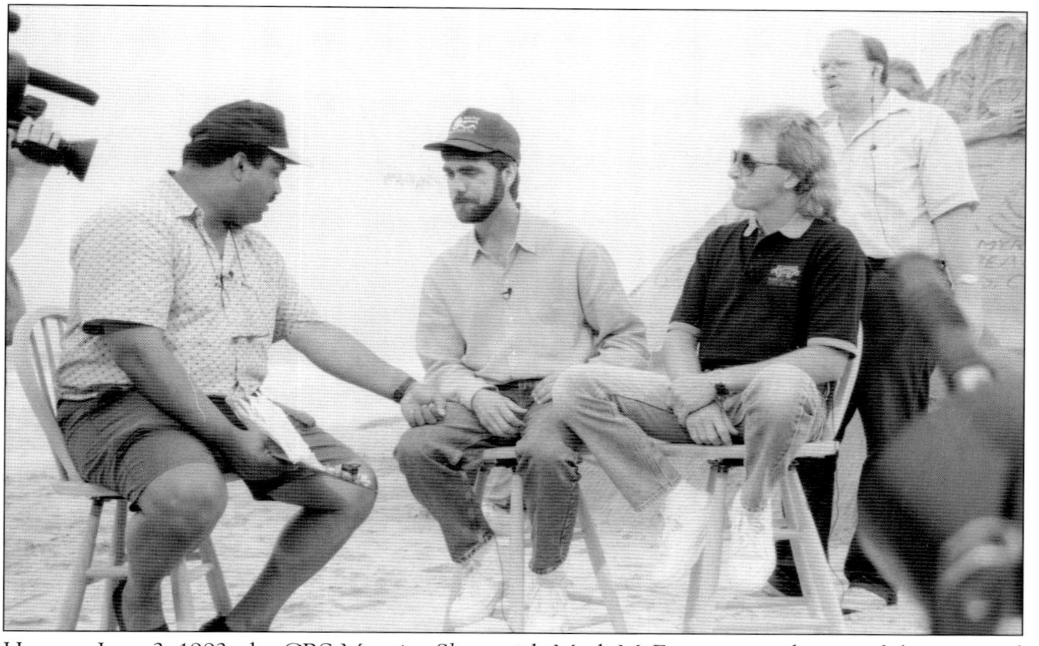

Here on June 3, 1993, the CBS *Morning Show* with Mark McEwen was only one of the national television shows that broadcast live from the Pavilion. Over the years, every major network sent crews to cover events at the Pavilion. The Travel Channel regularly listed the Pavilion as a top family travel destination. (Courtesy MBCC.)

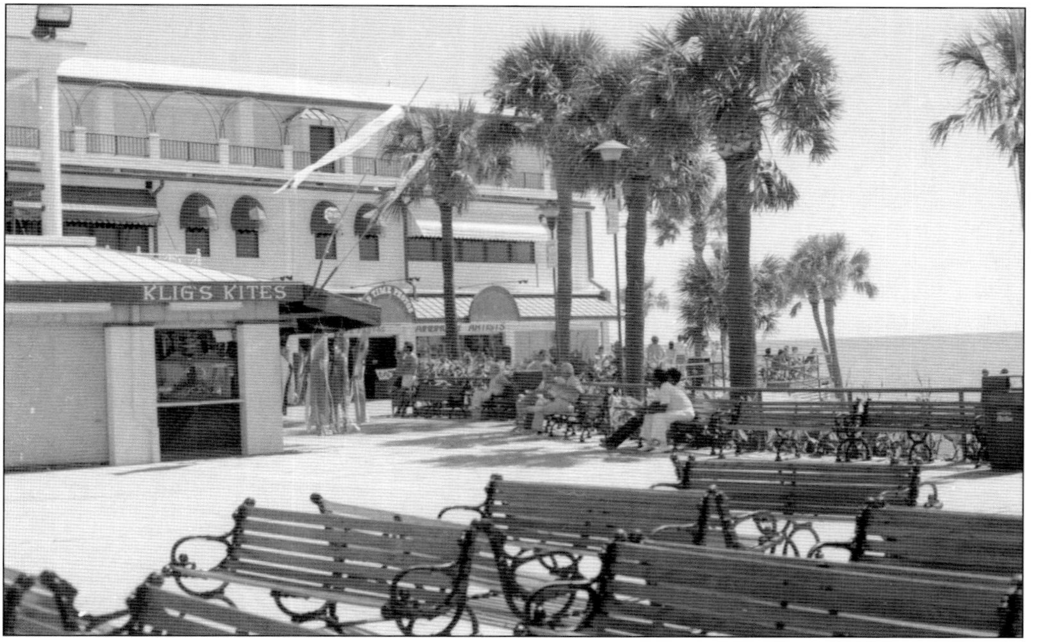

The arcades and amusements of the Pavilion were not restricted to those housed inside its huge structure. This photograph from the 1990s shows how over the years vendors such as Klig's Kites, the Silver Mine, and other souvenir businesses had opened shops lining the exterior walls of the Pavilion's courtyard area. (Courtesy MBCC.)

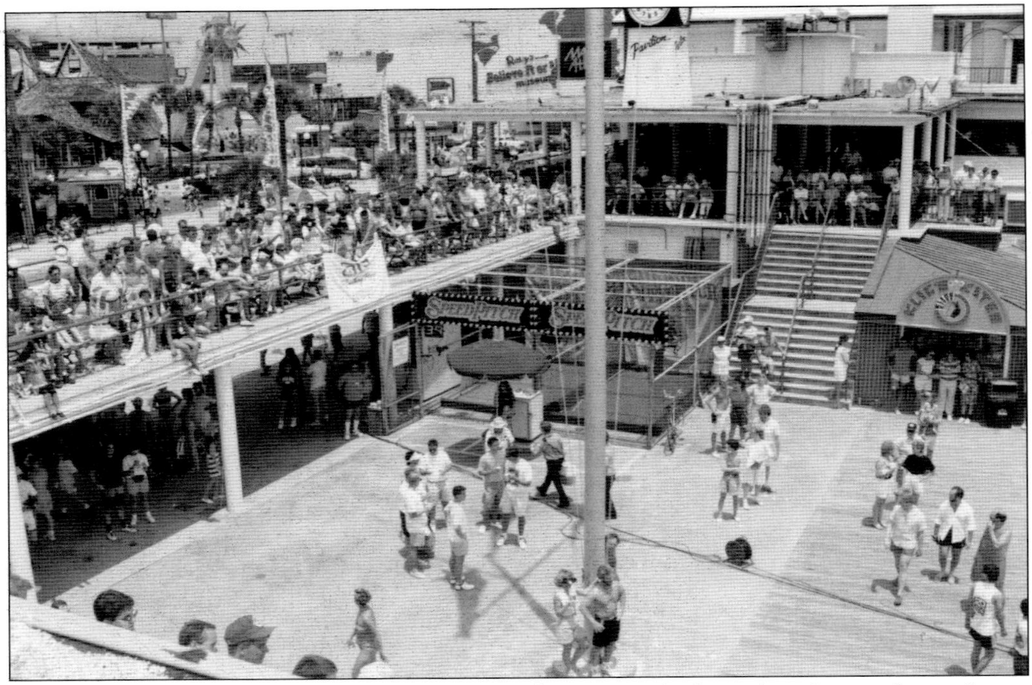

Part of the enduring appeal of the Pavilion was how it was laid out, based on architect James Cooney's design for optimum entertainment opportunities. Having the U-shaped upper deck allowed people on two levels to enjoy events taking place on either side of the building. The boardwalk area at the back of the Pavilion was always a coveted place to stage events. (Courtesy Jimmy Lathan.)

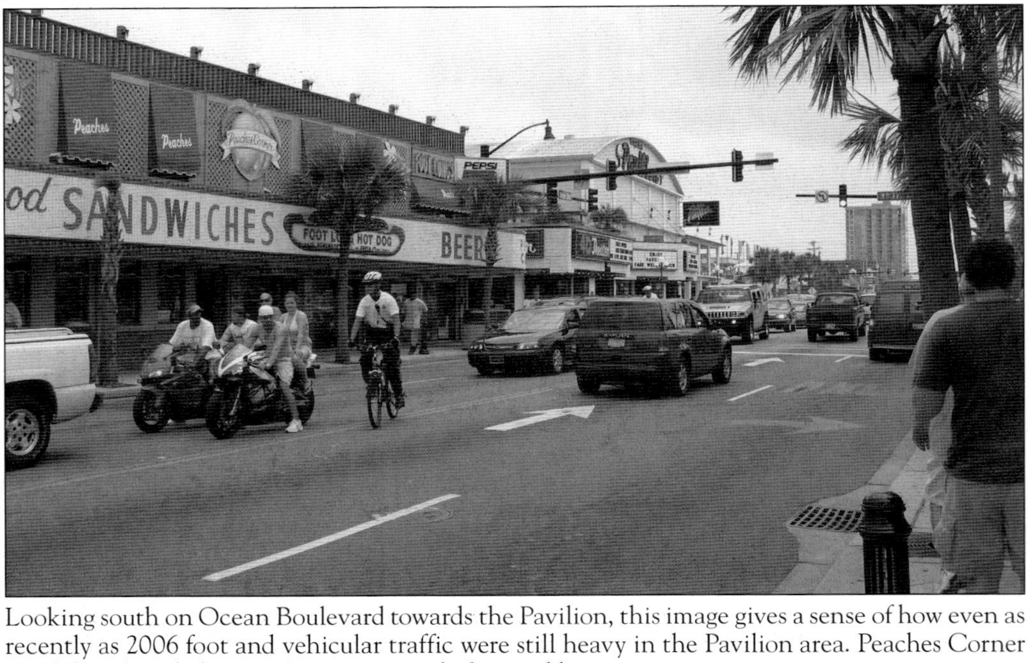

Looking south on Ocean Boulevard towards the Pavilion, this image gives a sense of how even as recently as 2006 foot and vehicular traffic were still heavy in the Pavilion area. Peaches Corner snack bar, founded in 1935, is prominently featured here.

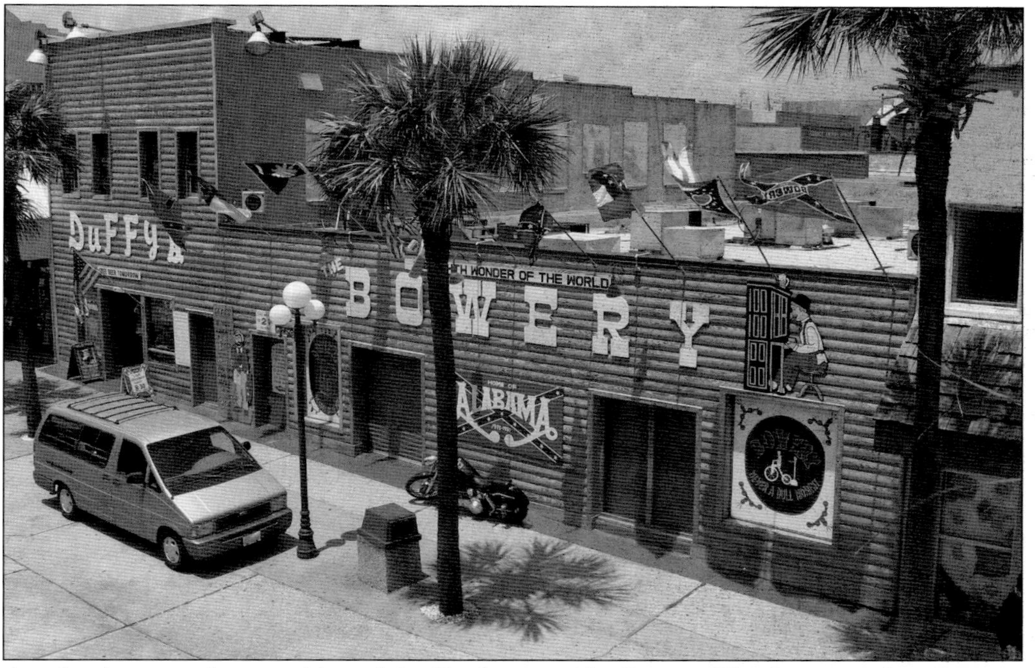

Another long-standing neighbor of the Pavilion was the Bowery. This bar opened its doors in 1944 and has hosted countless bands and served innumerable drinks. Its claim to fame, however, is that country music hall-of-famers Alabama got their start here as a house band in the 1970s.

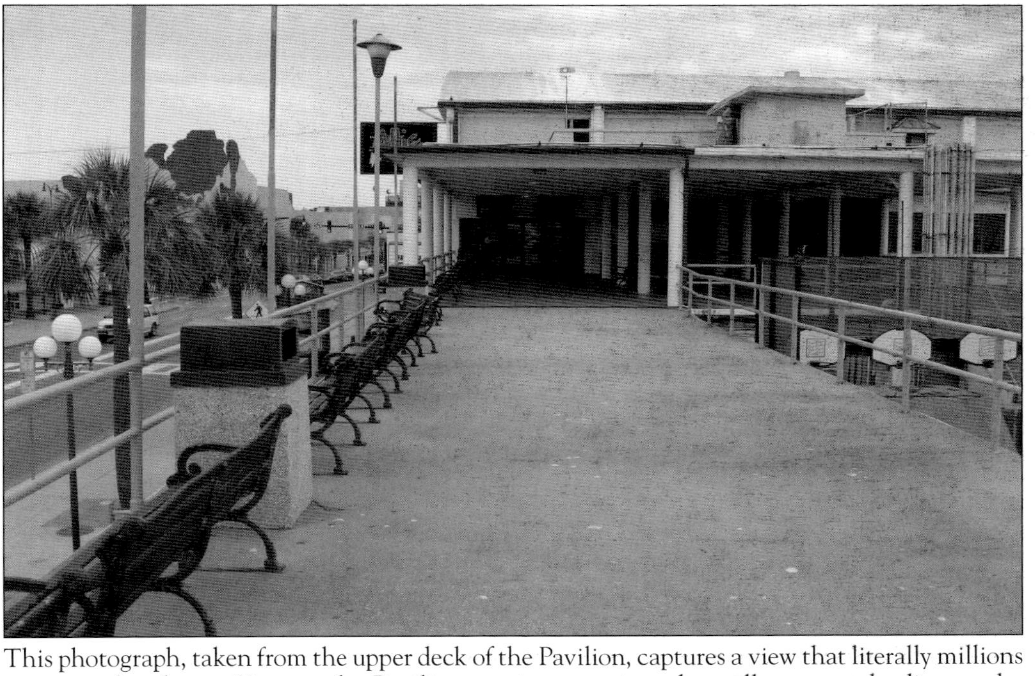

This photograph, taken from the upper deck of the Pavilion, captures a view that literally millions saw over the almost 60 years the Pavilion was in operation: the walkway area leading to the entertainment venue known as the Magic Attic (later the Attic). Over the decades, hundreds of bands performed here. (Photograph by Wayne Aiken.)

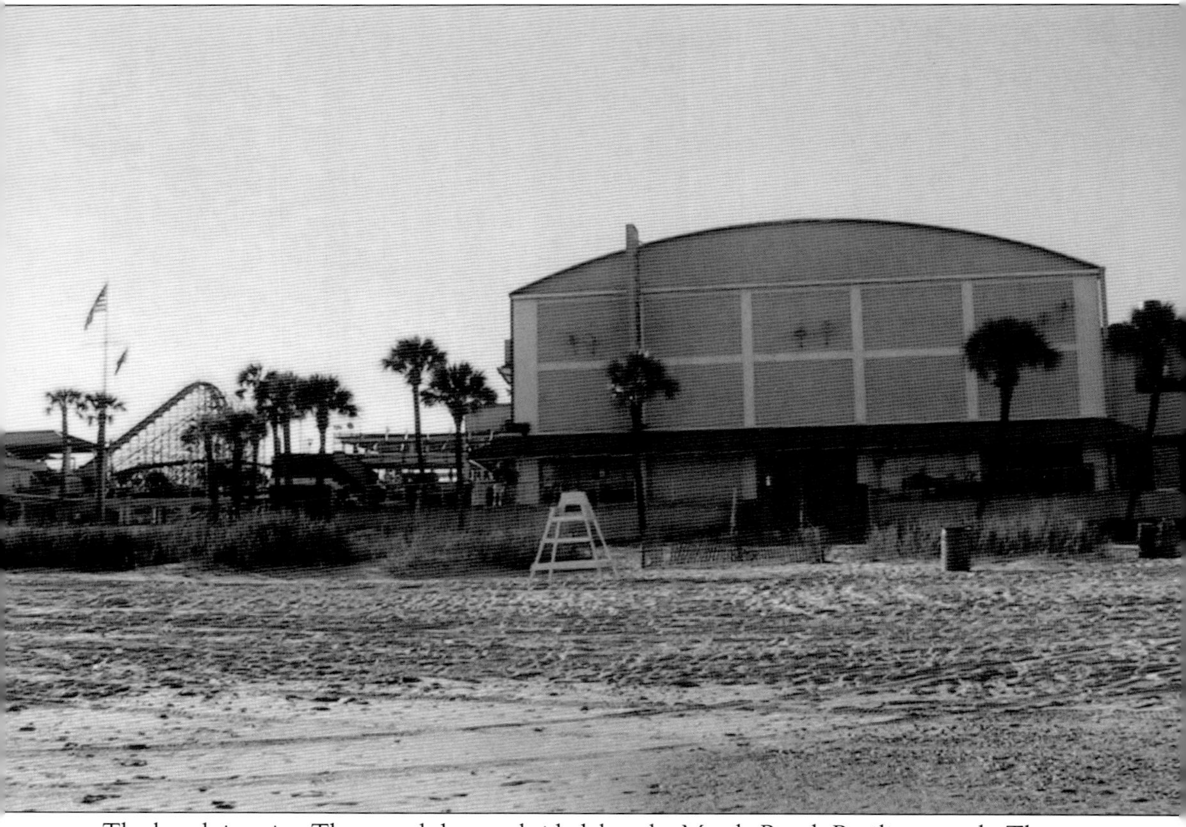

The beach is quiet. The crowds have subsided, but the Myrtle Beach Pavilion stands. The empty beach foreshadows what lies in store for this iconic structure. Some talked of the building as if it were a living and breathing thing. By the time this photograph was taken, the Pavilion was being readied to say good-bye. (Photograph by Wayne Aiken.)

Three
The Rides

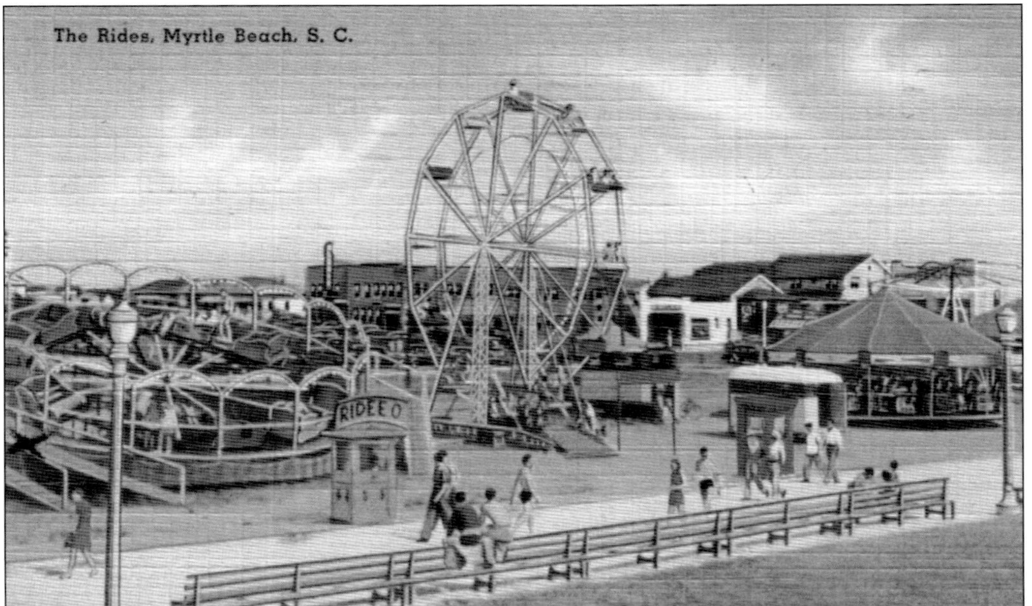

This postcard from 1943 shows some of the early amusements associated with the Pavilion. They included a Ferris wheel, carousel, a car ride, and bumper cars. Even in the 1940s after the third Pavilion burned, the rides remained in operation and were a popular attraction for beachgoers, whose numbers were increasing with each season.

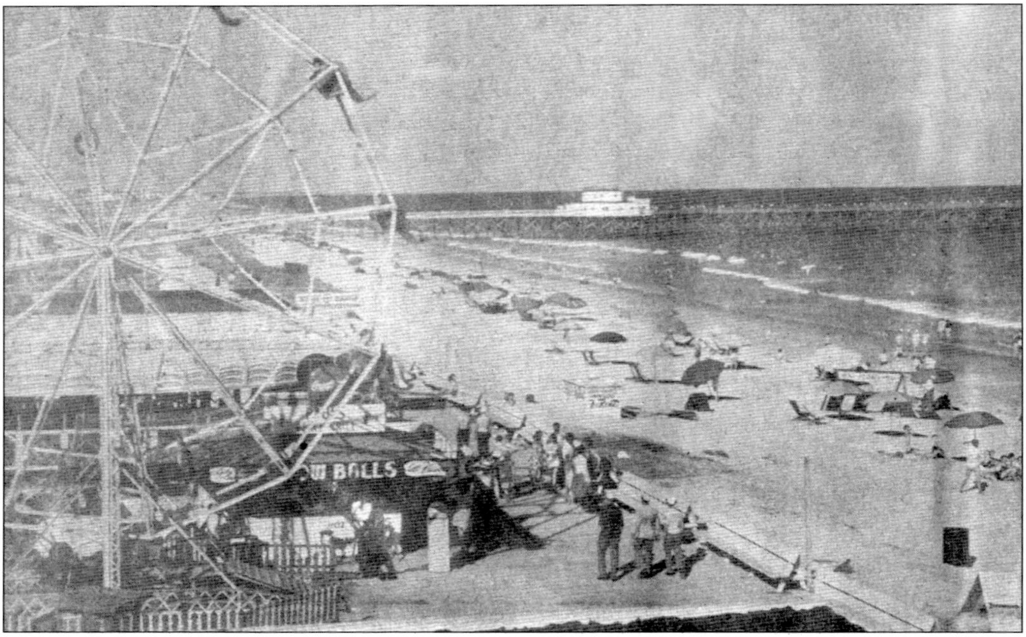

The Pavilion rides that were becoming so increasingly popular in the 1940s did not belong to Myrtle Beach Farms. They belonged to Harry Beach, who paid the company a commission for using the land. While the next and final Pavilion was being built, plans were being laid for Myrtle Beach Farms to own its own rides. (Courtesy HCHS.)

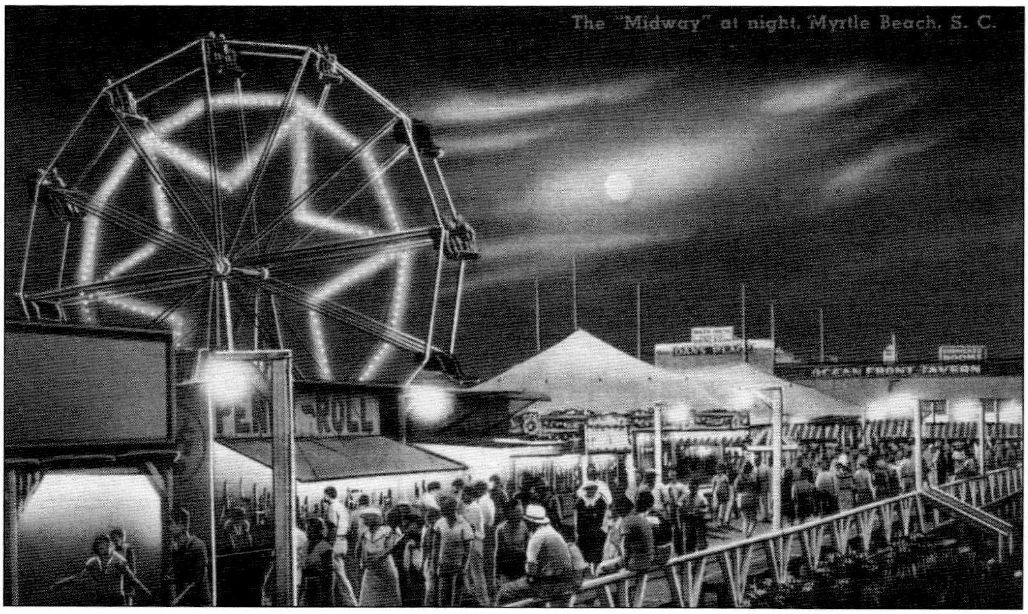

At night, the midway of the amusement park would come alive. Without a Pavilion for listening to music and dancing, visitors found themselves here instead. The arcades depicted in this rendering were makeshift booths and not permanent fixtures. Myrtle Beach was growing, but for many, this amusement area was still within walking distance. (Courtesy Burroughs and Chapin Company, Inc.)

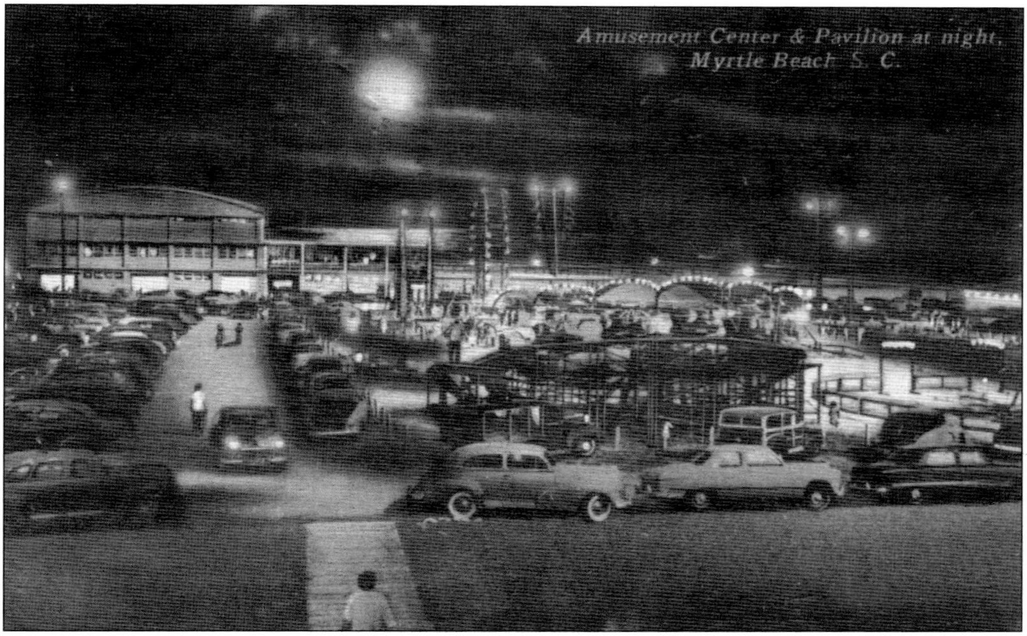

This photograph was likely taken in 1948, during the Pavilion's first season in operation. It reflects the layout of the rides at that time. While the Pavilion was being constructed, Edward Burroughs had discovered a traveling carnival at the Tobacco Festival in Conway. He made a deal with owners Earl and Sherwin Husted to relocate their carnival and rides to the Pavilion. (Courtesy Burroughs and Chapin Company, Inc..)

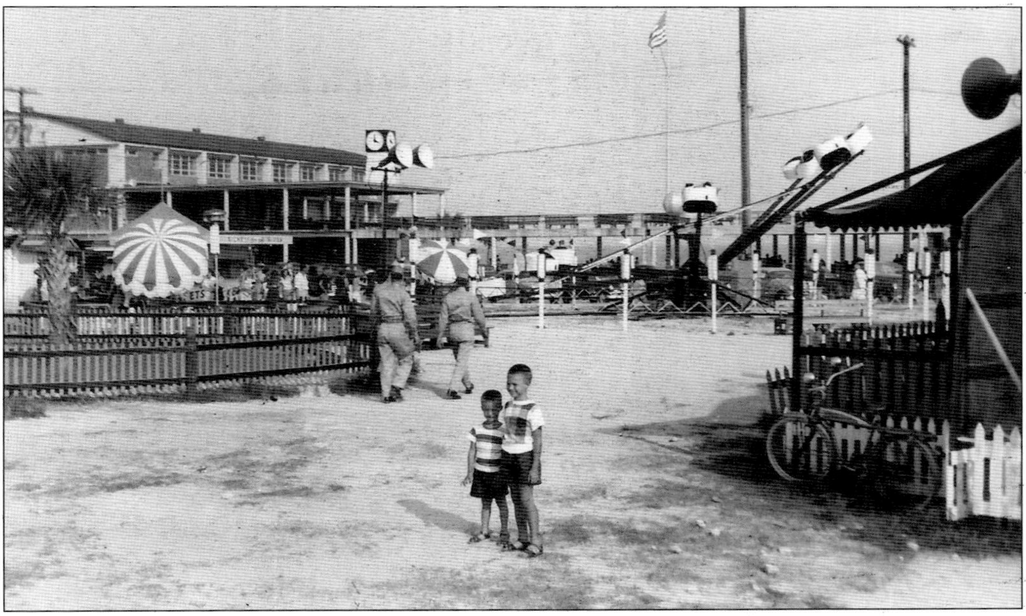

The Pavilion and its park were just a few years old when Carl and Weyman McDonald made this visit. Even though the Husteds' rides movement to the Pavilion site was considered permanent, many of those rides were moved from year to year within the park to accommodate the addition of the new amusements. (Courtesy Dorothy McDonald.)

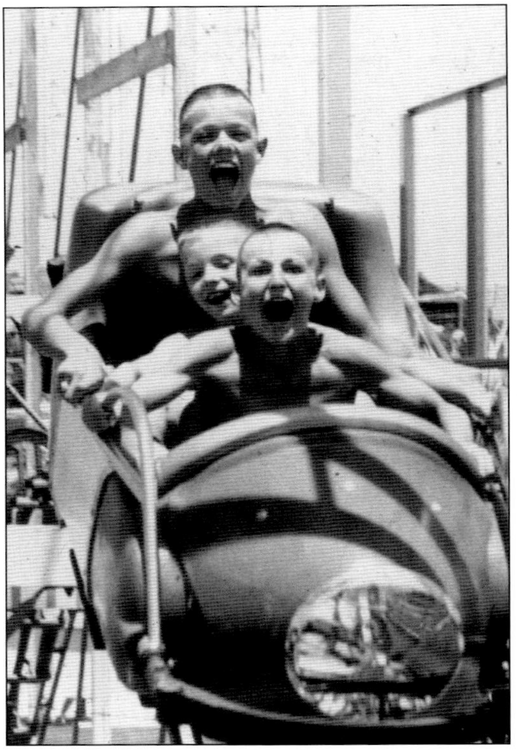

The Comet, the first roller coaster at the Pavilion, was added in 1950. By then, Myrtle Beach Farms had bought out the Husted brothers' Central Amusement Company (CAC). The CAC's 14 rides were brought in to enlarge the amusement park, which had been given the name "Kiddie Land." It took 38 trucks to relocate the rides, and Earl Husted was hired to manage the Pavilion. (Courtesy MBCC.)

The Herschell-Spillman carousel below was among the first permanent fixtures at the park. (Courtesy CML.)

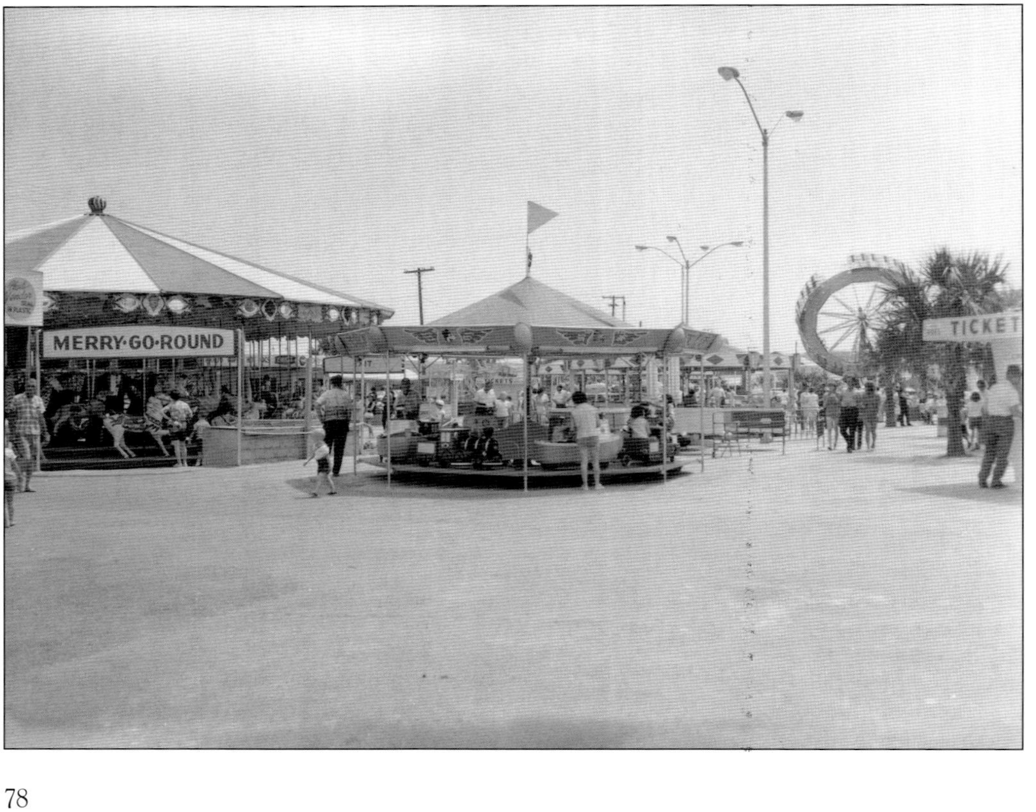

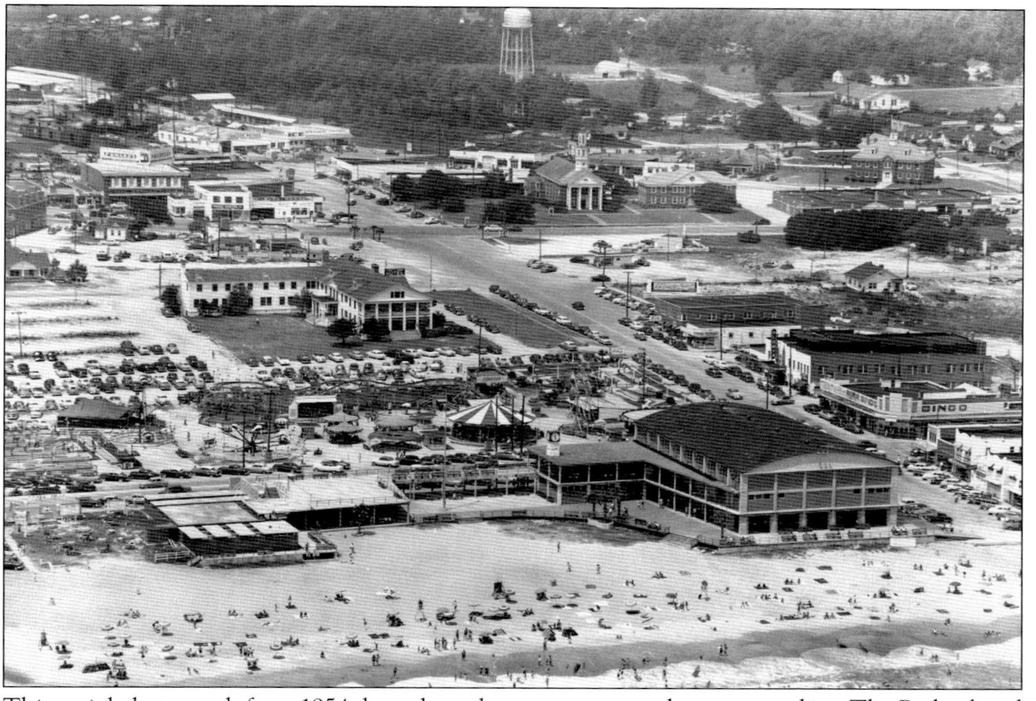

This aerial photograph from 1954 shows how the amusement park was expanding. The Baden band organ and Herschell-Spillman carousel are both visible. Mark Garner, who took the photograph, was the publisher of the Myrtle Beach *Sun News* and a big promoter of Myrtle Beach. Garner also served as the first executive secretary of the Myrtle Beach Chamber of Commerce in 1948 and later was mayor. (Courtesy CML.)

This lion water fountain was added to the park after the area was paved in the early 1950s. Before then, the grounds were dirt to accommodate the fact that most of the rides were still considered portable. The lion fountain moved several times but was always a feature that visitors would seek out. There were also hippo and alligator fountains. (Courtesy CML.)

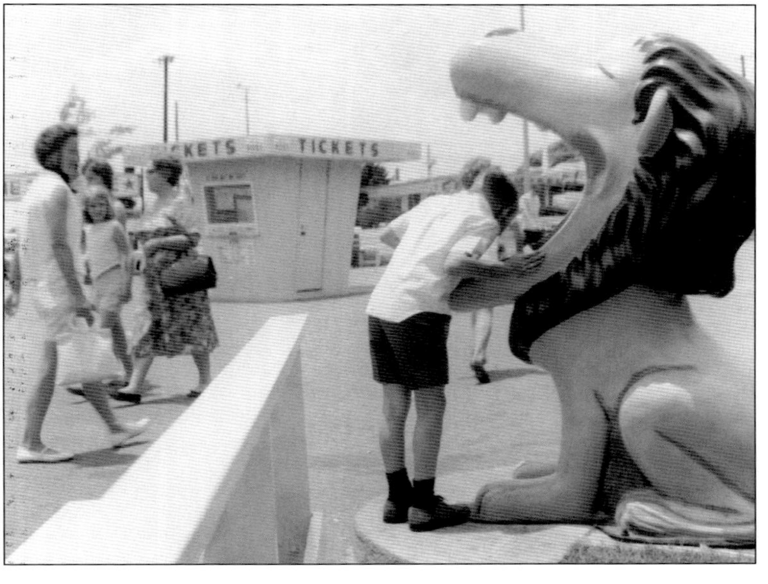

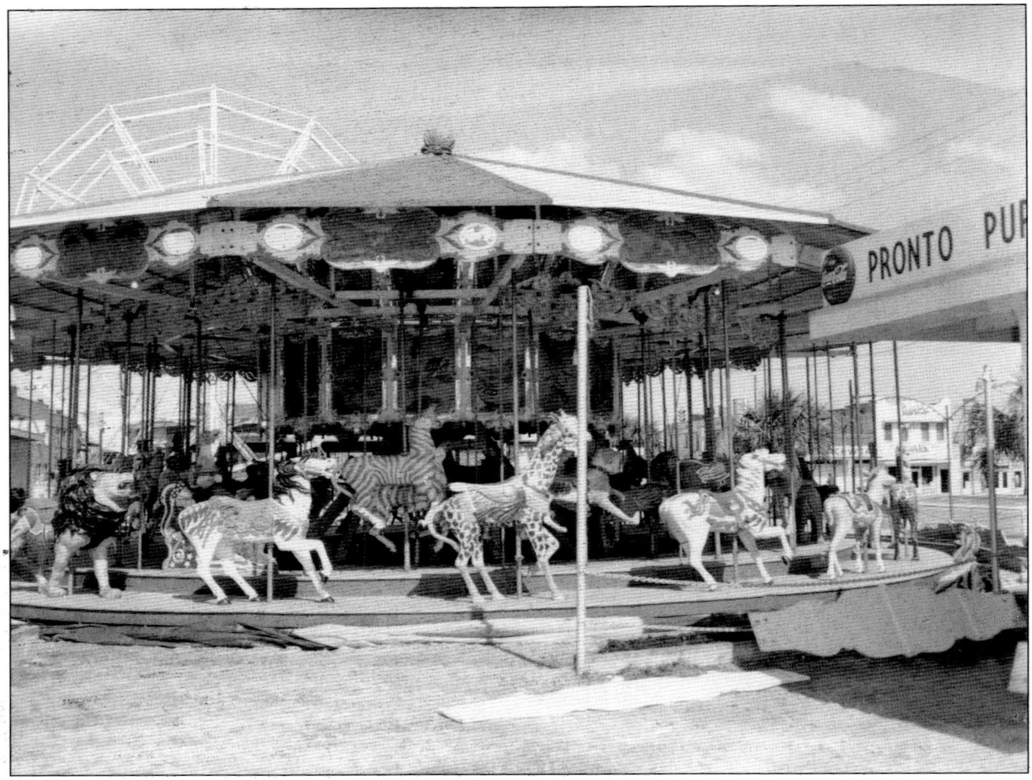

When it first arrived in Myrtle Beach in 1950, the Herschell-Spillman carousel was simply referred to as the "merry-go-round." It replaced a smaller carousel that had been part of the earlier midway on the oceanfront. Built in 1912, the original owners are not known. Myrtle Beach Farms purchased it from Oxford Lake Park near Anderson, Alabama. Each of the 50 figurines and two chariots on the two-tiered carousel was hand carved. (Courtesy CML.)

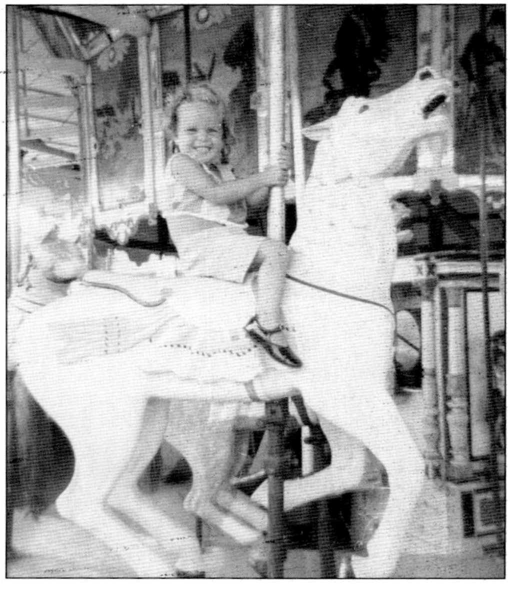

Horses on the carousel consist of 16 jumpers and 11 standers. The 23 menagerie figures include pairs of elephants, dogs, pigs, roosters, ostriches, cats, frogs, and zebras, as well as a tiger, a giraffe, a camel, a deer, a dragon, a lion, and an elk. By the ringing of a bell, riders would be warned that the carousel was about to start. A 1920s Wurlitzer organ provided the music. (Courtesy Susan Nuckles Williams.)

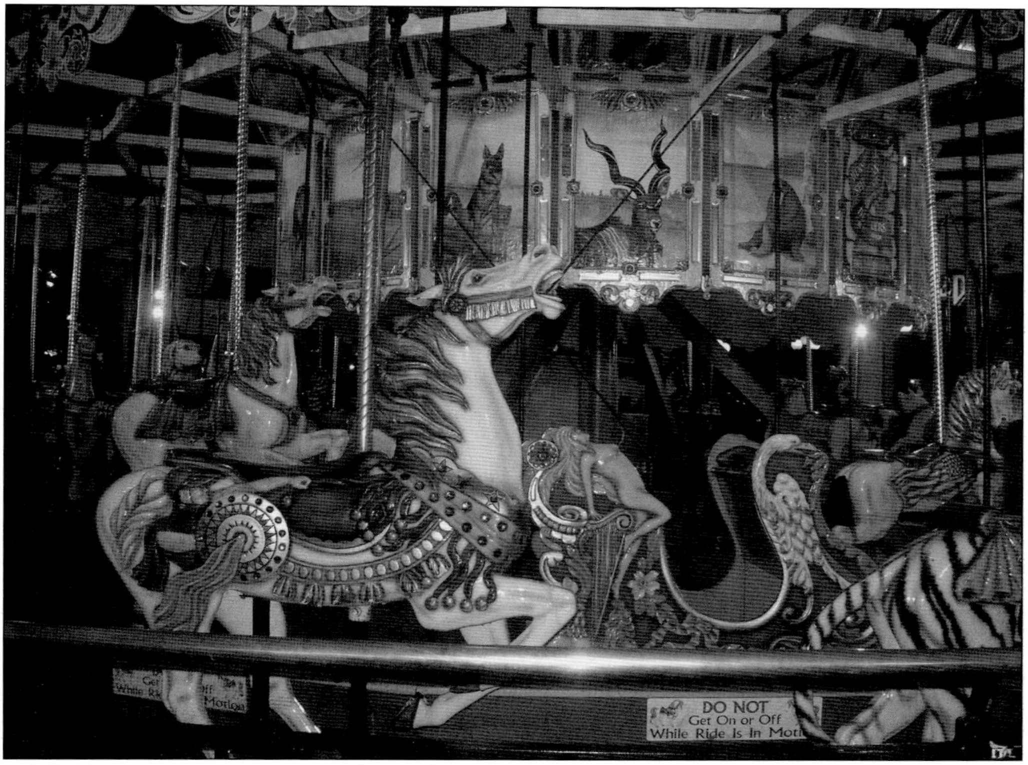

While there may not seem an order to this series of animals, there is, in fact, a lead horse to be followed. Carousel tradition dictates that the lead horse be found on the outside row. For the Pavilion's carousel, the elaborately decorated lead horse sports a jeweled breast plate and a shield. (Photograph by Anna Boyce.)

The Herschell-Spillman Company employed about 300 artisans who hand carved all of the figures for its carousels. Operating between 1900 and the mid-1920s, the company was said to produce a carousel a day. There are only 15 Herschell-Spillman carousels still in operation in the United States, and the Pavilion's was considered the most elaborate. The Pavilion's carousel is now located at the Pavilion Nostalgia Park at Broadway at the Beach.

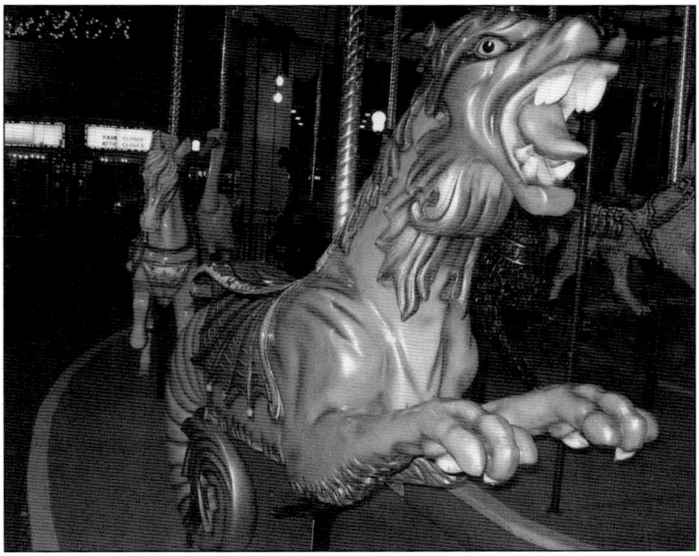

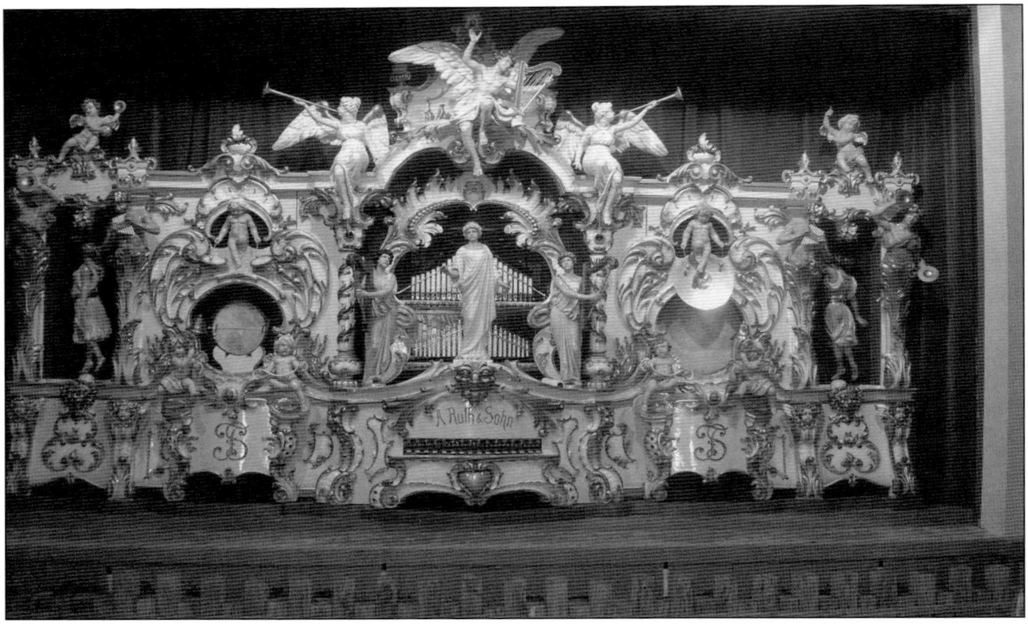

An enduring favorite of the Pavilion Park from 1954 was the Baden band organ. Constructed in 1900 at Waldkrich in Bayden, Germany, by A. Ruth and Sohn, it was a featured attraction of the World Exposition in Paris, France. After returning to Germany, it was used as traveling entertainment throughout the countryside. Carried on a large wagon drawn by six horses, the organ would play music as townspeople listened and danced. (Courtesy Burroughs and Chapin Company, Inc.)

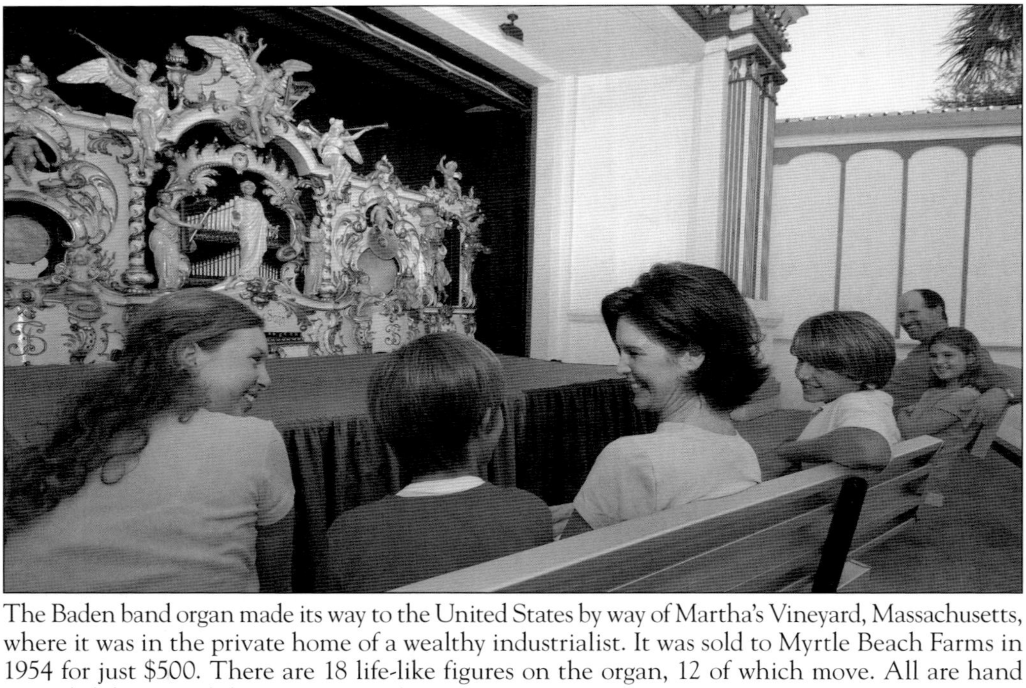

The Baden band organ made its way to the United States by way of Martha's Vineyard, Massachusetts, where it was in the private home of a wealthy industrialist. It was sold to Myrtle Beach Farms in 1954 for just \$500. There are 18 life-like figures on the organ, 12 of which move. All are hand carved. (Photograph by Anna Boyce.)

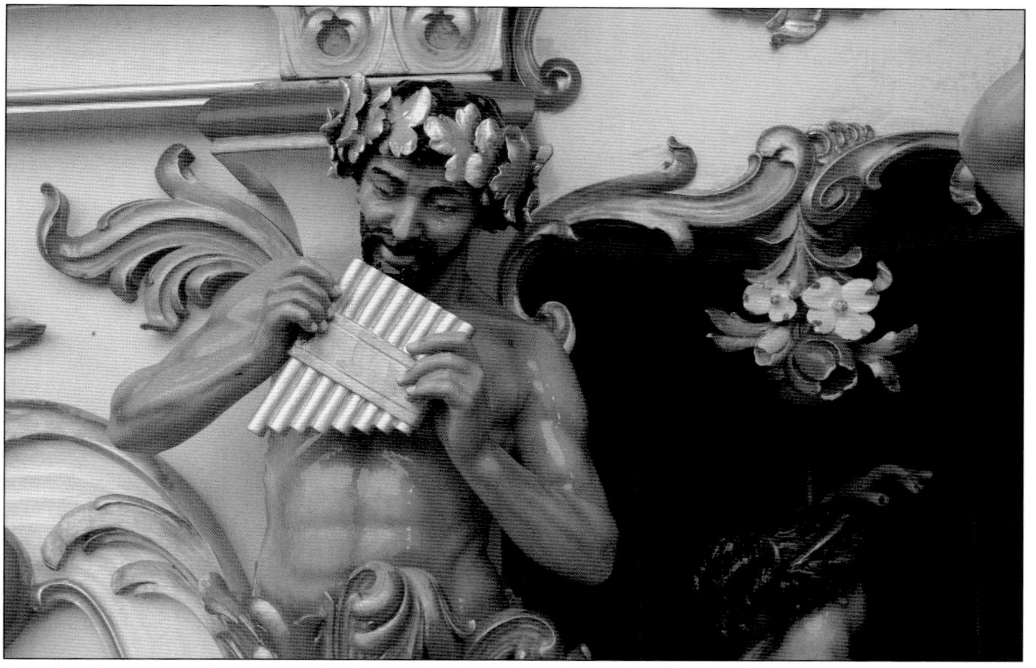

A mile of music cards came with the Baden band organ, and it still uses the same original cardboard sheet music that arrived with it in Myrtle Beach in 1954. The organ weighs approximately 2 tons. It stands 11 feet high, is 20 feet long, and 7 feet deep.

The 400 pipes, 98 keys, and 12 moving figures of the organ originally operated by a massive hand-turned wheel. The compressed air that plays the music and twirls the dance figures now runs by electric motor. Listed on the National Register of Historic Places, the organ was relocated to the Pavilion Nostalgia Park.

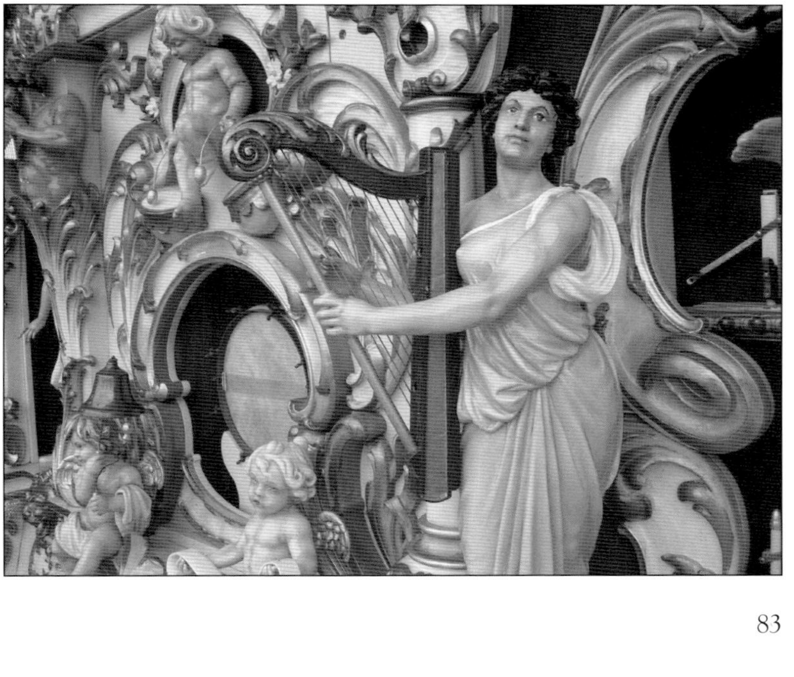

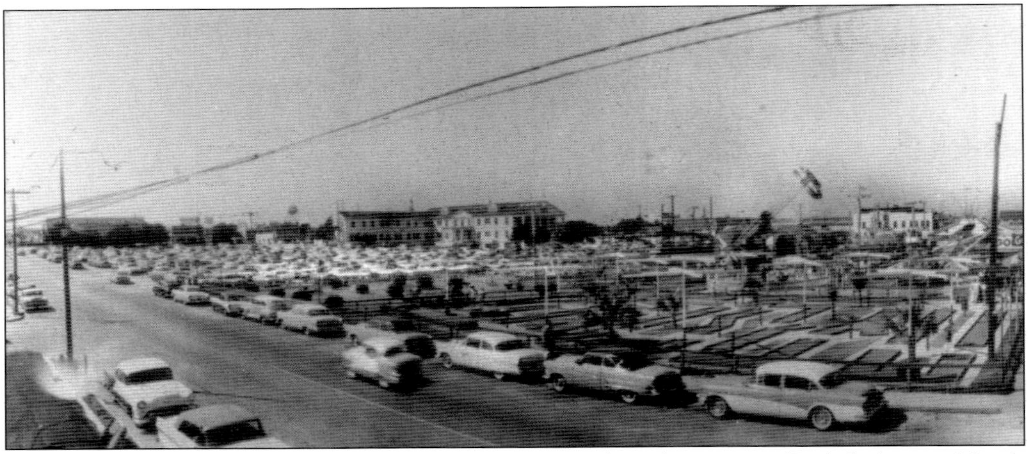

A miniature golf course was added to the amusement park at the corner of Eighth Avenue North and Ocean Boulevard soon after the ride expansion. The first carpet golf course in town had been on the corner of Ninth Avenue North and Kings Highway. The Pavilion course was simply called Putt-Putt Golf, and admission to golf was separate from riding the rides. (Courtesy MBCC.)

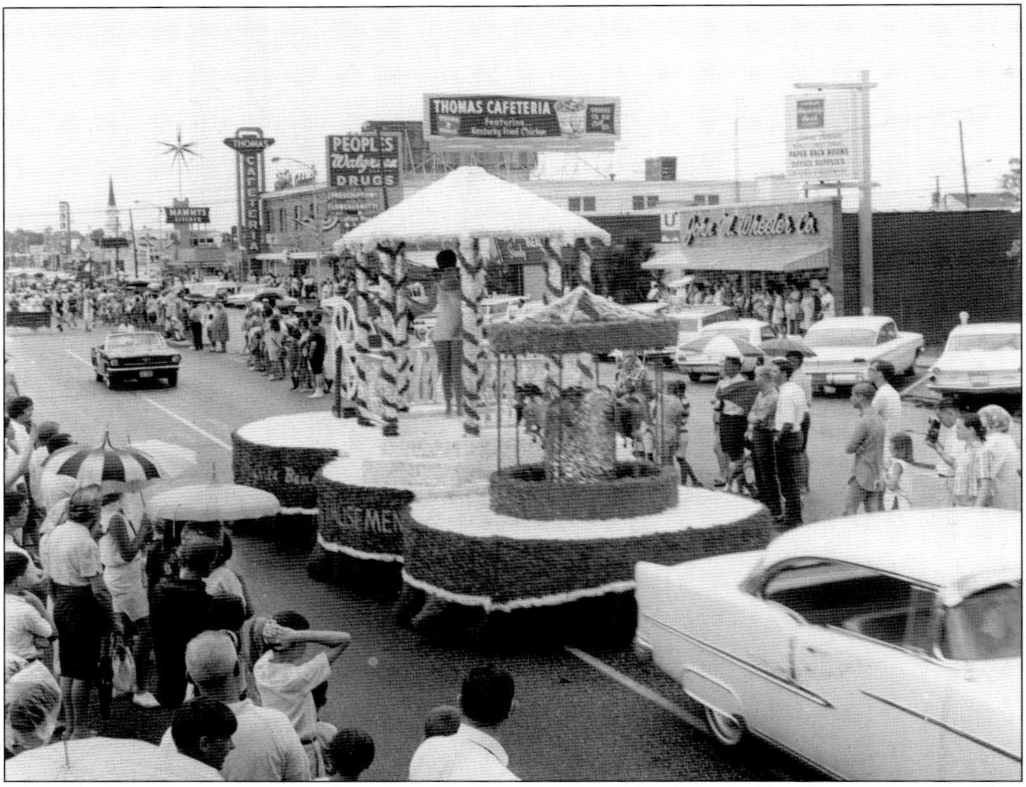

The Pavilion Amusement Park was very much a part of the Myrtle Beach community. This Pavilion float is shown during one of the first Sun Fun Parades in the mid-1950s. The location of the picture was on Kings Highway between Ninth and Tenth Avenues North, just three blocks from the park itself. (Courtesy CML.)

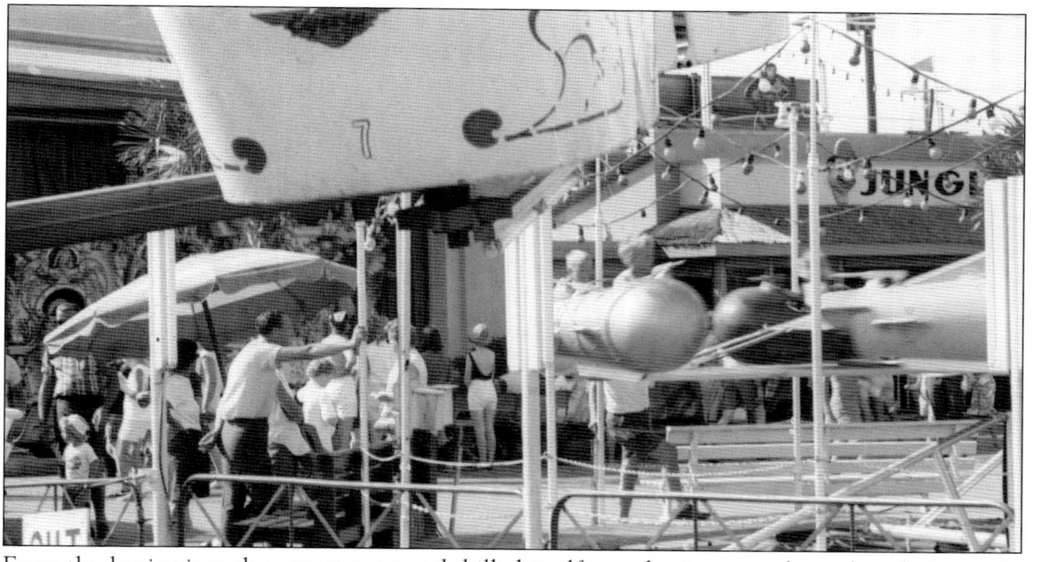

From the beginning, the amusement park billed itself as a destination where the whole family could have fun. For much of the late 1950s and 1960s, the amusement or ride area was simply called "Kiddie Land." While the more daring rides like the roller coasters, the Scrambler, and the Tilt-a-Whirl were for teens and adults, a handful of rides were dedicated entirely to the younger set. They included this boat ride and spaceship ride, along with a miniature roller coaster and even—at one time—a kid-sized Ferris wheel. The boat ride was one of the most enduring and has been relocated to the Pavilion Nostalgia Park at Broadway at the Beach. (Below, courtesy Susan Nuckles Williams.)

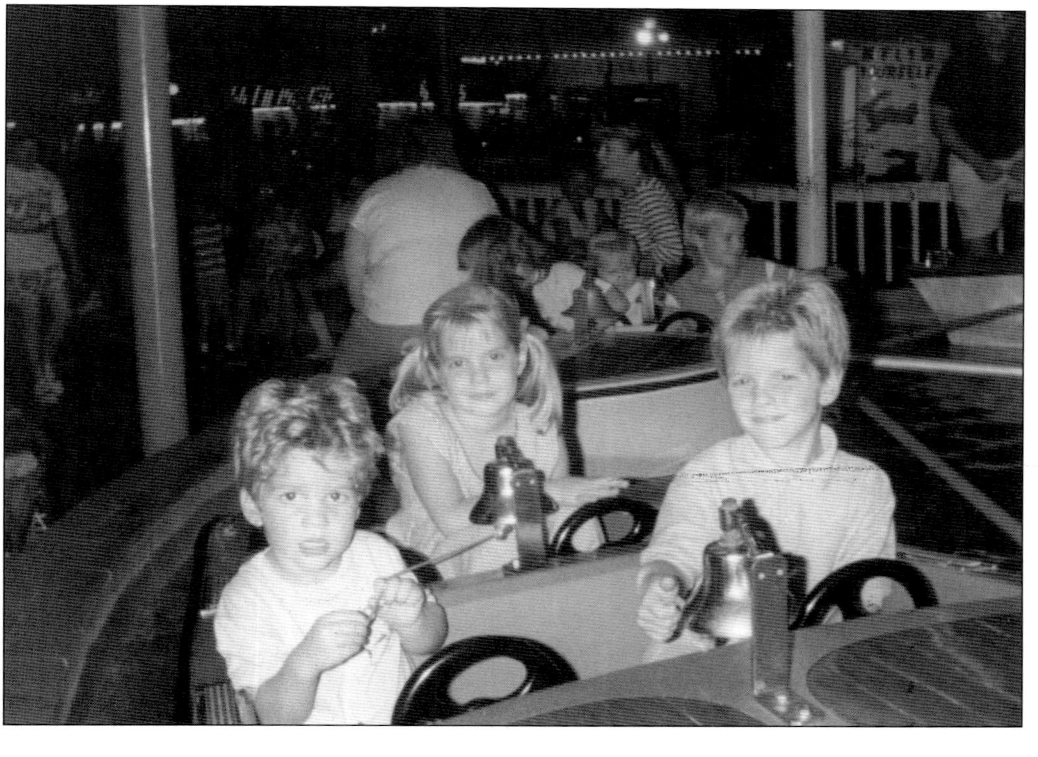

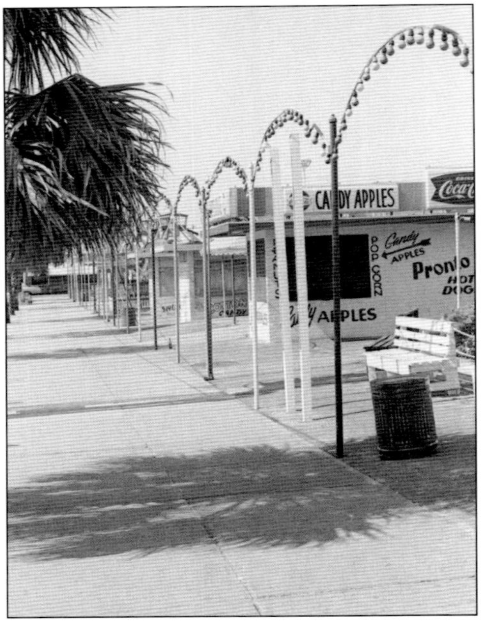

The bulbs on the arches lining the perimeter of the early park may seem obsolete, but they show how keeping the lights bright on the midway was important even in the 1950s. Entire rides were lined with flashing colored orbs. In 1985, a full-time light changer was hired to keep the more than 700,000 lights burning. The Caterpillar ride alone was estimated to have 13,000 lights in various colors. (Courtesy MBCC.)

There were a few concession "musts" for anyone visiting the rides. First and foremost was cotton candy. Patrons could watch as the vendor poured sugar into the center of the round, tub-like machine. The cotton confection would then shoot out as he took his cardboard cone and twirled it into a big puff of pink or blue cotton candy. Other favorites were candied apples, caramel apples, and Pronto Pup corn dogs. (Photograph by Mary Catherine Hardee.)

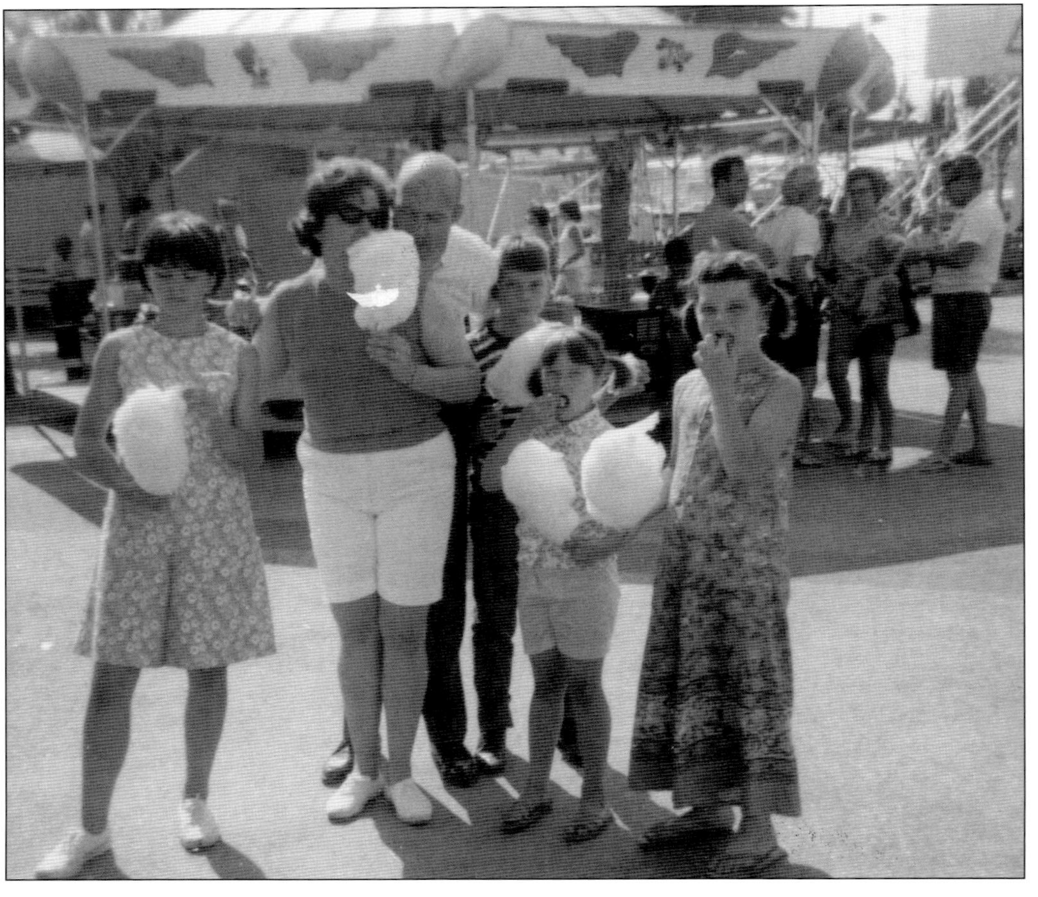

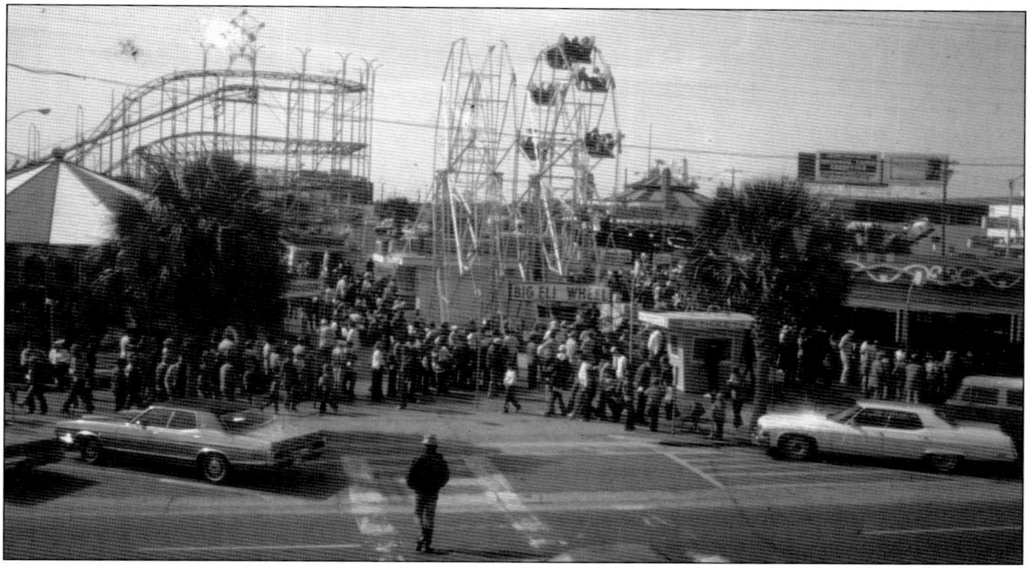

For almost two decades, these dual "Big Eli" Ferris wheels were positioned right along the boulevard, to the delight of both the riders and passersby. Ferris wheels were an ever-evolving aspect of the Pavilion rides. The early boardwalk had a Ferris wheel that was later moved to the boulevard location. Made by the Eli Bridge Company, the dual wheels were later replaced by the single, much-taller Big Eli, which had 18 seats. This Big Eli was 57 feet high, tall enough so that riders could see the ocean beyond the Pavilion building as they crested the top. The Big Eli was removed following a fatal accident in 1991. (Above, courtesy MBCC; below, courtesy CML.)

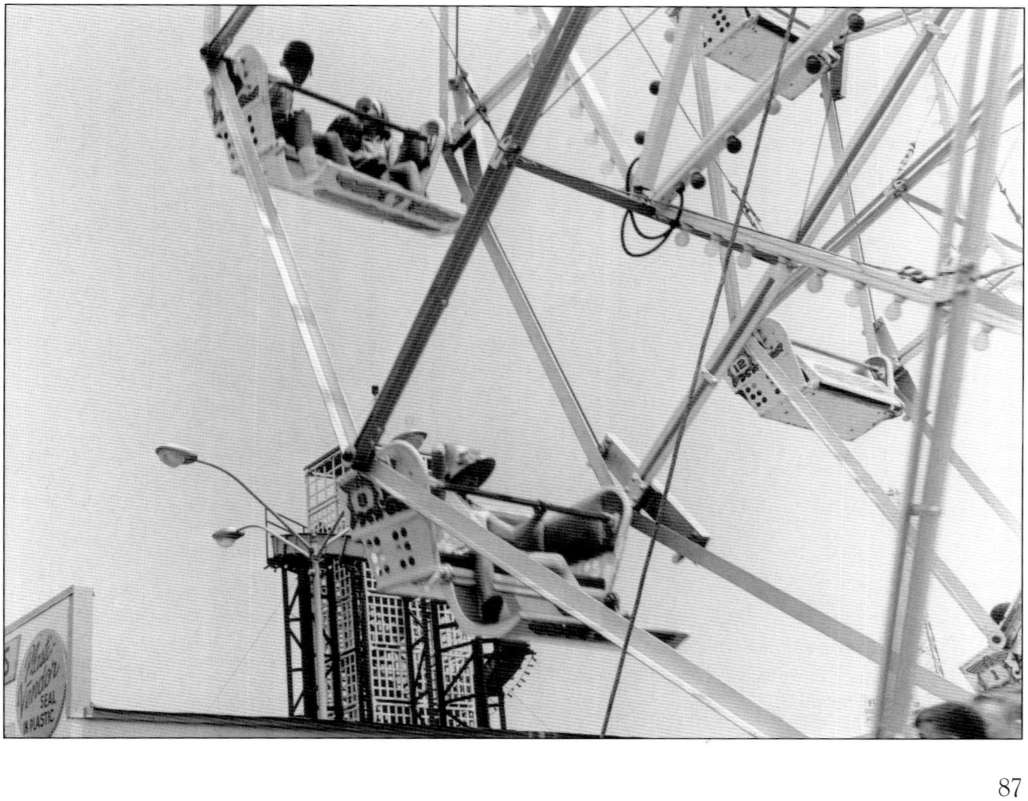

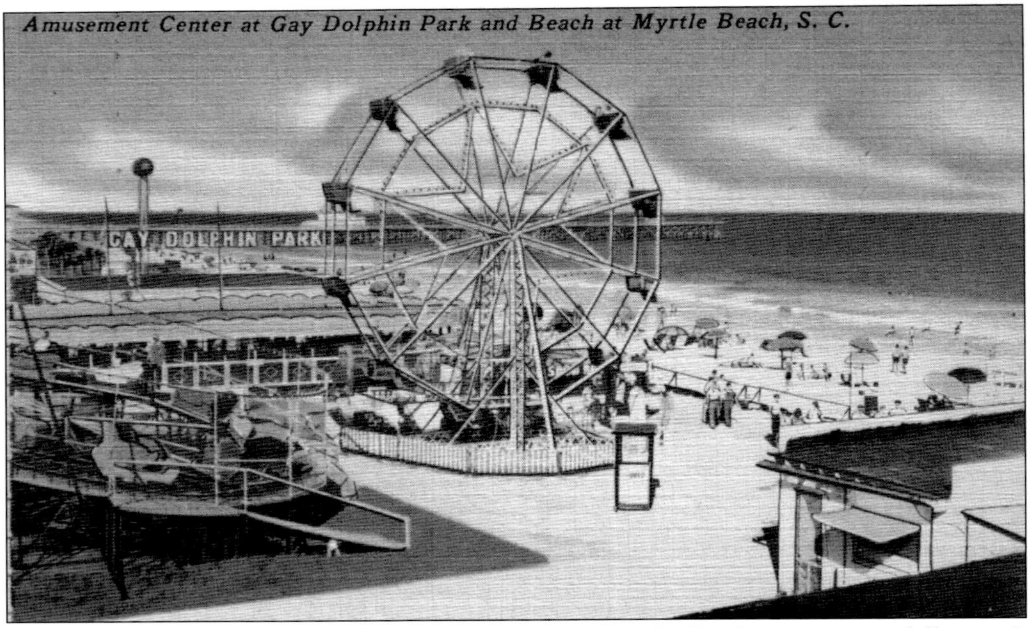

Popularity breeds competition, and for the amusements at the Pavilion, it was no different. A neighbor to the north along the beach, the Gay Dolphin Gift Shop began its own amusement park in the 1950s, which remained in operation until 1968. The gift shop itself, which for a while proclaimed itself the world's largest, is still in operation. (Courtesy Burroughs and Chapin Company, Inc.)

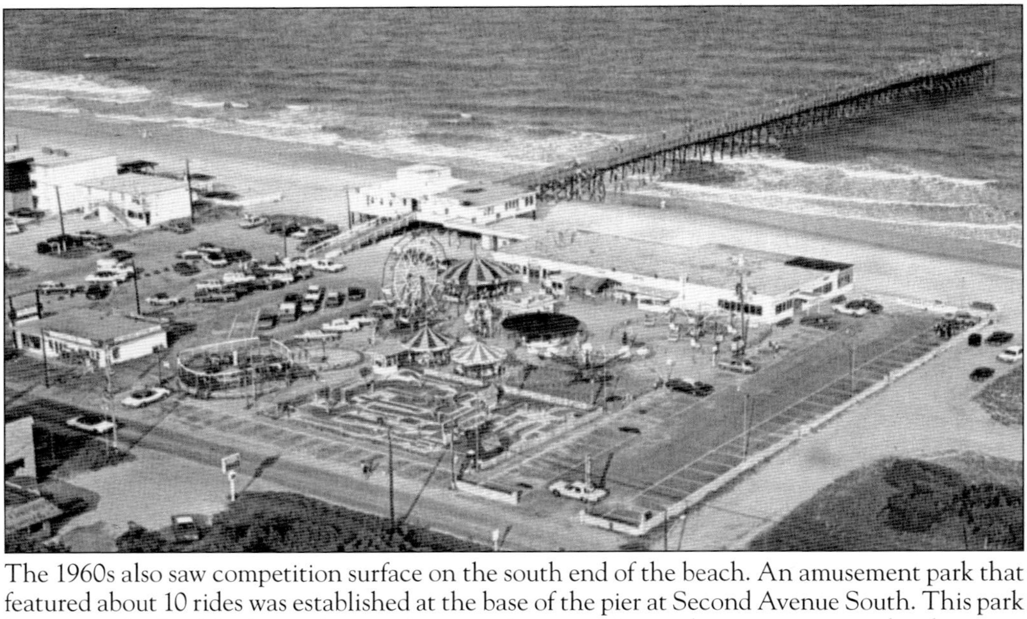

The 1960s also saw competition surface on the south end of the beach. An amusement park that featured about 10 rides was established at the base of the pier at Second Avenue South. This park later moved a few blocks south to make room for expansion and now operates under the name Family Kingdom. (Courtesy Burroughs and Chapin Company, Inc.)

Arcade games and games of skill were an important part of the midway from the beginning. This game challenged players to pitch pennies into a variety of containers. If a penny landed and remained in one of the containers, its pitcher won a prize—likely a small stuffed animal. (Courtesy Mary Catherine Hardee.)

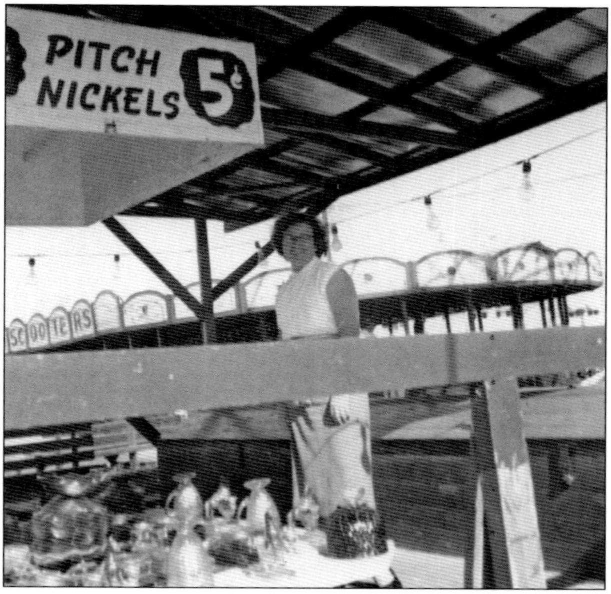

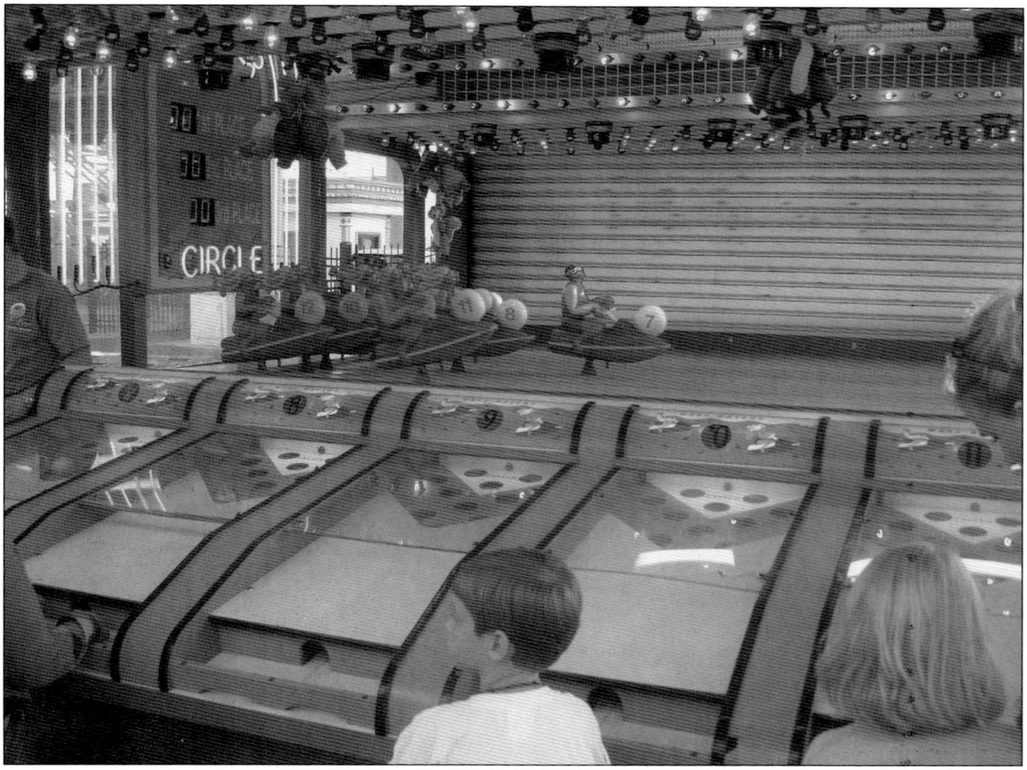

Over the years, some of the games on the midway stayed pretty much unchanged while others became more technologically complex. In the game pictured here, players aimed a stream of water at a small target. So long as their stream hit the target, their horses would continue moving slowly along a track. The player whose horse reached the finish line first won a stuffed animal. (Courtesy Lauchlan McKay.)

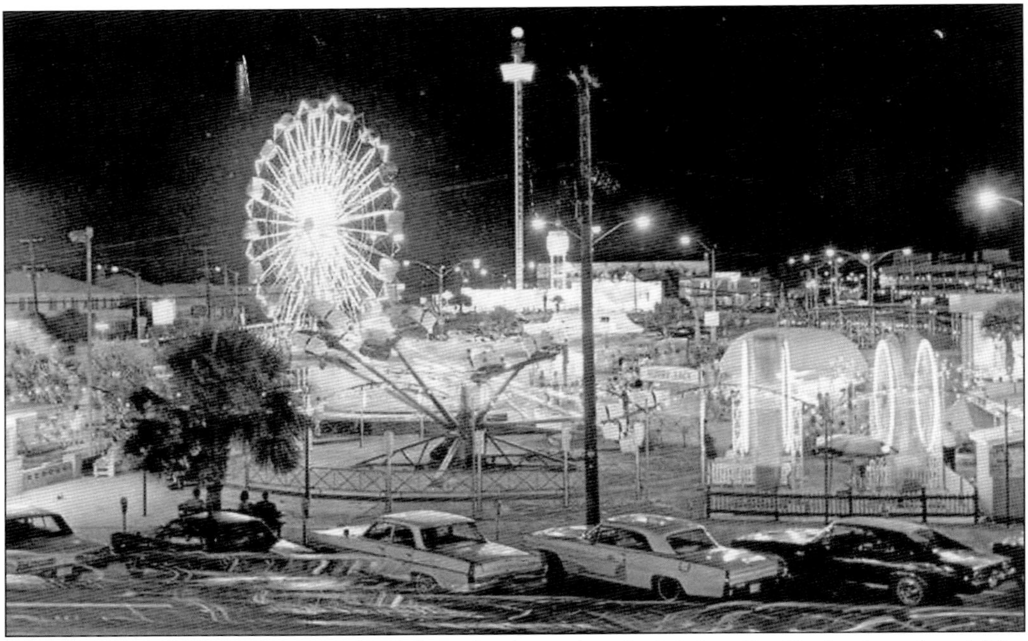

This 1970s time-lapse photograph of the rides was taken by Mickey Brafford, whose band (the Imperials Rock and Roll Combo) performed at the Pavilion in 1963 and 1964. It shows not only the dual Ferris wheels and Sky Diver ride in the foreground, but the 200-foot-tall Astro Needle in the background. (Photograph by Mickey Brafford.)

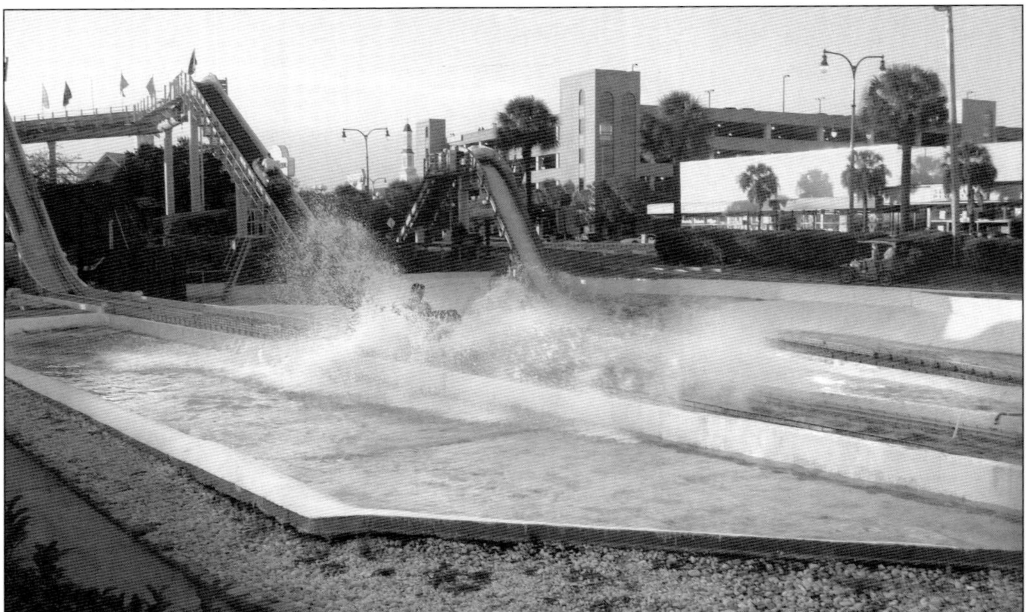

The 1984 summer season opened with a splash. The Pavilion inaugurated what at the time was the largest log flume ride in the Carolinas. With more than 1,500 feet of hills and thrills, guests rode inside fiberglass log replicas that would travel through tunnels and up and down hills. The longest drop was 35 feet, which assured that riders would get wet. (Courtesy Lauchlan McKay.)

The Astro Needle Amusement Park was located on the corner of Chester Street and Eighth Avenue North. Covering less than a block, it was hardly competition to the much-larger Pavilion. But it did offer guests something they could not get anywhere else on the Grand Strand. The ride would take riders 200 feet into the sky for an incredible view of Myrtle Beach. The small amusement park that included the needle operated across the street from the Pavilion park between 1970 and 1981. In addition to the giant needle, it also included a 10,000 square-foot nightclub. The Astro Needle Amusement Park was sold to Burroughs and Chapin in 1981 for redevelopment.

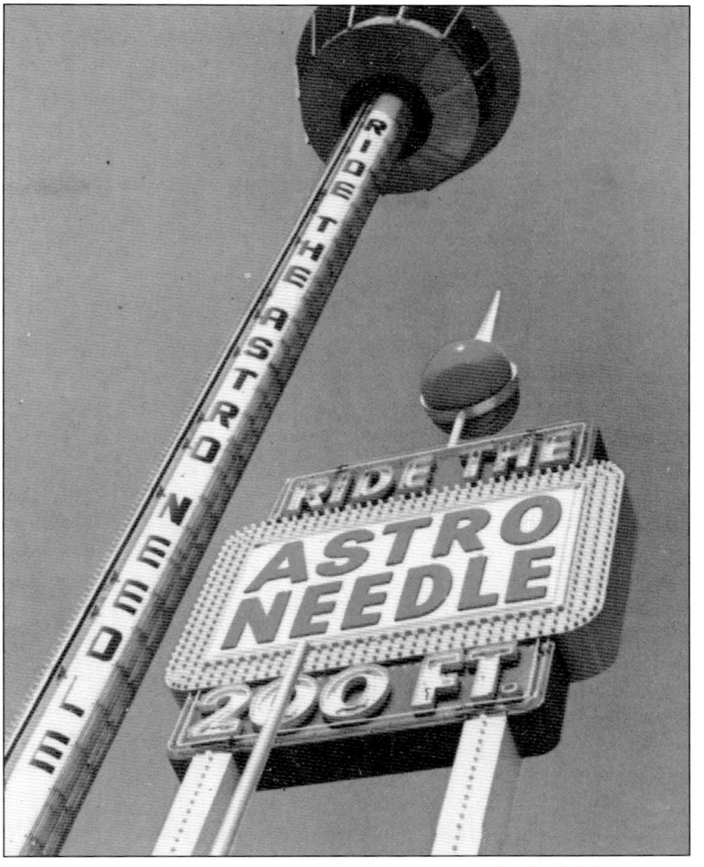

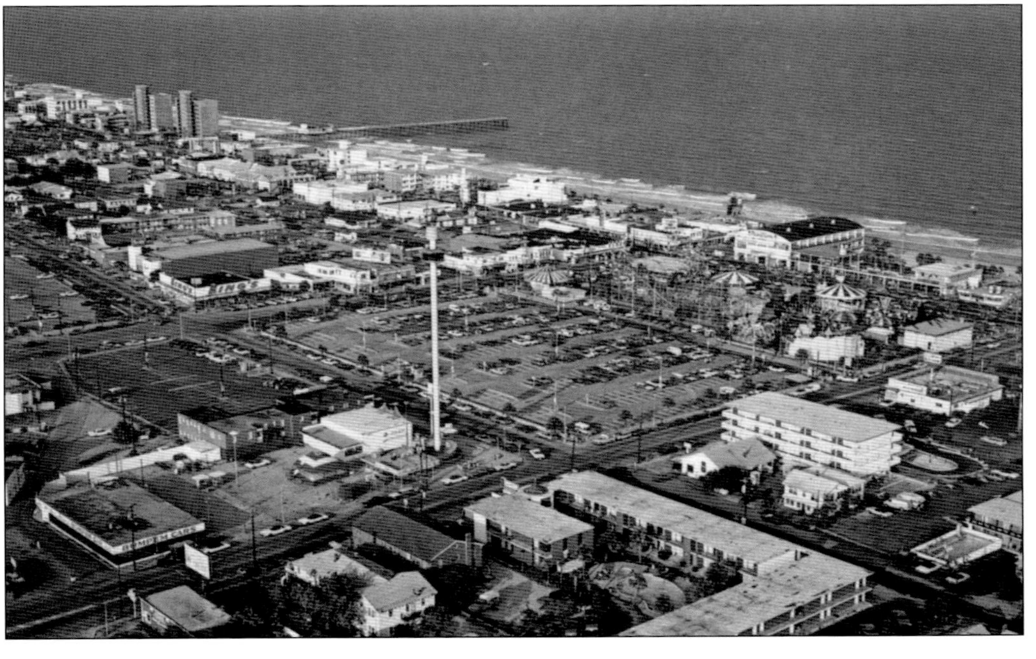

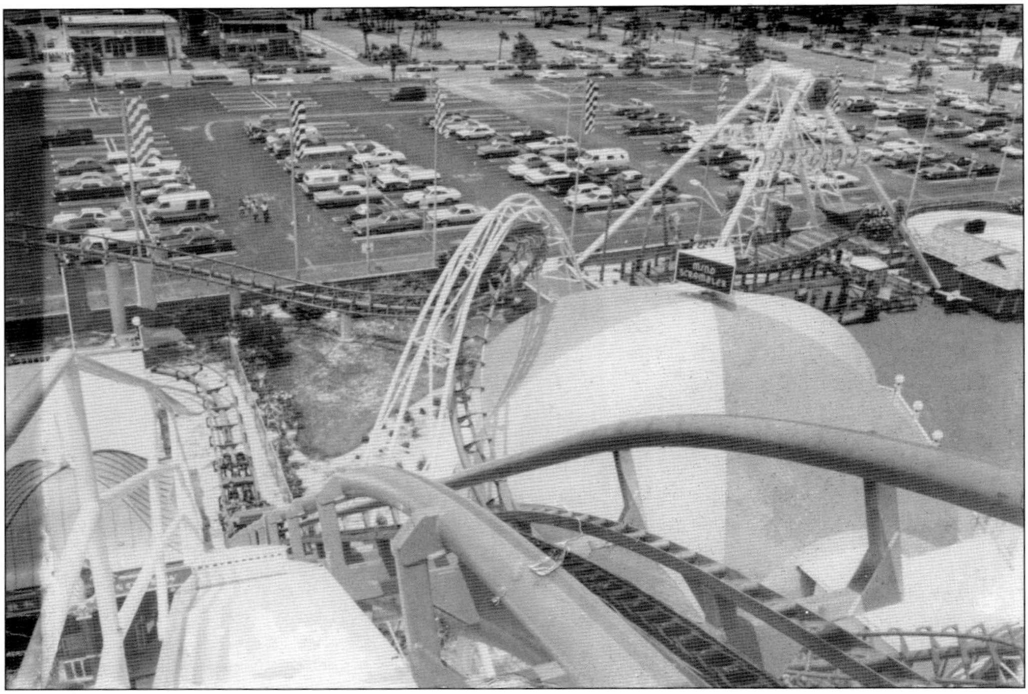

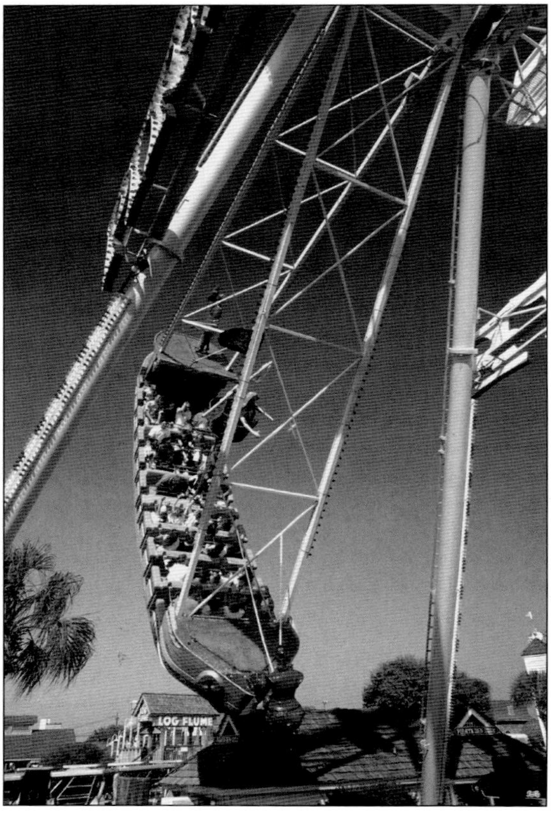

The Corkscrew roller coaster moved to the Pavilion Amusement Park in 1979. The six-car ride cost an estimated $1.5 million when it was first built and had originally been in operation at another Myrtle Beach amusement park known as Magic Harbor. When Magic Harbor went out of business, Myrtle Beach Farms bought the Corkscrew and moved it to the Pavilion. (Courtesy Jimmy Lathan.)

In 1981, the amusement park added two new rides, bringing the total to 25. The Pirate was a huge boat swing built in Germany with a back and forth swinging radius, peaking at 75 degrees. The other attraction added was Sky Tracker, a rotating ride like the Scrambler that was run in a darkened enclosure with flashing lights at its center. The Pirate is among the rides that are preserved at the Pavilion Amusement Park at Broadway at the Beach. (Courtesy Burroughs and Chapin Company, Inc.)

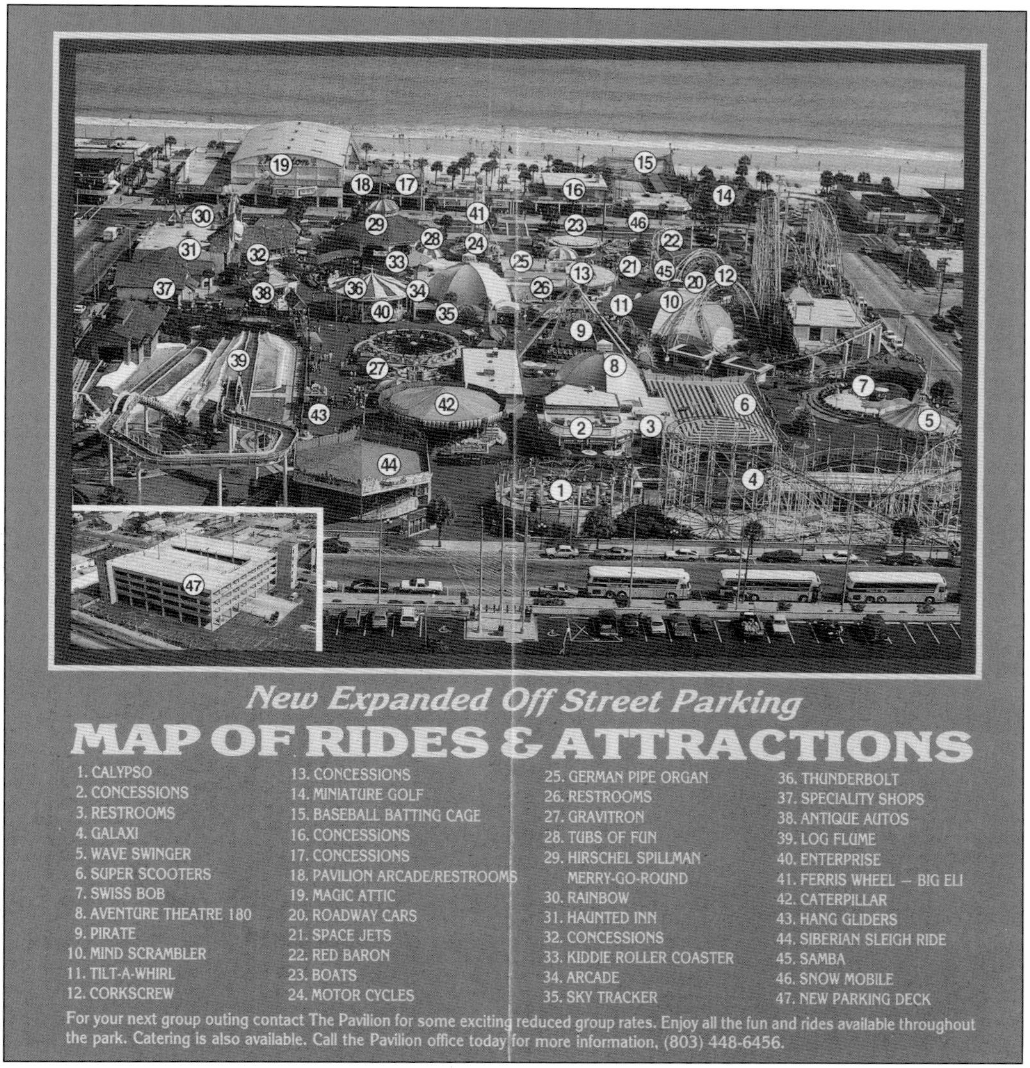

This brochure from the mid-1980s shows the layout of the Pavilion Amusement Park at that time. By now, Burroughs and Chapin had built a new parking deck at the corner of Ninth Avenue North and Kings Highway to accommodate visitors as the park continued to expand its way towards the highway. Each year, more rides were being added, and street parking was getting harder to come by. In 1993, the park made the final push and took over Chester Street where buses are seen parked in this view. (Courtesy MBCC.)

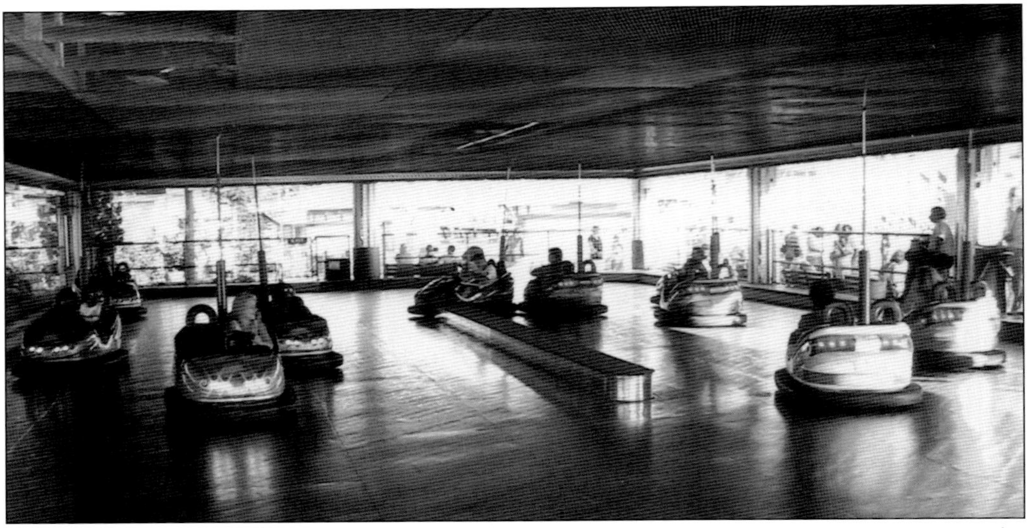

There had been some sort of bumper cars at the park since almost the beginning, but in 1985, the park spent $4.5 million for a major expansion. The Super Scooter bumper cars included 32 cars to allow more riders to take part in the fun at any given time. (Courtesy Wayne Aiken.)

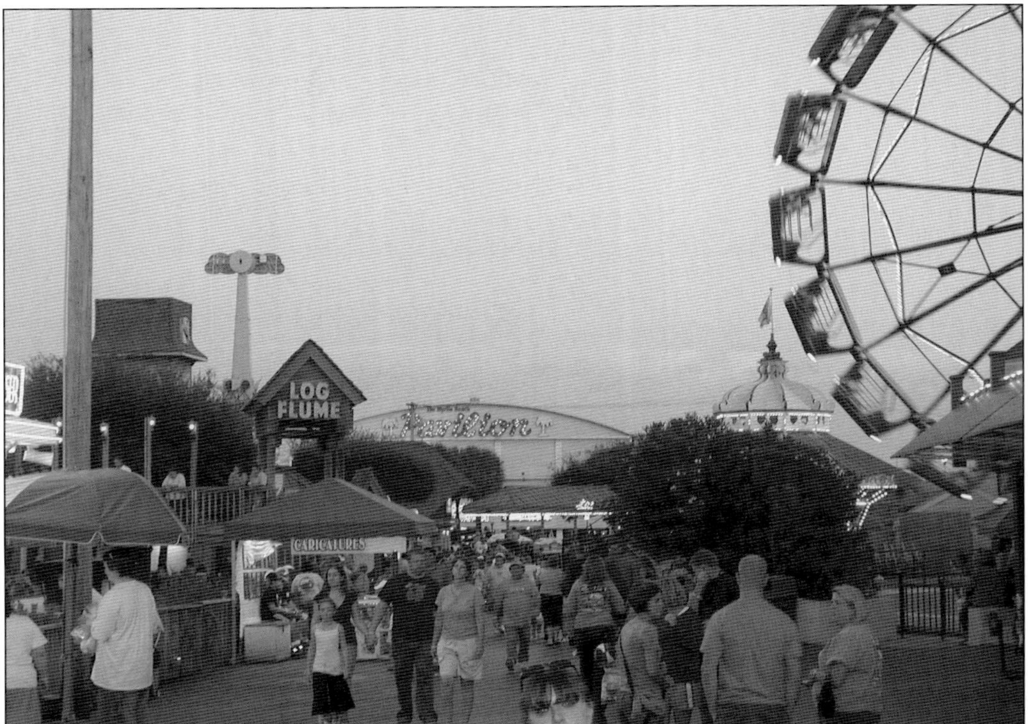

The first rumblings that the Pavilion might close were heard in 1996. Burroughs and Chapin had just built their Broadway at the Beach complex on the Highway 17 Bypass and announced they would be moving the rides to the new development in 1998. The City of Myrtle Beach felt the Pavilion complex was vital to the town and its visitors and convinced them to stay and help revitalize the area. (Courtesy Lauchlan McKay.)

Appropriately named, the Chaos ride looked tame enough to begin with, but once it got started, it soon became a thrill a minute. Riders would get in their swings, which would start swinging outward as the ride spun faster and eventually turned on its side. (Courtesy Burroughs and Chapin Company, Inc.)

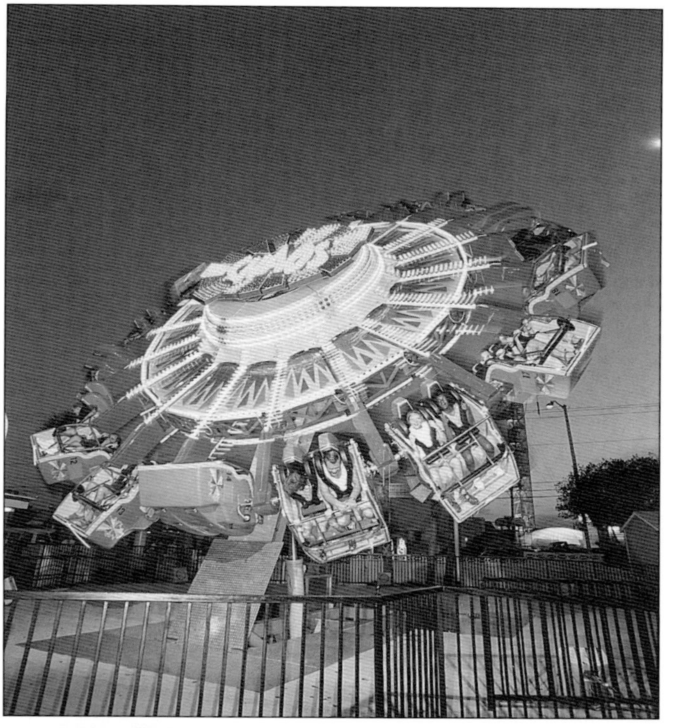

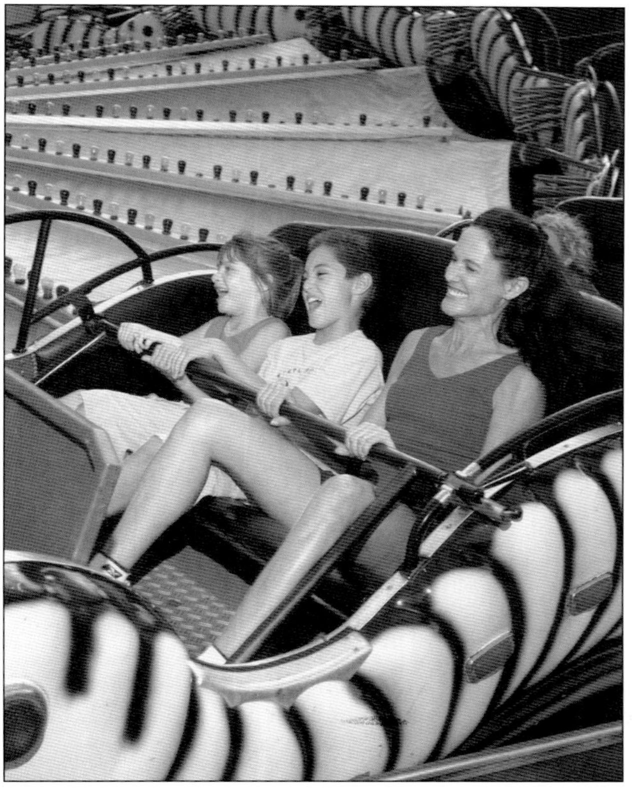

The spinning and flashing Caterpillar that came to the Pavilion was a remake of a ride that was first manufactured in 1925 for New York's Cooney Island Amusement Park. Engineering was by Allen Herschell, who also built the Pavilion's classic carousel. The Caterpillar is so named because halfway through the ride, a cocoon goes over the cars and riders spin around in the dark. (Courtesy Burroughs and Chapin Company, Inc.)

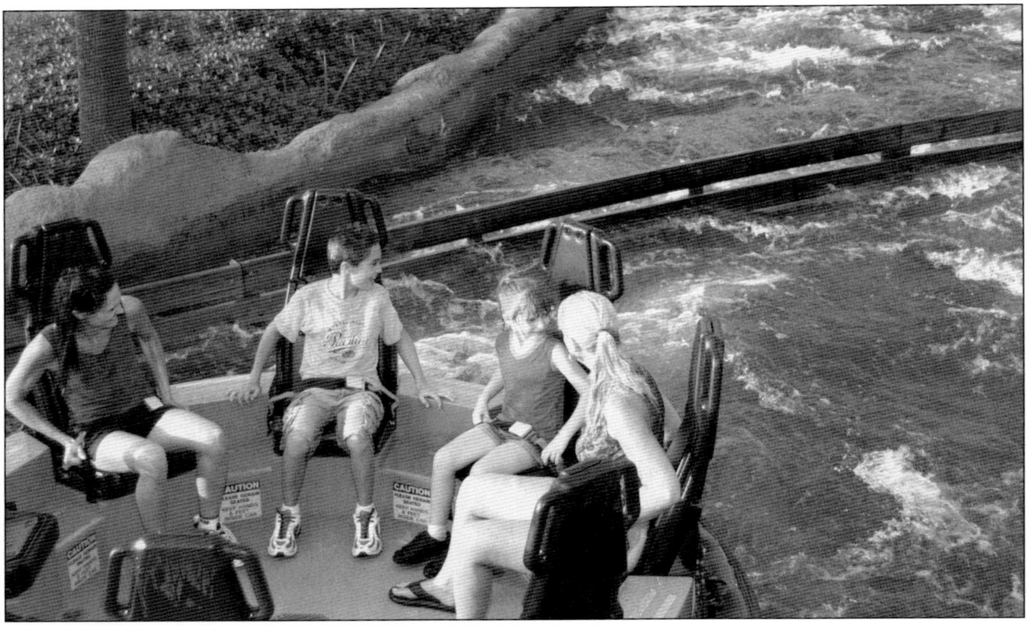

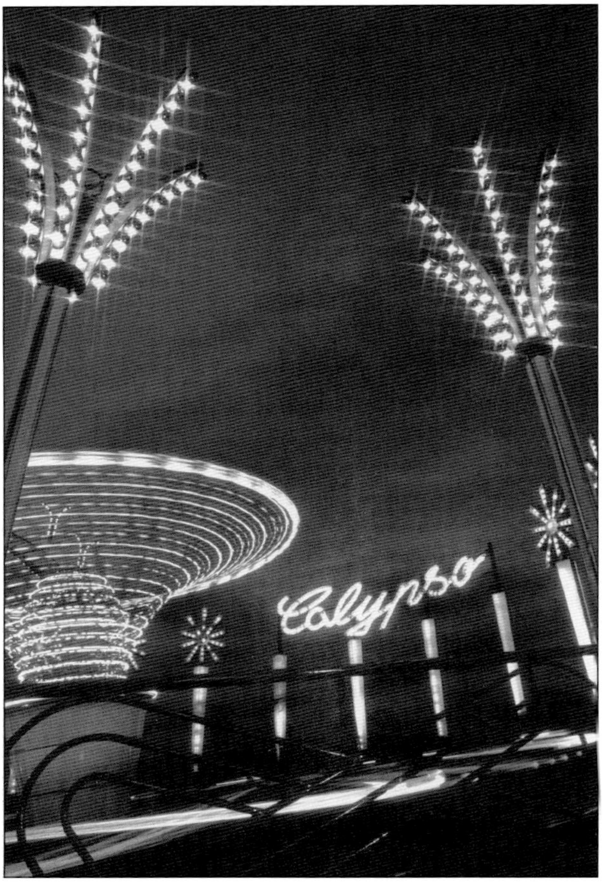

Staying dry was not an option for anyone who chose to ride the Hydro Surge, which opened in 1993. This 1,100-foot water ride took riders from the beach to a raging river. Riders would board their eight-person raft and find themselves in the middle of a white-water experience that recreated the excitement of rafting down a wild river. (Courtesy Burroughs and Chapin Company, Inc.)

The Mack Calypso or simply Calypsos was a whirling dervish with lights, spinning its 50 passengers at incredible speeds. The ride spun in two degrees of motion at once. It was akin to the Scrambler, only on an incline. Both rides were considered "flat rides" because they were easily made operational and only needed a flat surface for their set up. (Photograph by Tim Ribar.)

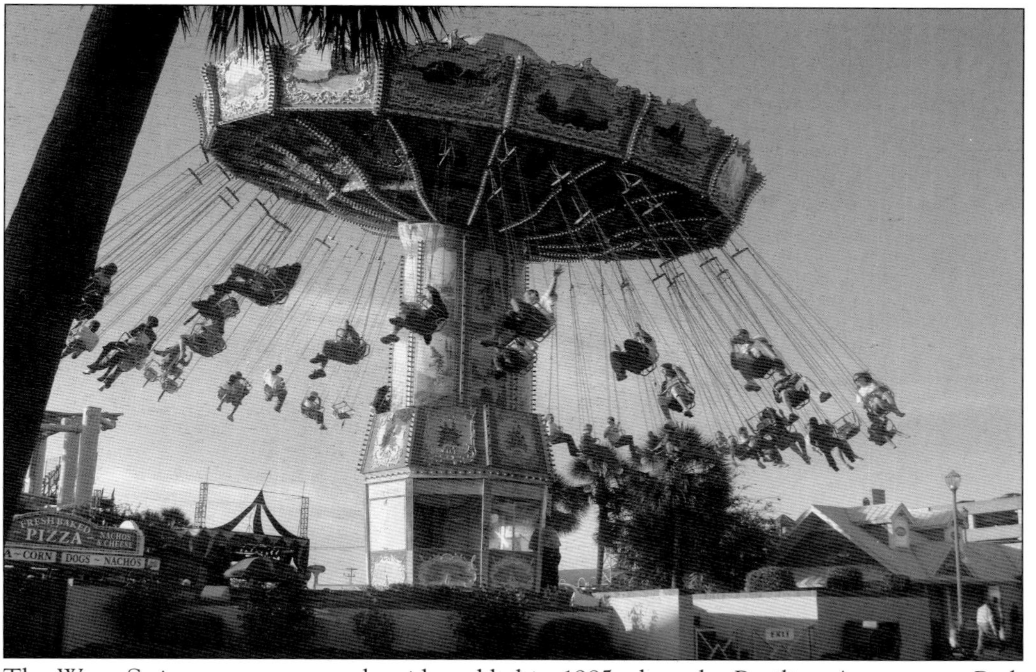

The Wave Swinger was among the rides added in 1985 when the Pavilion Amusement Park underwent a major overhaul. Other additions that year included a 180-degree cinema screen called Adventure Theater and an updated Galaxie roller coaster. Park vice president Earl Husted predicted the 30 million tickets he ordered for the season would not be enough. (Courtesy Lauchlan McKay.)

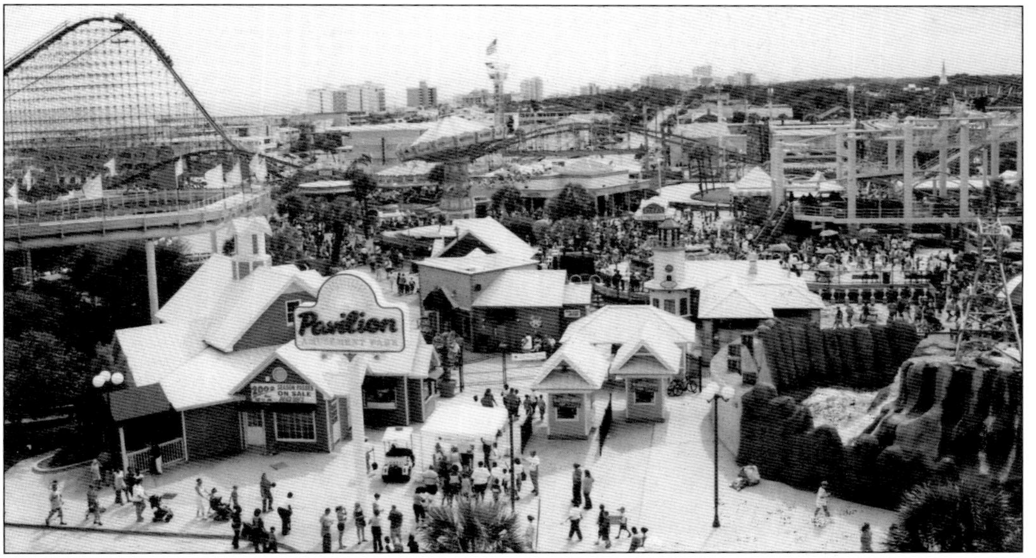

The Pavilion's popular Hurricane Category Five roller coaster is seen on the horizon of this overview photograph of the amusement park. The coaster made its debut in Myrtle Beach in April 2000. Costing $5 million to build, it was custom-designed for the Pavilion Amusement Park and had been on the drawing boards for four years while awaiting word of whether the Pavilion would stay in its oceanfront location or move to Broadway at the Beach. (Courtesy Burroughs and Chapin Company, Inc.)

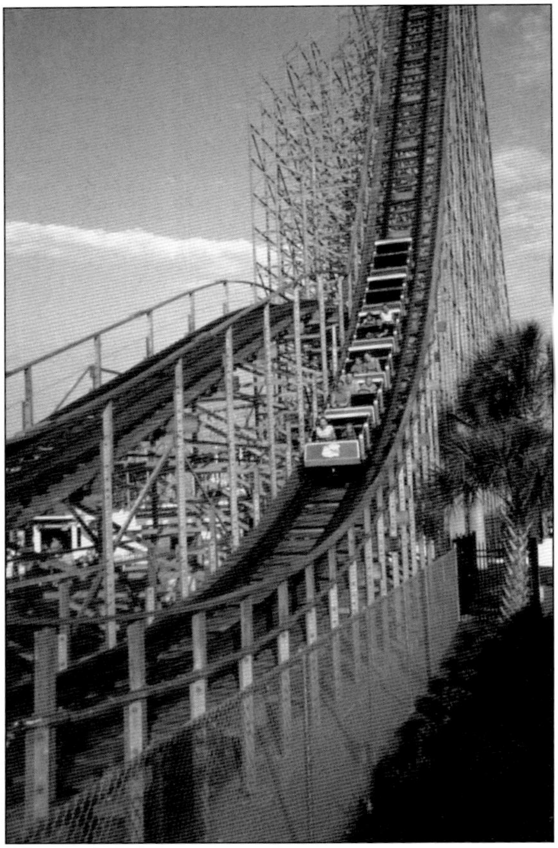

The first drop of the Hurricane could take one's breath away. The 100-foot vertical descent would send the cars screaming along the track at speeds of 55 miles an hour. The coaster had 12 turns in all and operated two 24-passenger trains. (Courtesy Burroughs and Chapin Company, Inc.)

Eight different rides had to be moved to make way for the Hurricane. The 110-foot-tall wooden coaster was the tallest in South Carolina and stretched the length of the park along Eighth Avenue. With more than 3,800 feet of track, the ride lasted about two minutes. (Courtesy Burroughs and Chapin Company, Inc.)

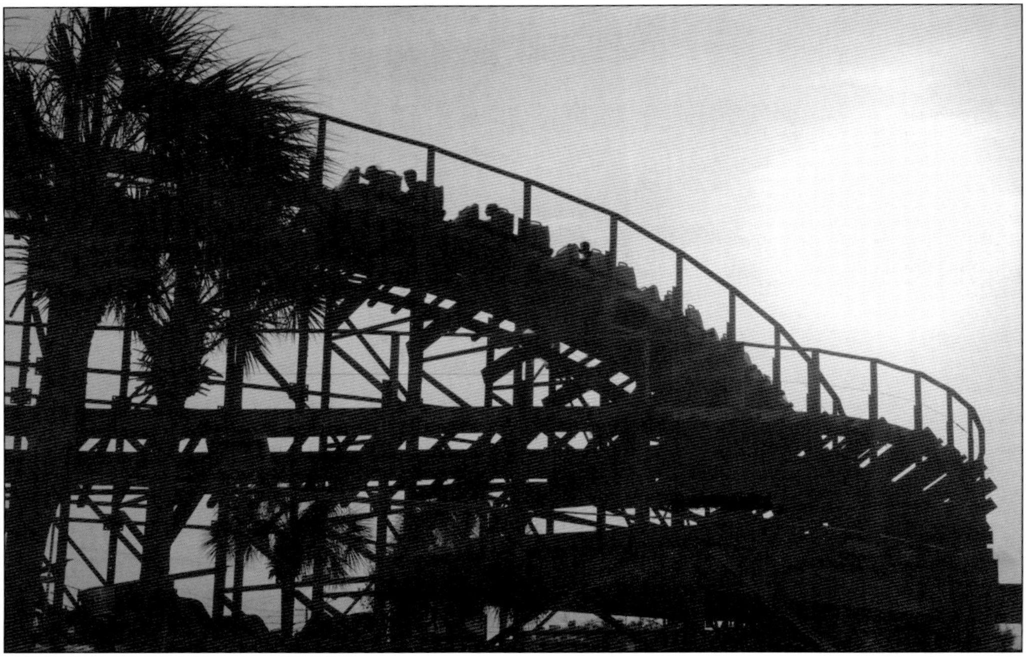

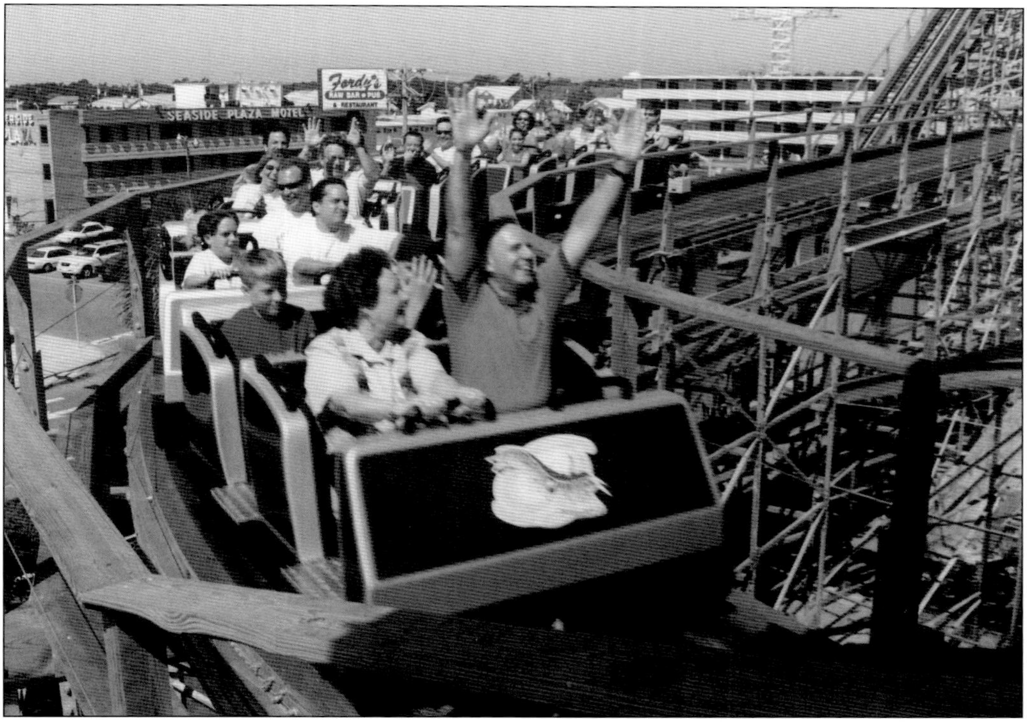

To celebrate the arrival of the Hurricane, Burroughs and Chapin Company, Inc., threw a party and invited company officials and VIPs on its inaugural ride. Seated in the front car for this ride are company chairman Douglas P. Wendel and his wife, Paula. (Courtesy Burroughs and Chapin Company, Inc.)

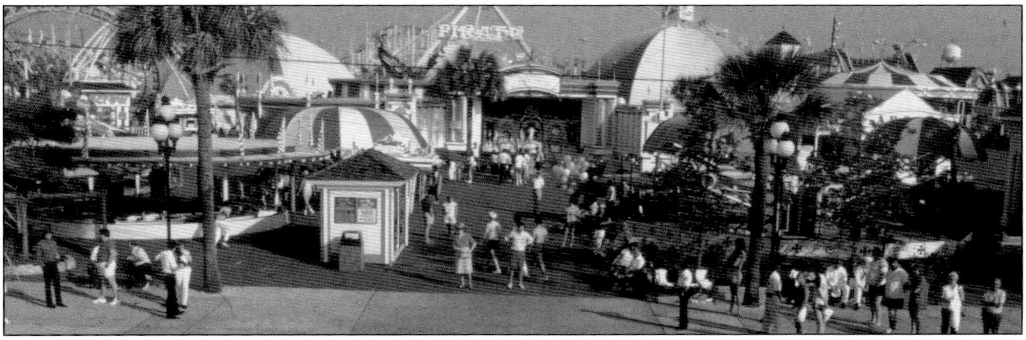

The rides at the Myrtle Beach Pavilion Amusement Park changed constantly throughout the park's nearly 60-year history. The constants were the Baden band organ and Herschell-Spillman carousel. The original park had about five or six rides, including a Ferris wheel, a slide, and a merry-go-round. By the time of the final season in 2006, the number of rides had peaked at 49. Part of the allure of visiting the Pavilion area was to wander among its rides. In preparation for the 2000 season, Burroughs and Chapin decided to put a fence around the rides and charge a park admission fee of $5. Restricting access to the area proved very unpopular, and the admission fee was dropped by 2003. (Courtesy MBCC.)

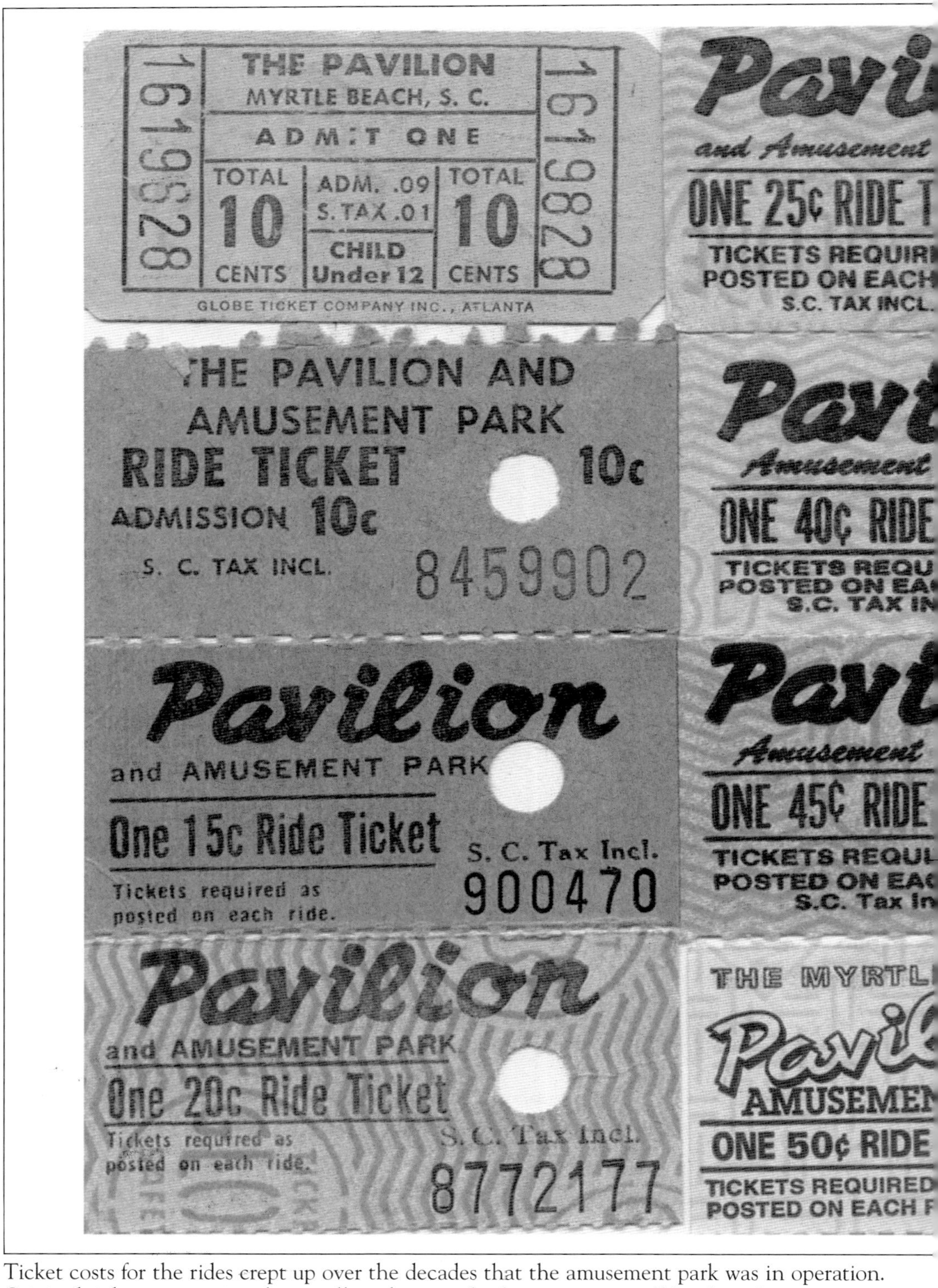

Ticket costs for the rides crept up over the decades that the amusement park was in operation. Original tickets were printed in a roll, and strips of tickets were torn off for the riders to present

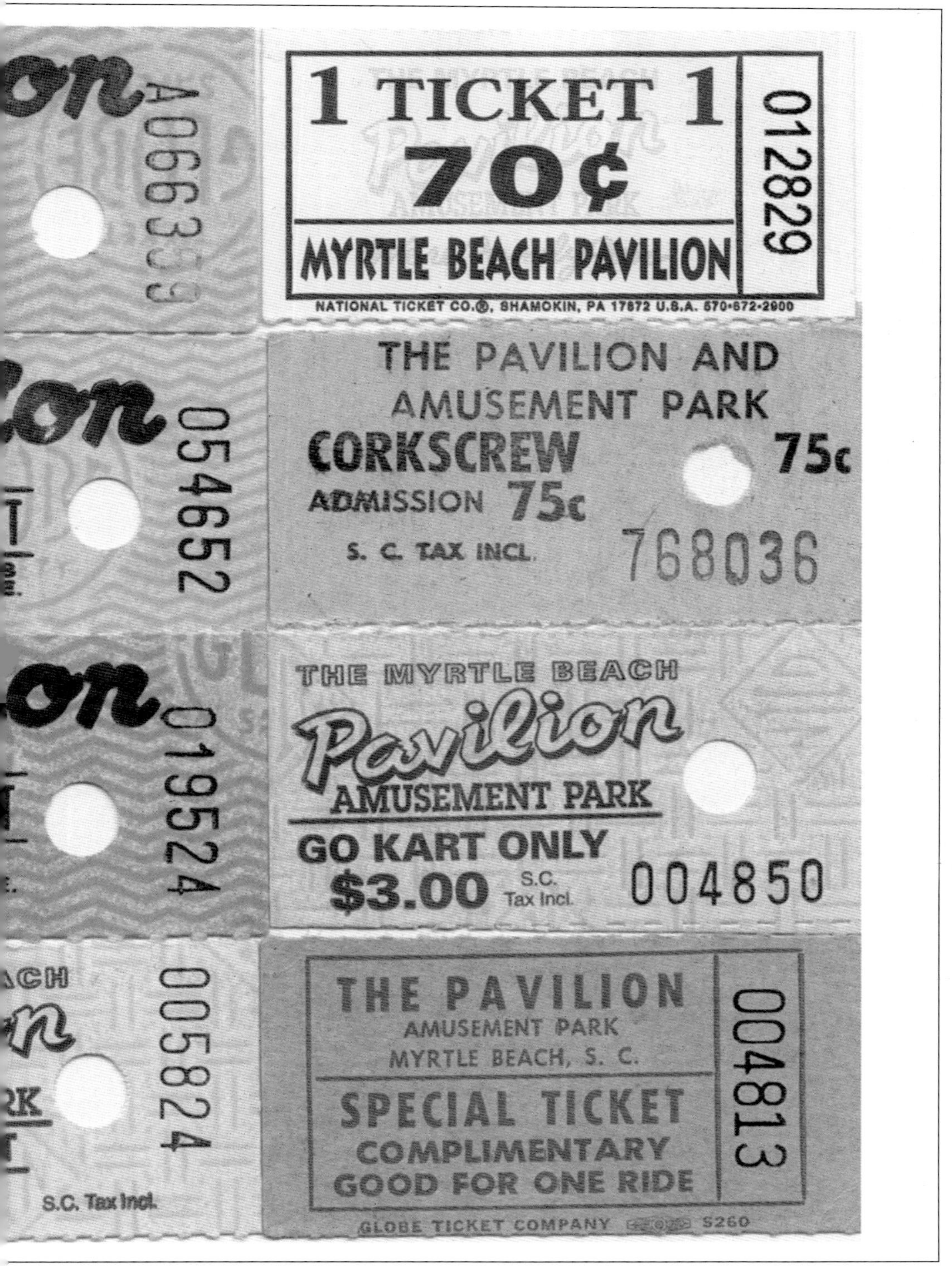

to the operators. One dollar would buy the opportunity to ride 10 rides at 10¢ each. By the time the park closed in 2006, the cost was $1 per ride. (Courtesy Jimmy Lathan.)

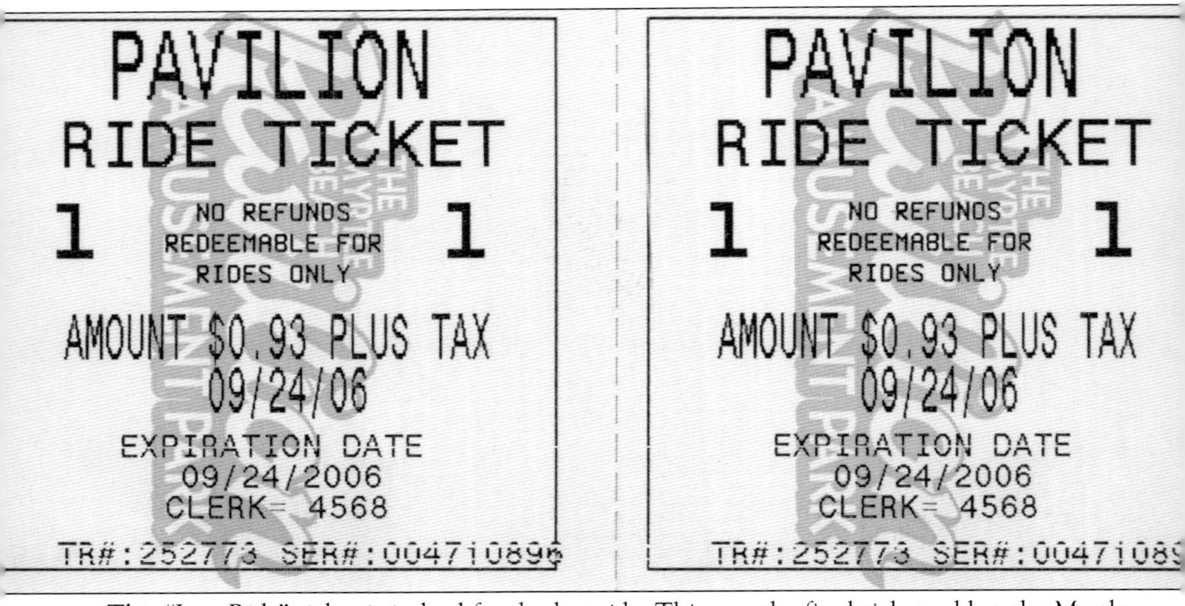

This "Last Ride" ticket is indeed for the last ride. This was the final ticket sold at the Myrtle Beach Pavilion Amusement Park. Having worked at the Pavilion for decades, former Magic Attic manager Jimmy Lathan says he knew which ticket booth was the last to close and purchased five tickets just as it was preparing to shut down on the park's final evening, September 24, 2006. (Courtesy Jimmy Lathan.)

Four

The 2006 Farewell Season

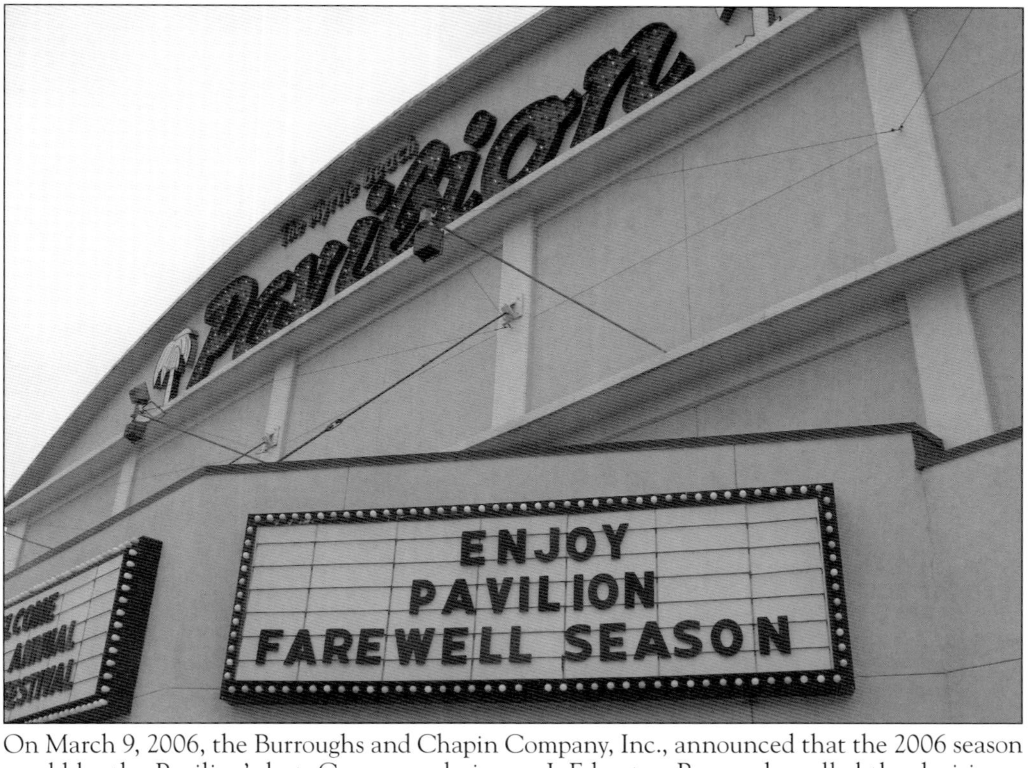

On March 9, 2006, the Burroughs and Chapin Company, Inc., announced that the 2006 season would be the Pavilion's last. Company chairman J. Edgerton Burroughs called the decision a difficult one but said it was based on economics and not emotions. While admitting Myrtle Beach's downtown area needed a focal point to remain viable, he felt that this "focal point" business would need to be a year-round venture. The company announced plans for the Pavilion's farewell season.

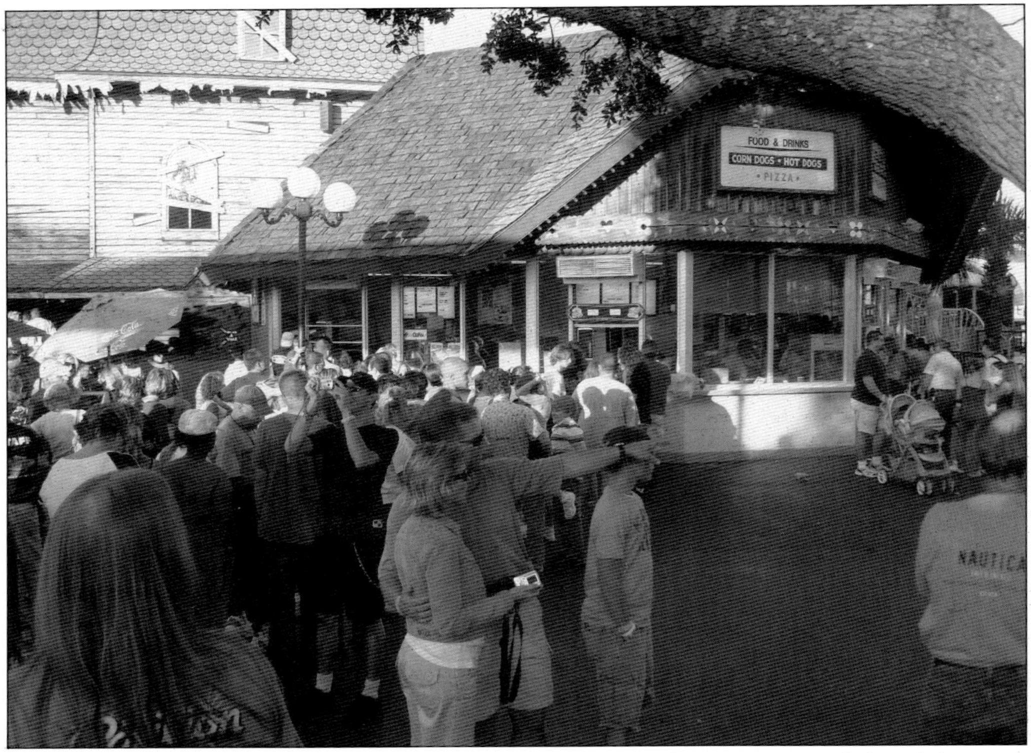

Reaction to word that the Pavilion was closing after almost 60 years was immediate and emotional. Petitions were launched in an attempt to reverse the plans, which had been set in motion long before the announcement was made. The decision stood firm, and people flocked to be a part of the beloved landmark's last few months of existence. (Courtesy Lauchlan McKay.)

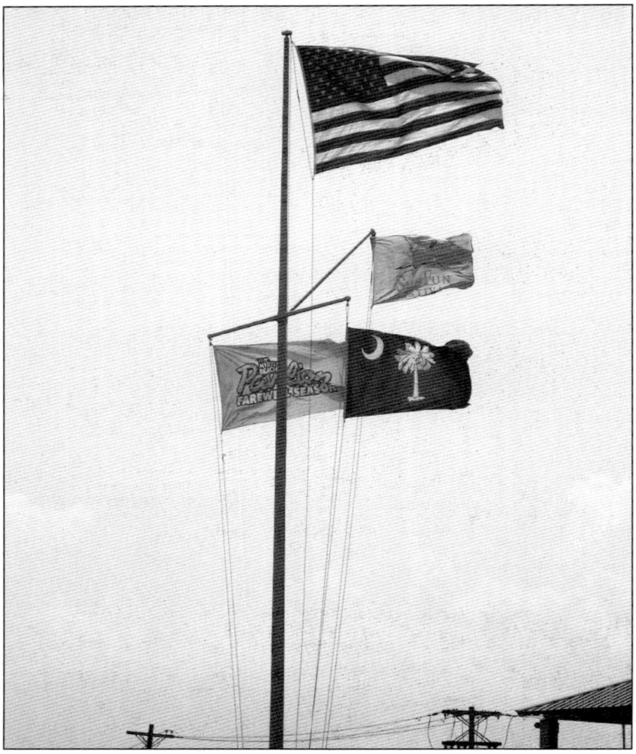

A farewell season logo was designed to commemorate the Pavilion's last year. A flag displaying the logo replaced the old Pavilion flag that flew over the boardwalk along with the U.S. flag and that of South Carolina. The farewell logo was included on almost everything associated with the final season, including tickets and T-shirts.

The 55th Annual Sun Fun Festival kicked off Myrtle Beach's 2006 summer season on the first weekend in June. This would be the last year that spectators could sit at the Pavilion and enjoy the bands, floats, and cars. What spectators did not know was that it would also be the last Sun Fun Parade. With the favorite viewing area no longer in existence, the Sun Fun Parade ceased to be.

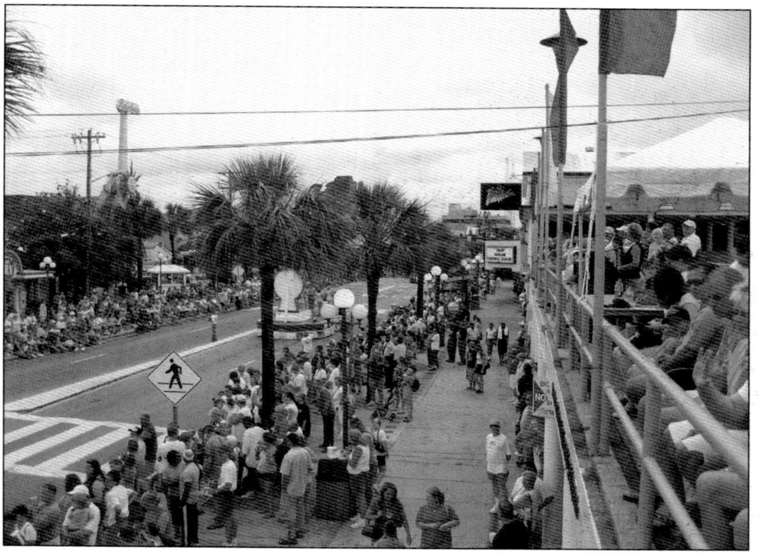

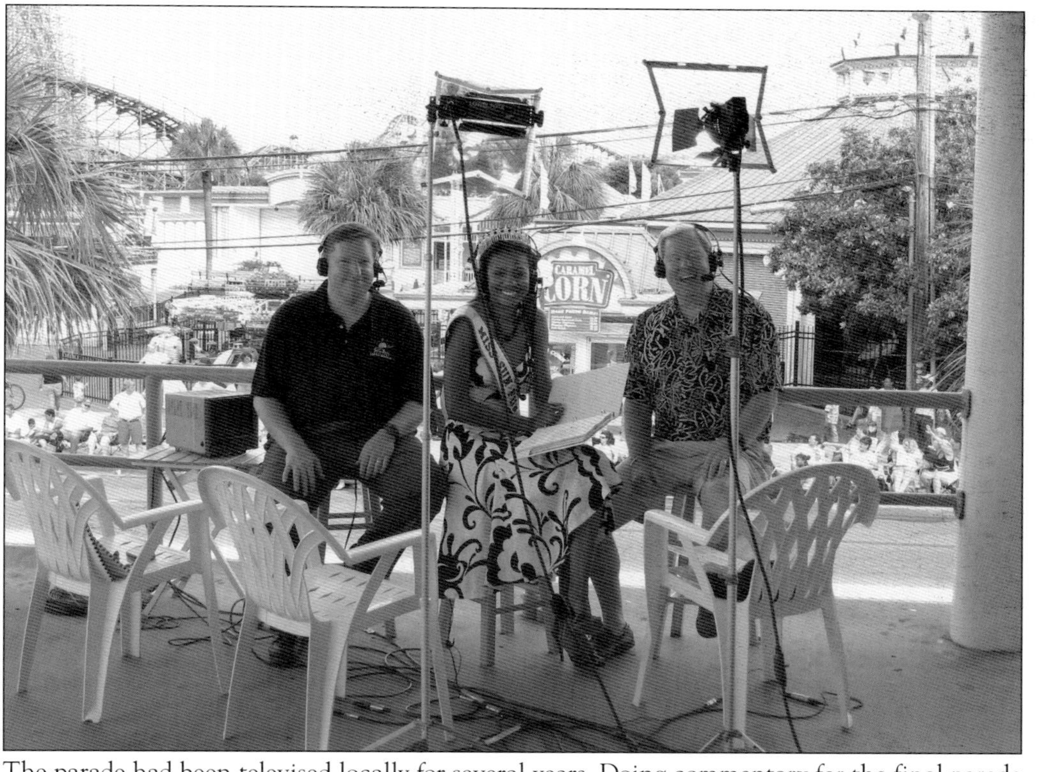

The parade had been televised locally for several years. Doing commentary for the final parade were the president of the Myrtle Beach Chamber of Commerce, Brad Dean; outgoing Miss Sun Fun, Joycelyn McElveen; and television personality Joe Pinner. Pinner, a weatherman as well the host of the show *Mr. Knowzit* on WIS-TV in Columbia, had been involved in the Sun Fun Festival for more than three decades.

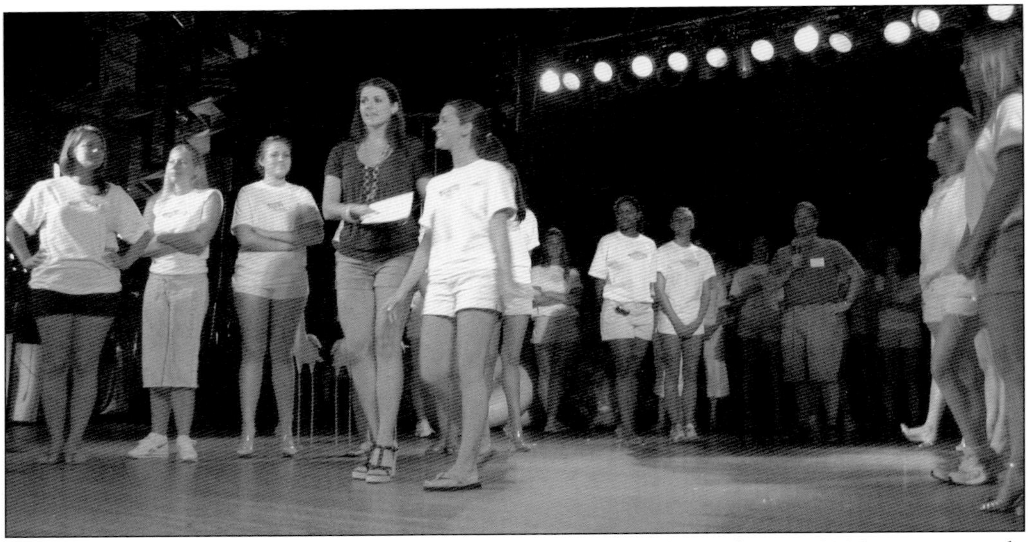

The Miss Sun Fun Pageant had returned to the Myrtle Beach Pavilion in 2005 so it was only appropriate that it would also host the pageant for the Pavilion's final season. Miss USA 2005, Chelsea Cooley, who was also grand marshal for the Sun Fun Parade, helped emcee the pageant. Miss Sun Fun had by now returned to its Miss Universe roots and was again a Miss Universe preliminary. Girls from across the state competed in both the Miss and Teen divisions to help represent Myrtle Beach's tourism industry for the coming year. Megan Radvansky was crowned Miss Sun Fun USA 2007, and Meredith Hoffman became Miss Sun Fun Teen USA.

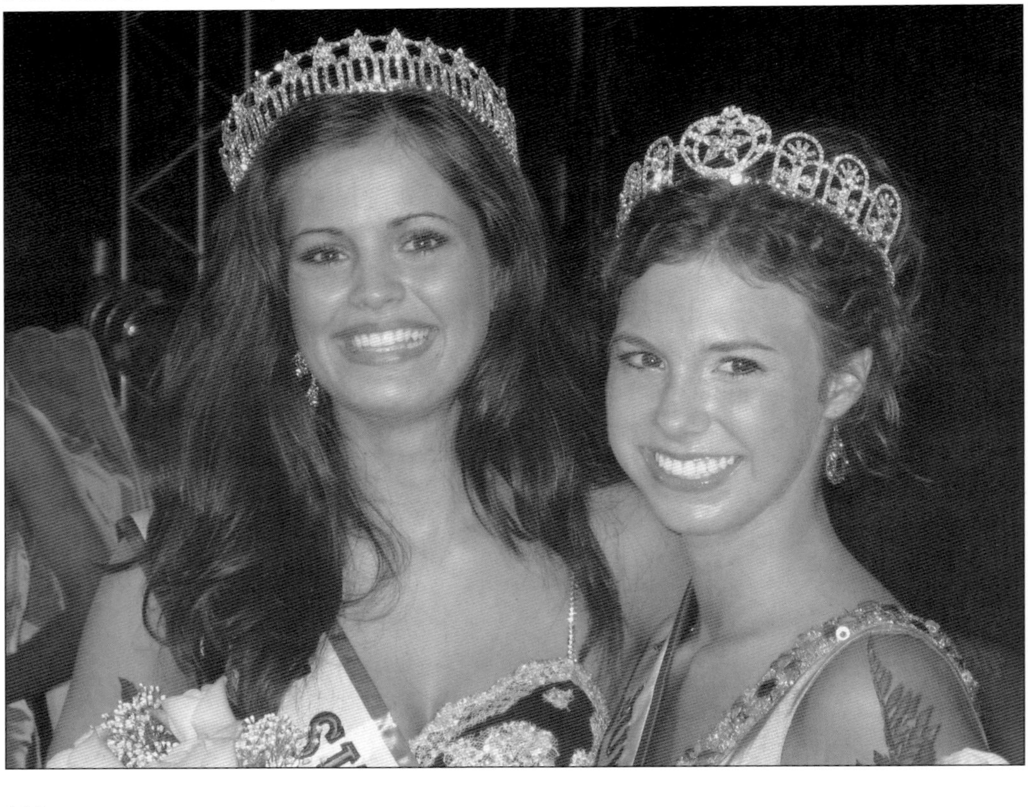

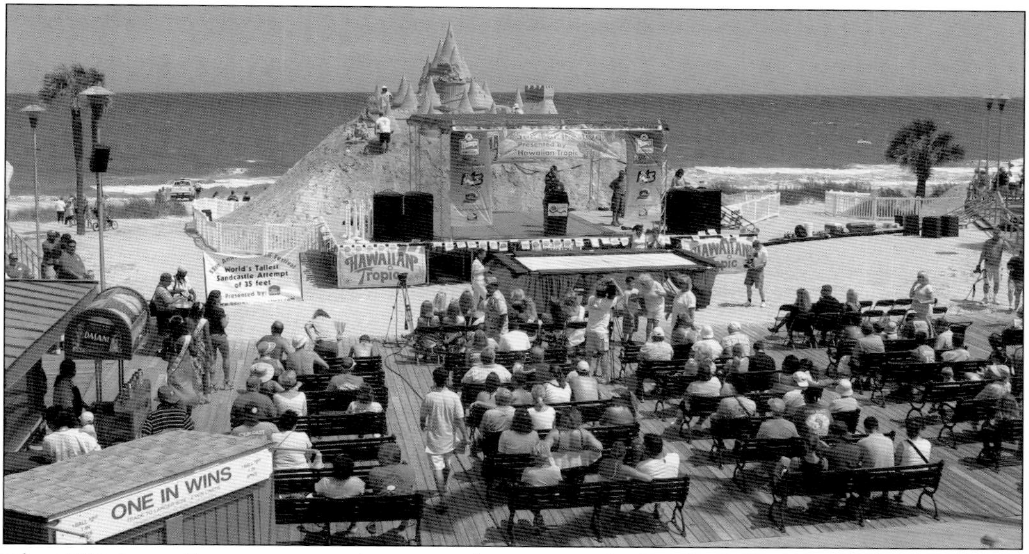

The 2006 farewell season meant huge crowds again on the Pavilion's boardwalk for the annual Miss Bikini Wahine beauty pageant. The sun tan lotion company Hawaiian Tropic, which continued to promote the free oceanfront event, had established this bikini and beauty pageant in 1971. In 2006, the event also took place in front of the world's tallest sandcastle, built for the Sun Fun Festival. The photograph below shows outgoing queen Reid McLeod crowning her successor, McKenzie Redmond. McLeod's own mother, Judi McAllister McLeod, had been Miss Bikini Wahine in 1979.

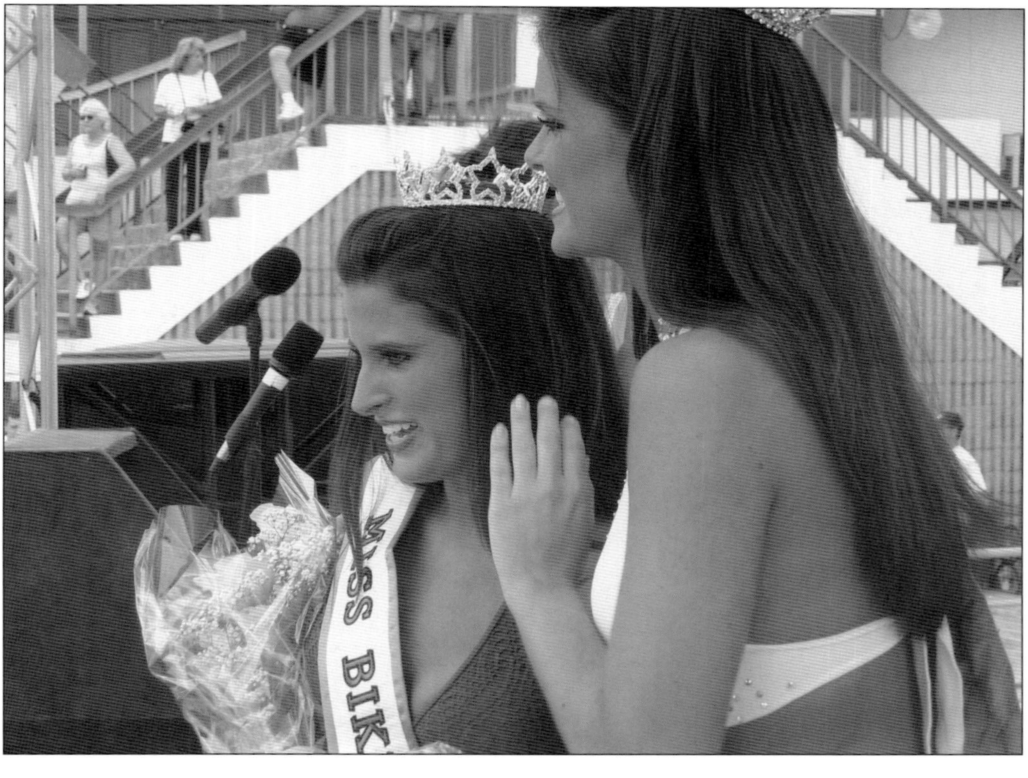

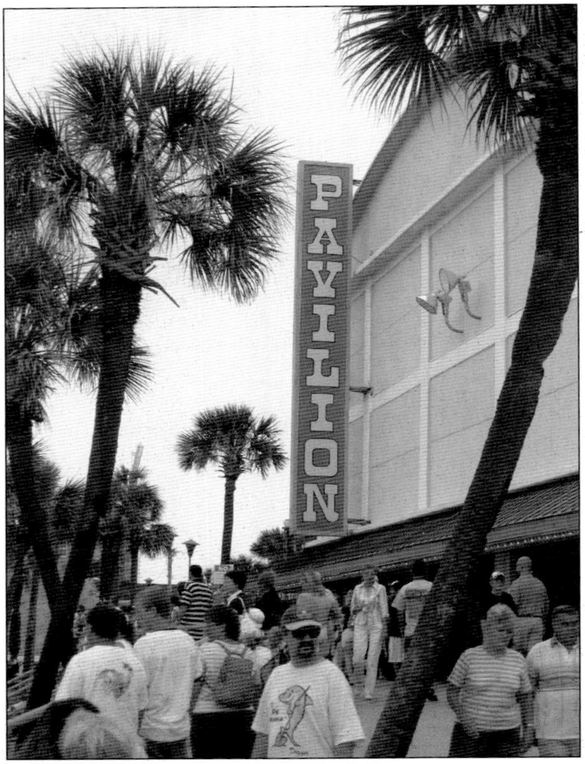

While the Sun Fun Festival was always a huge draw for tourists to Myrtle Beach, the 2006 season was even more so. The Pavilion was again the epicenter of all of the activities and the boardwalk remained crowded for the entire summer as people came to say good-bye.

The Pavilion had been home to Myrtle Beach's ongoing effort to lay claim to as many world's records as possible when it came to building sandcastles. The 2006 season was no different. A mind-boggling 130 truckloads of sand were brought in and dumped behind the Pavilion for that year's goal. A team of workers from Sandtastic of Florida was brought in to construct the World's Tallest Sandcastle.

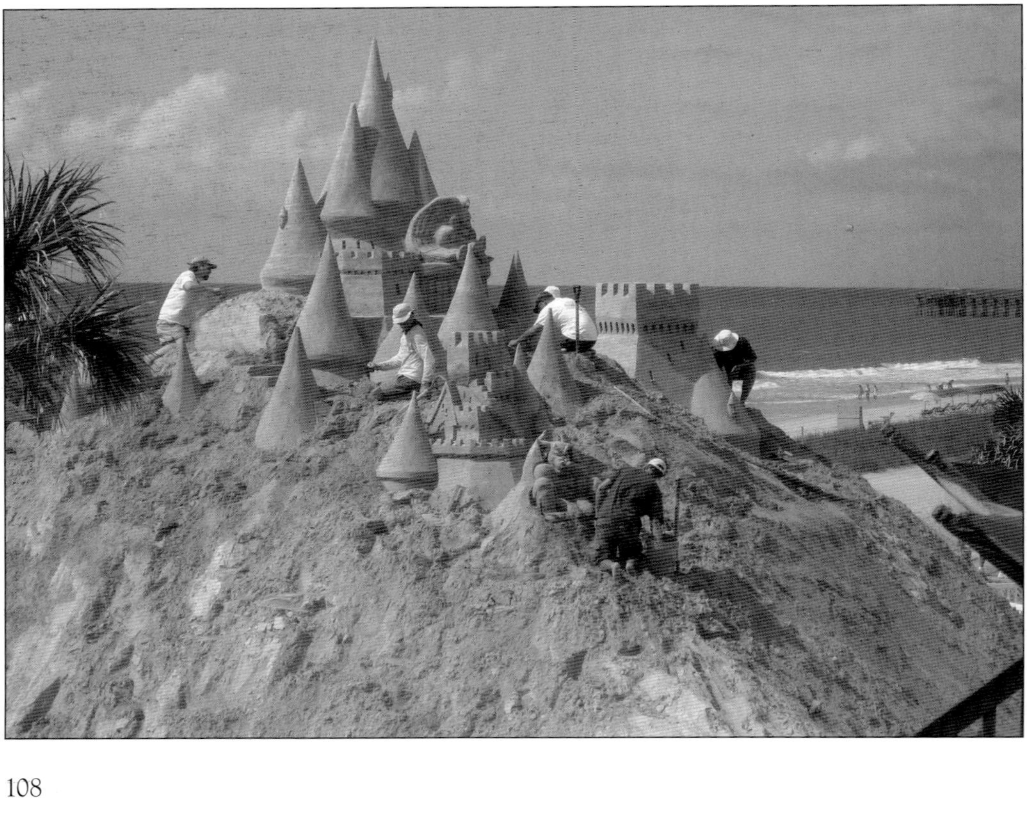

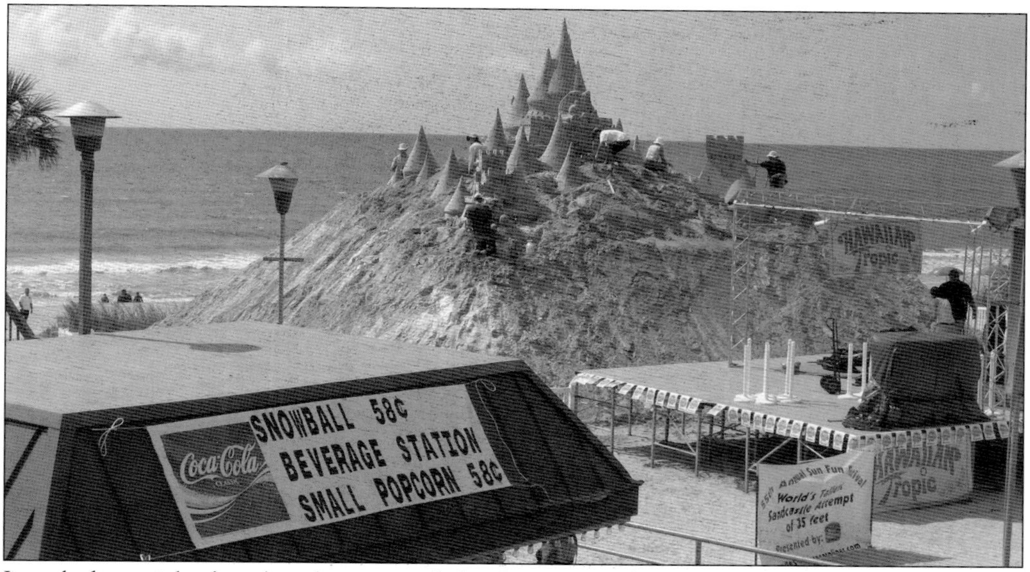

It took them eight days, but they succeeded in being accredited by the Guinness Book of World Records with a castle measuring 32.5 feet high. Myrtle Beach already held a record from 1991 for the world's longest sandcastle, measuring 10.5 miles long. This photograph showing the progress of the giant sandcastle also depicts some of the changes in prices of some of the concessions. Snowballs, soft drinks, and popcorn were each 58¢ in honor of the 58 years that the Pavilion had been in operation. In another nod to nostalgia, a cardboard sandcastle cutout was erected so tourists like Stacy Meschke of Florida and her daughters Annabel and Sabina could mug for photographs.

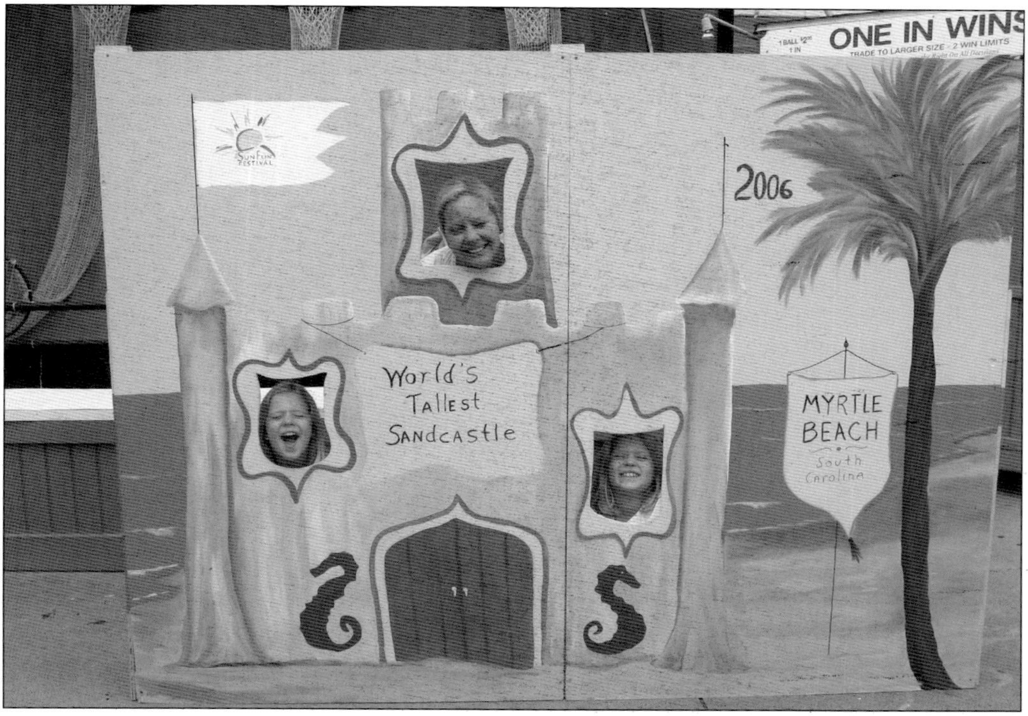

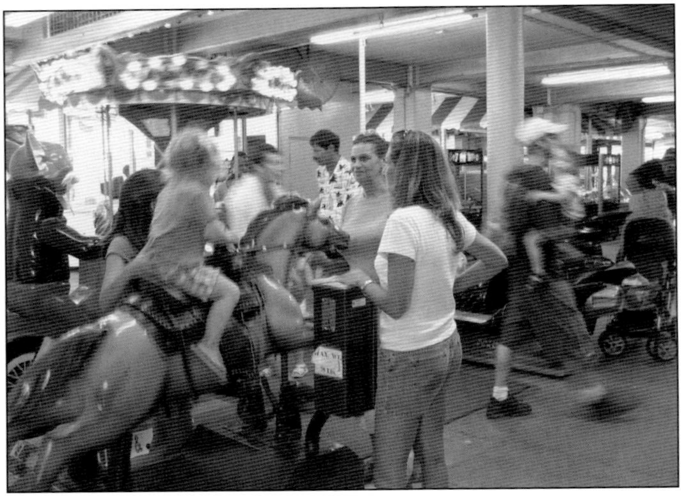

Except for some new digital games, the Pavilion's arcade area had maintained much of its old-fashioned charm over the decades. Patrons still enjoyed skee ball, fun mirrors, and kiddie rides. In a nod to the nostalgia theme, Burroughs and Chapin implemented a series of events that harkened back to the Pavilion's early days. There were pie-throwing and bubble gum–blowing contests, and some concessions reverted to 1950s prices.

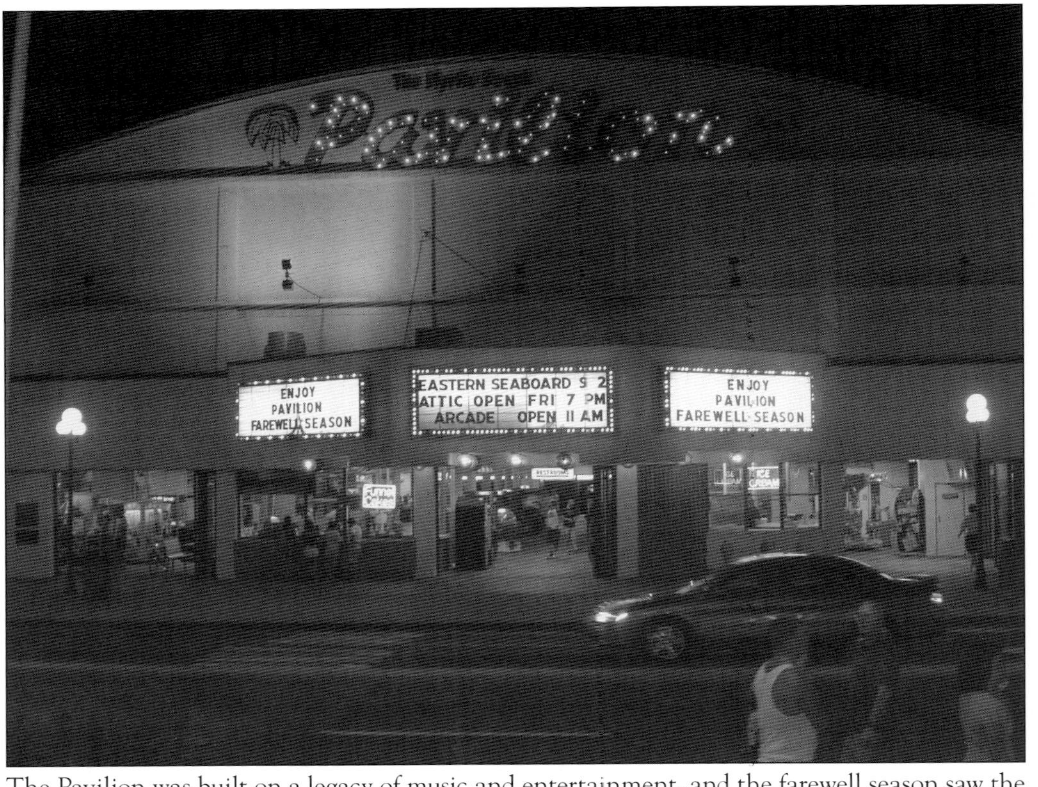

The Pavilion was built on a legacy of music and entertainment, and the farewell season saw the entertainment spill over from the upstairs Attic to the boardwalk. The Myrtle Beach Pavilion Farewell Season Sun Fun Concert Series brought back groups that had played the venue throughout the decades. Groups like Eastern Seaboard, Chairmen of the Board, and Sugar Creek once again drew crowds on the beach.

Until the very end, photographer Jack Thompson could be seen around the Pavilion with his camera, capturing memories. At the age of 13, Thompson had run away from home and come to Myrtle Beach. His first stop was the Pavilion, where he fell in love with the building and the energy that surrounded it. The Pavilion was his favorite subject and that love affair continued through the park's closure. (Courtesy Lauchlan McKay.)

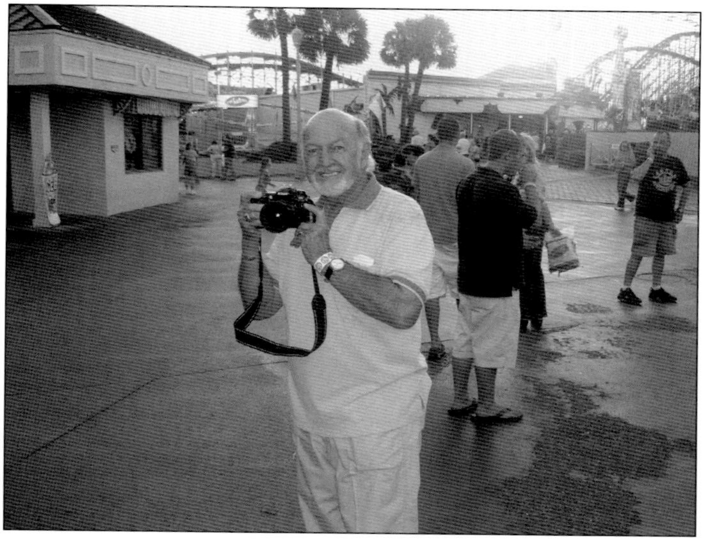

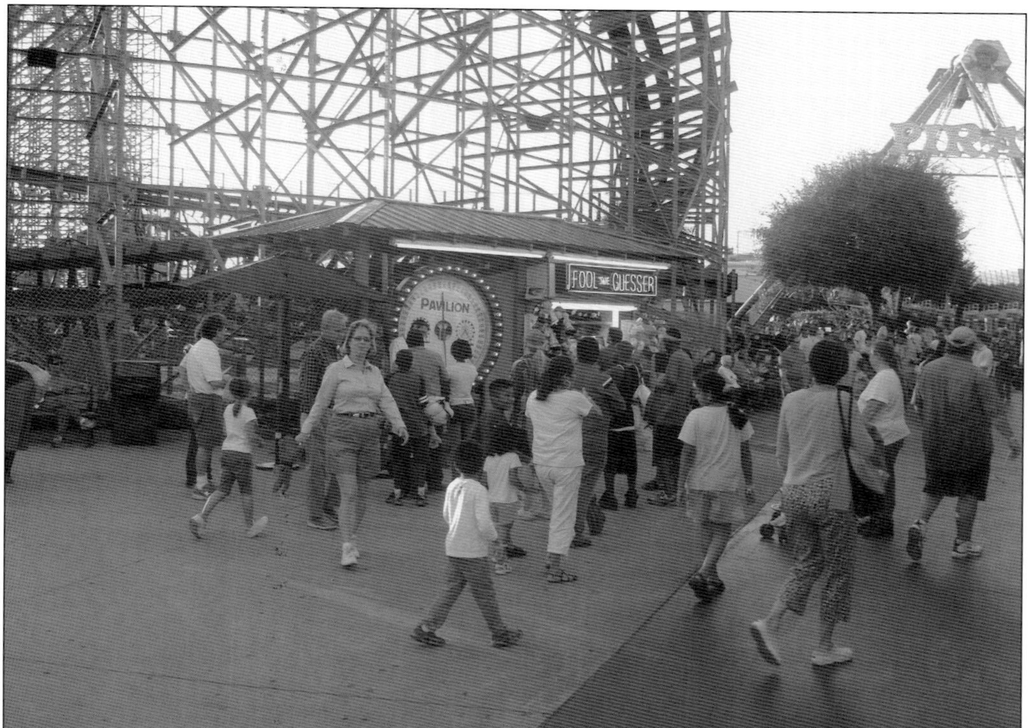

On September 17, the Pavilion Amusement Park hosted Family Appreciation Day. The theme was "Thanks for 58 years of Memories." Thousands flocked to the park to create some last memories of their own. An all-day ride pass cost just $10, and portions of the proceeds went to the United Way of Horry County. (Courtesy Lauchlan McKay.)

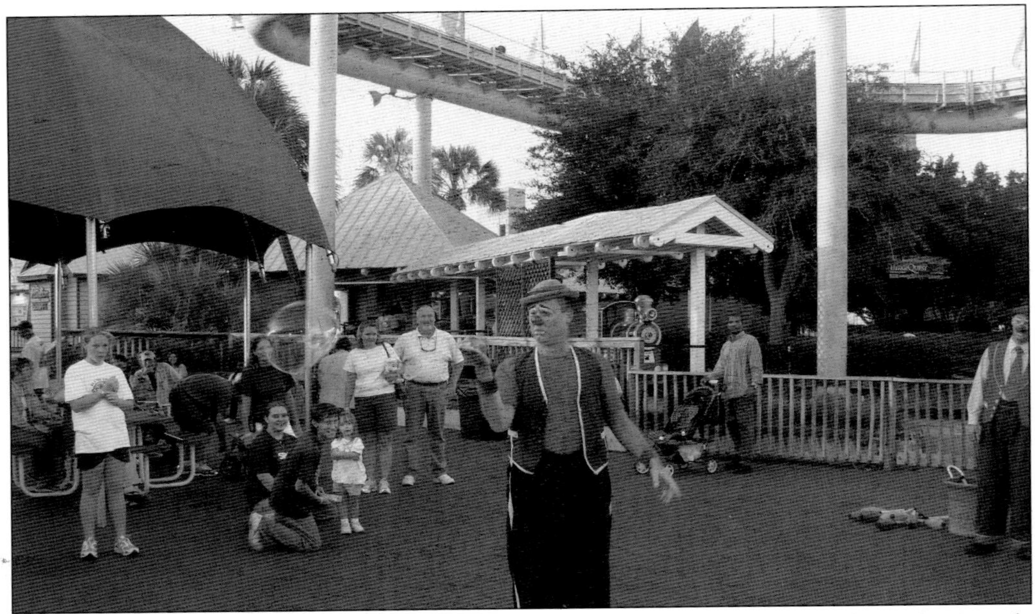

During the final years of the Pavilion Amusement Park, a regular feature had been the Seaside Clown Cavalcade. The troupe of clowns had regularly scheduled performances but also roamed the park to perform tricks for the kids. The final days were no different as crowds gathered to share a few last laughs together. (Courtesy Lauchlan McKay.)

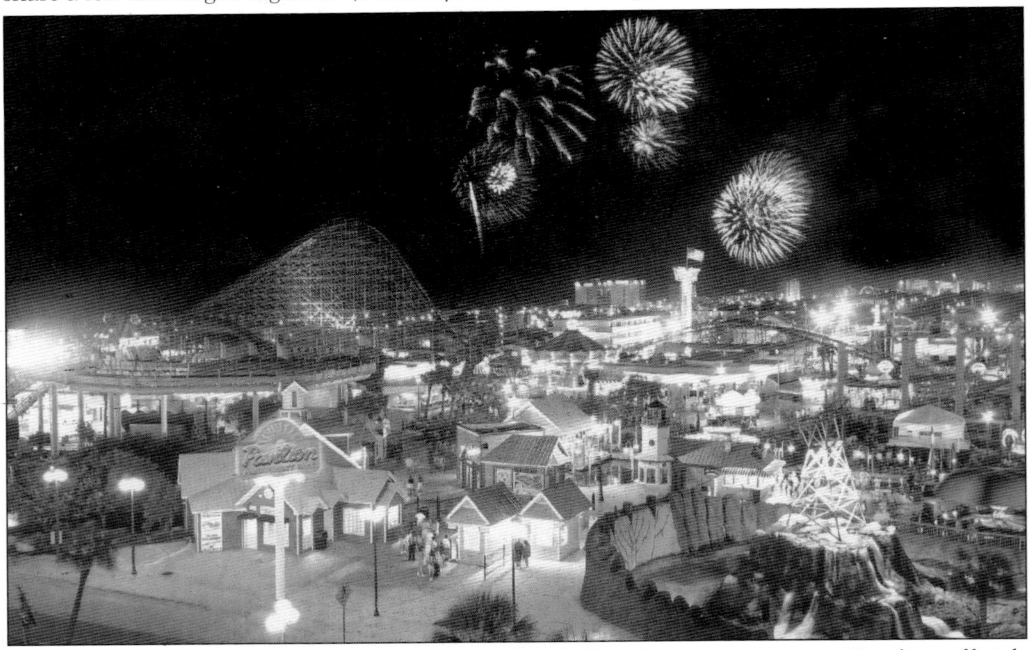

The Pavilion's farewell season proved an unparalleled, if not bittersweet, success. Pavilion officials had stated that the previous 2005 season had drawn fewer than 500,000 paying customers. They compared the final weekend's attendance for the 2006 farewell season to that of Fourth of Julys in days gone by with well more than 1.2 million tickets sold. (Courtesy Burroughs and Chapin Company, Inc.)

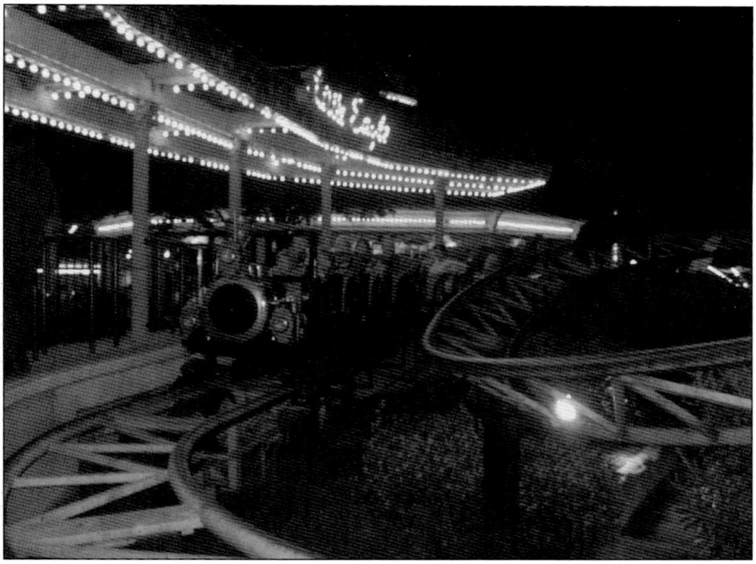

One week after the building and amusement park closed, a private party was held at the Pavilion for VIP guests, including city employees and employees of Burroughs and Chapin. Among them were the 38 people who had worked full time at the Myrtle Beach Pavilion. The party's theme was "Save the Last Dance." (Photograph by Allison Hardin.)

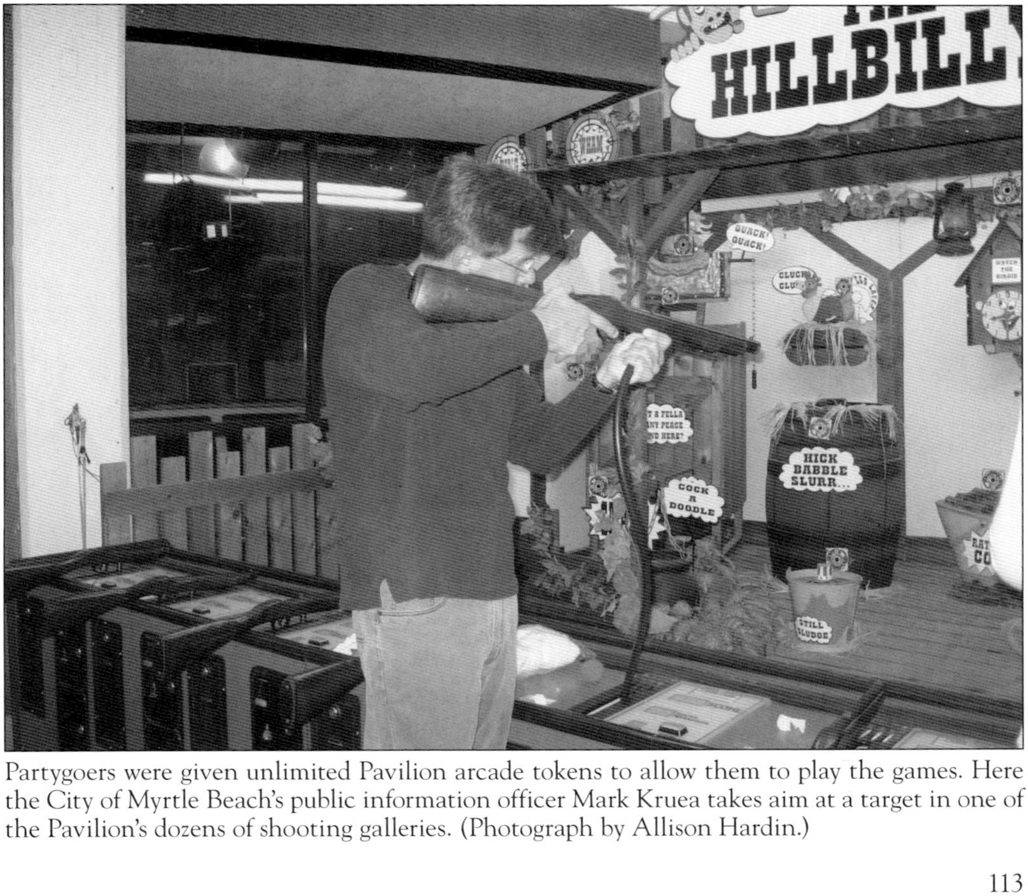

Partygoers were given unlimited Pavilion arcade tokens to allow them to play the games. Here the City of Myrtle Beach's public information officer Mark Kruea takes aim at a target in one of the Pavilion's dozens of shooting galleries. (Photograph by Allison Hardin.)

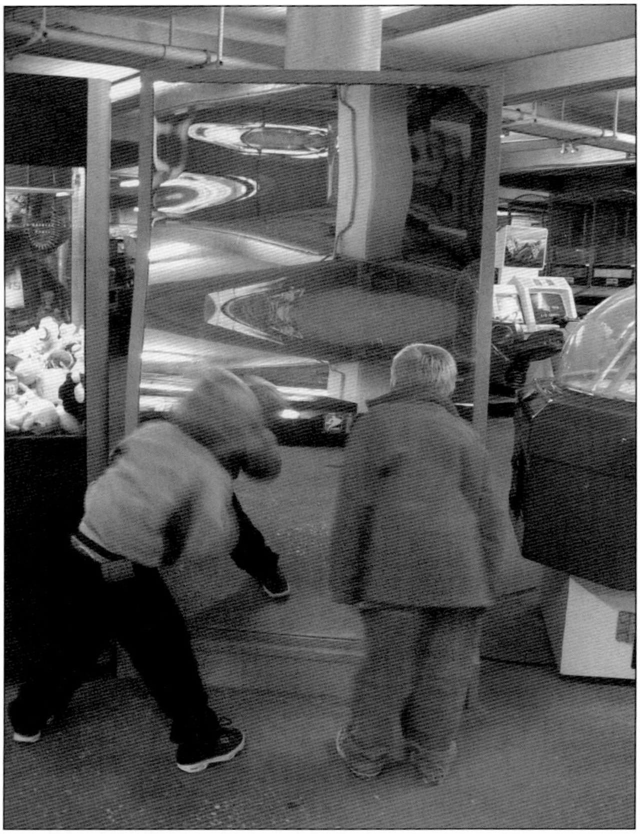

Even on the last night of the Pavilion, the fun mirrors were hard for kids to resist. The "Save the Last Dance" event was a family affair. Burroughs and Chapin Company's motto was "Family values since 1885," and the company wanted to make sure their employees' families could enjoy the Pavilion one last time. (Photograph by Allison Hardin.)

In addition to dinner and music, the guests at the "Save the Last Dance" party were allowed to ride the rides one last time, or, in some cases, several last times. Senior planner for the City of Myrtle Beach Planning Department Diane Moskow-McKenzie took this photograph of the amusement park sign just before it went dark for good. (Photograph by Diane Moskow-McKenzie.)

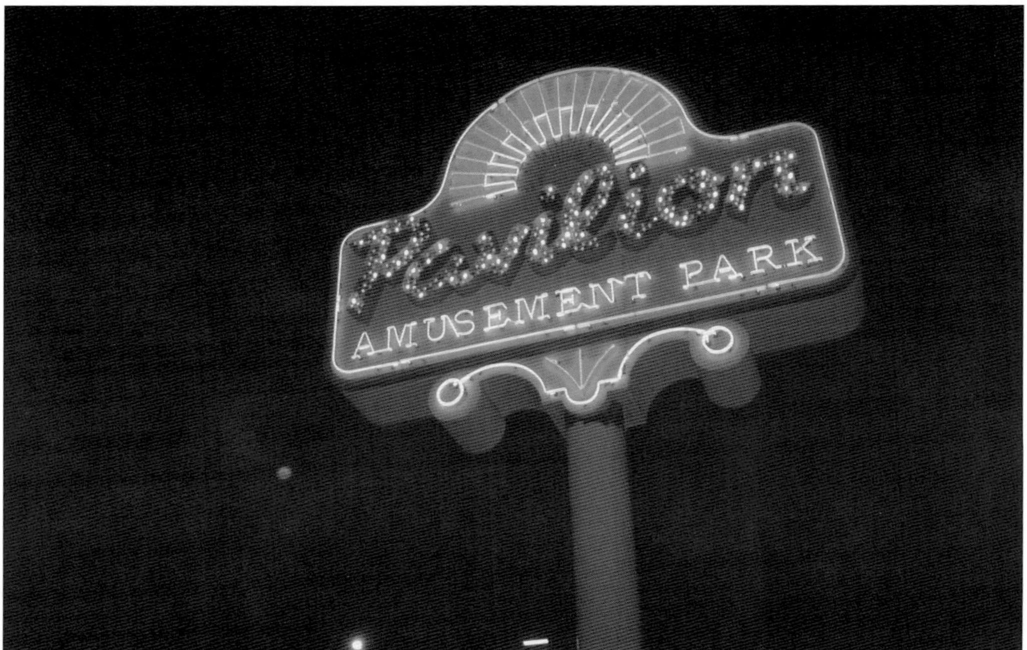

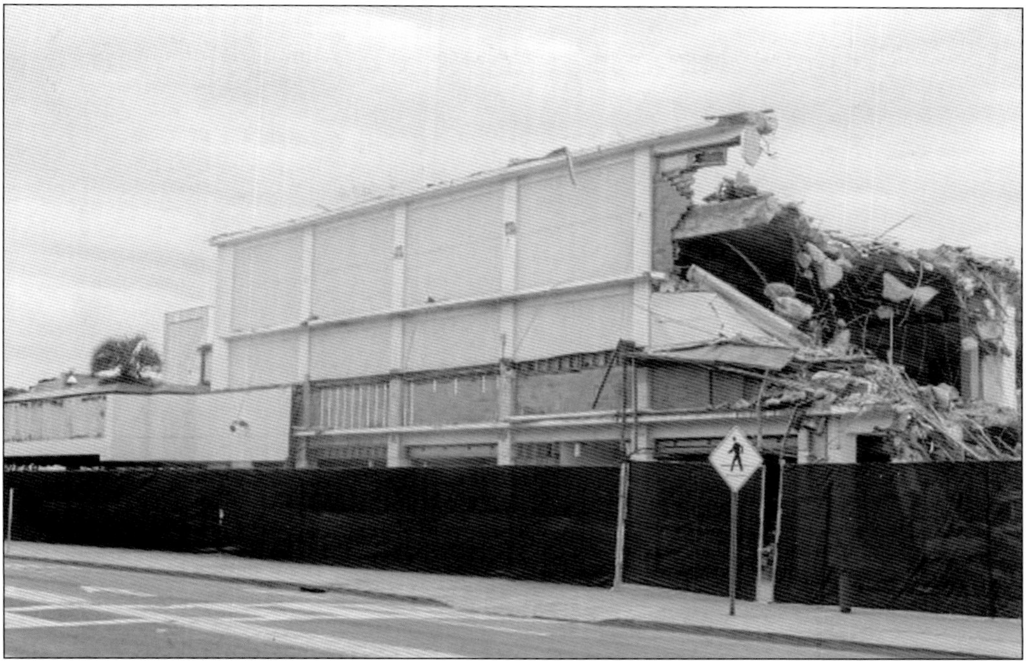

Within weeks of the Pavilion's closing, a construction fence was erected around both the Pavilion building and the amusement park across the street. An army of workers moved in to remove arcade machines, fixtures, trash cans, pipes, and just about anything that could be re-used before the wrecking machines came in. Most of the items salvaged were later sold at auction. A lot of the scrap and rubble itself was simply sold as souvenirs to people who wanted a piece, any piece, of their beloved Pavilion. For weeks, as the demolition crews worked, locals and a few tourists came by to watch the Pavilion be reduced to rubble and then removed. Many wept as they watched. (Above, courtesy Danny Caudle; below, courtesy Glenn Broach, City of Myrtle Beach Construction Services.)

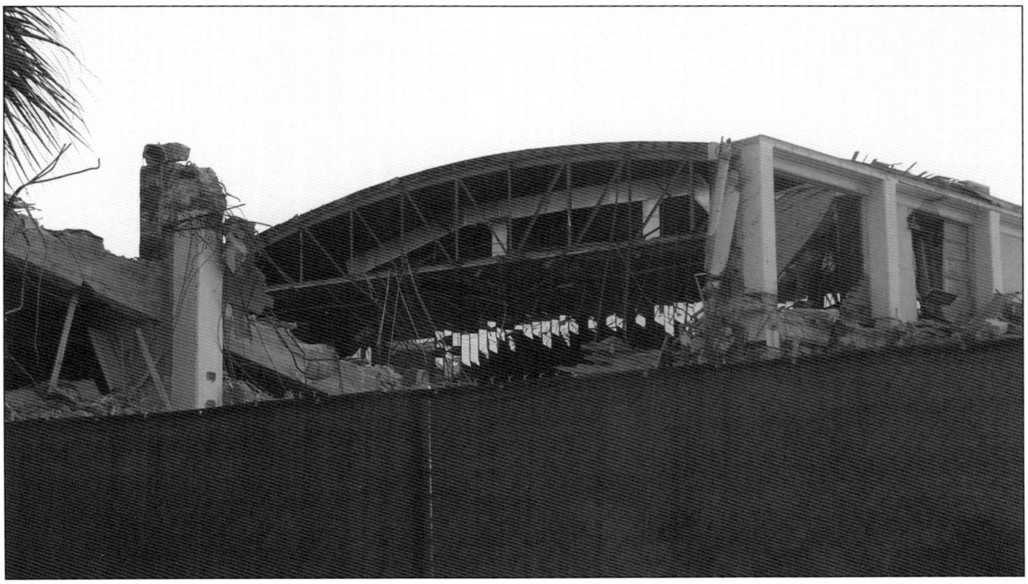

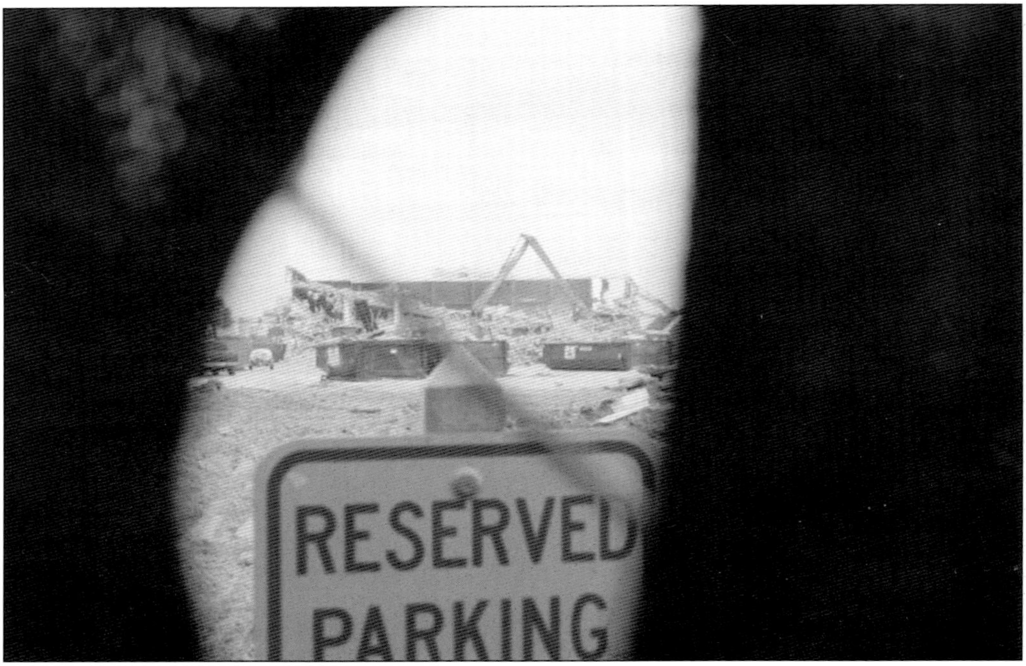

In 1949, when the Pavilion was built, it was designed to withstand just about anything, including 150-mile-an-hour winds. For almost 60 years, it had been battered by storms, undergone renovations, and seen the entire world change around it. All this the Myrtle Beach Pavilion had endured, but in the end, the bulldozers and wrecking crews won out. (Courtesy Danny Caudle.)

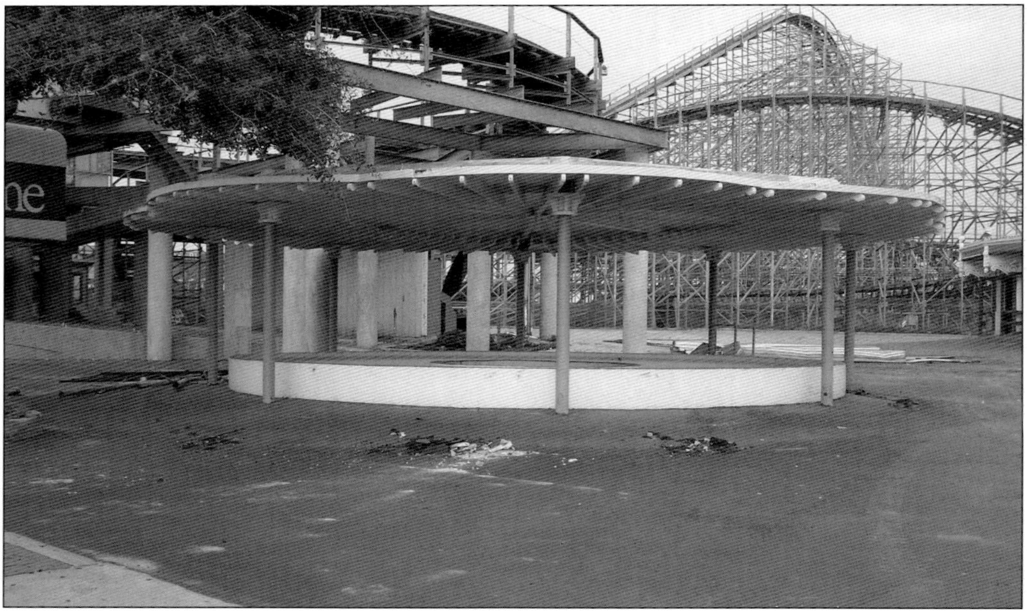

While demolition of the Pavilion was under way, bit by bit the amusement park was disappearing as well. This round concrete platform was once home to one of the park's kiddie rides where younger children could sit on a motorcycle and go around and around while lights flashed. The ride was relocated to Broadway at the Beach.

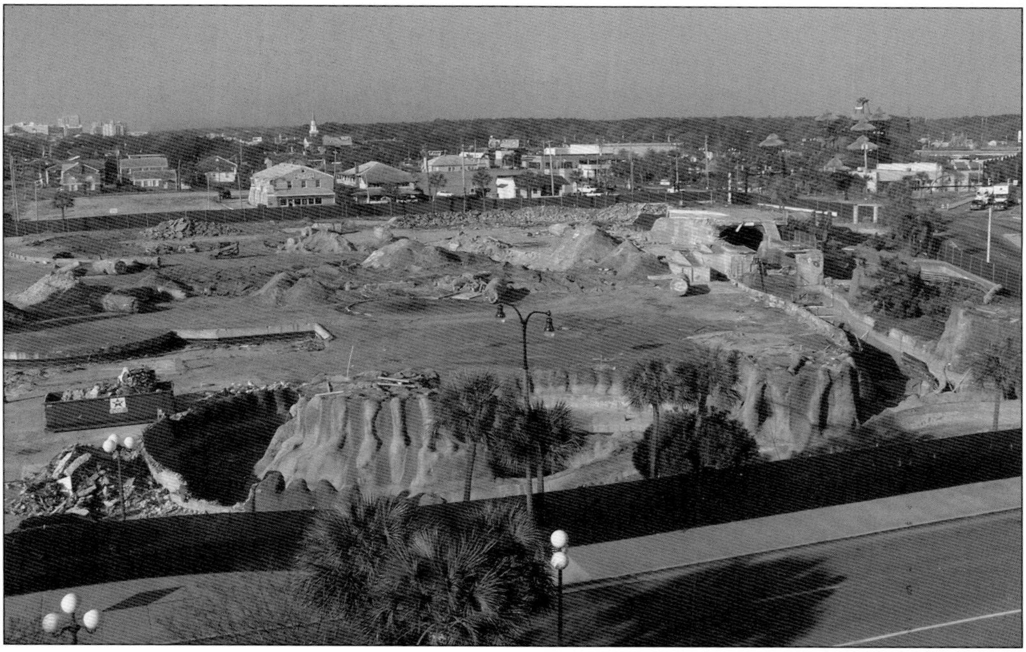

The Pavilion's 11-acre ride area took longer to dismantle than the Pavilion itself. Work began in late December 2006 and was done by April 2007. Some of the rides were moved to parks elsewhere in the area, including some to the new Pavilion Nostalgia Park at Broadway at the Beach. Among those preserved are several kiddie rides, the Pirate, the Caterpillar, the Herschell-Spillman carousel, and the 1900 Baden band organ. The Haunted Hotel and multimillion-dollar Hurricane roller coaster were demolished because they were too big to be reused. Some of the Hurricane's cars were sold to Kings Island in Mason, Ohio, to be used in their Son of Beast roller coaster.

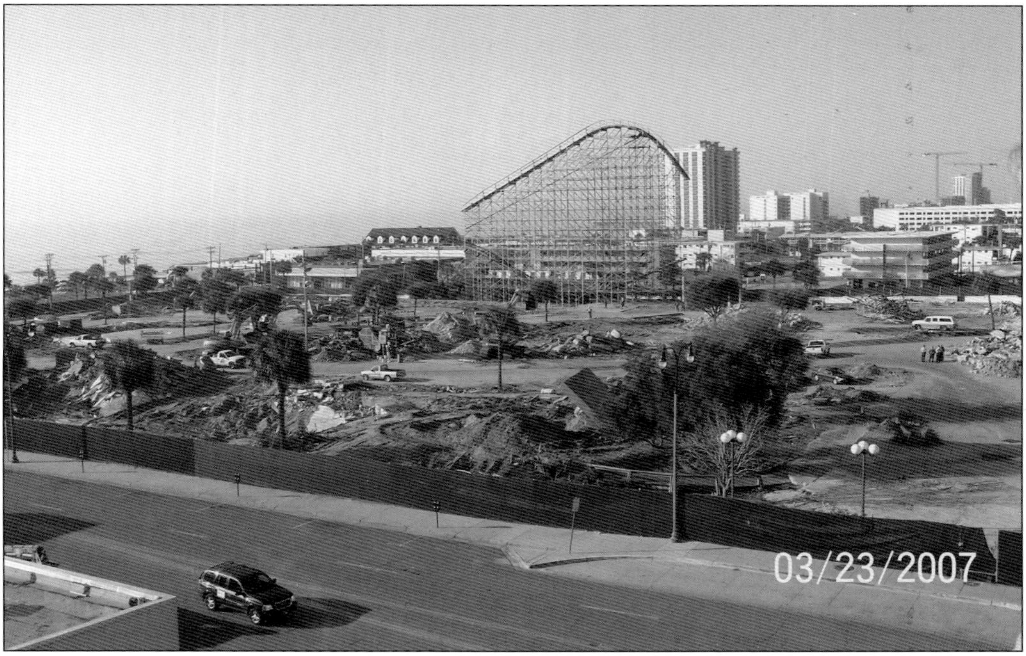

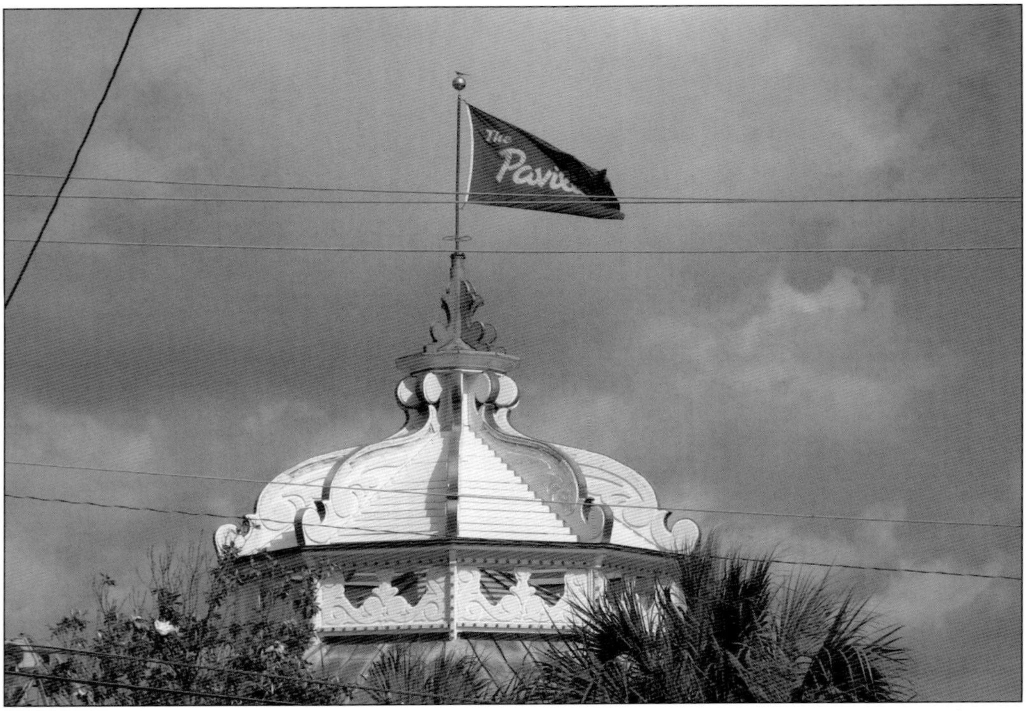

These two photographs are a stark contrast to one another. The top photograph was taken at the beginning of the farewell season on June 1, 2006, when the Pavilion's flag still flew atop the Herschell-Spillman carousel. The second photograph was taken less than 10 months later on the day the Hurricane roller coaster was brought down. The shelter for the carousel remained locked up tight while the demolition took place around it. Its new location at Broadway at the Beach had yet to be built. This series of demolition photographs were taken from on top of the Pavilion garage. Its height advantage made it a prime location for people to watch the destruction and say their final farewell.

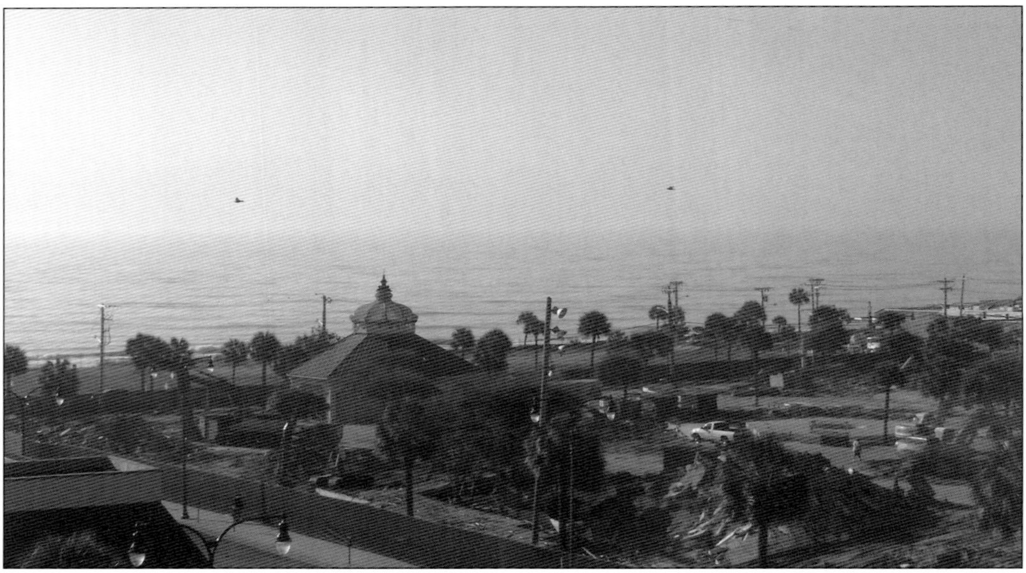

Five
Pavilion Ever After

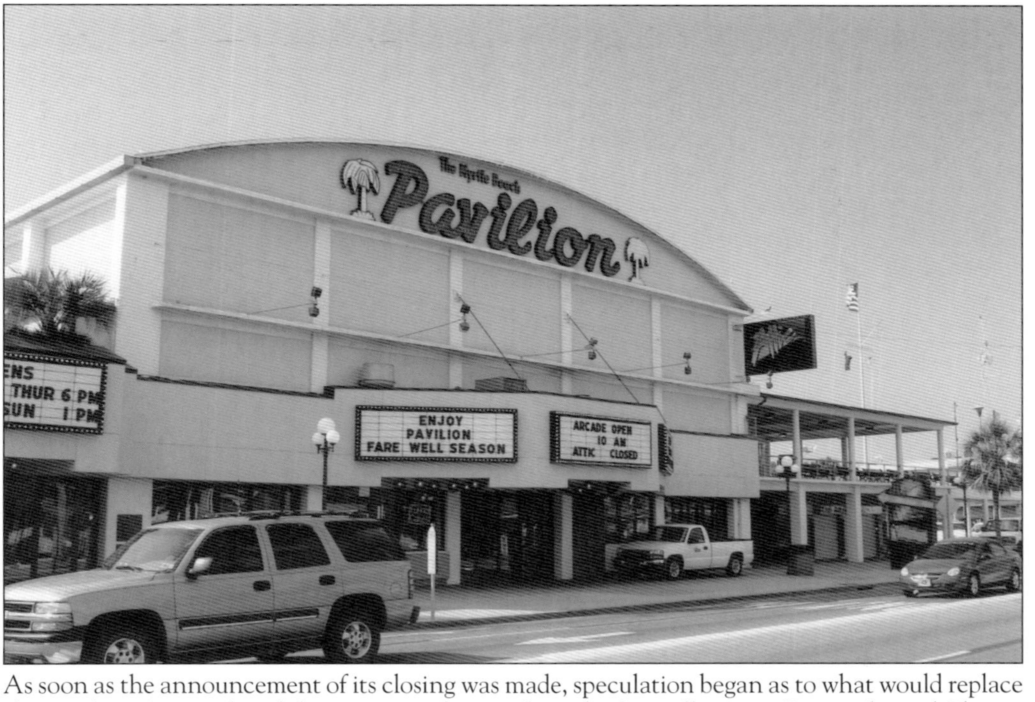

As soon as the announcement of its closing was made, speculation began as to what would replace the Pavilion. Saying they did not want to distract from the farewell season, Burroughs and Chapin promised to announce plans for redevelopment by October 2006. The announcement did not come, but several of the best-loved rides were relocated to a new Pavilion Nostalgia Park at the company-owned Broadway at the Beach.

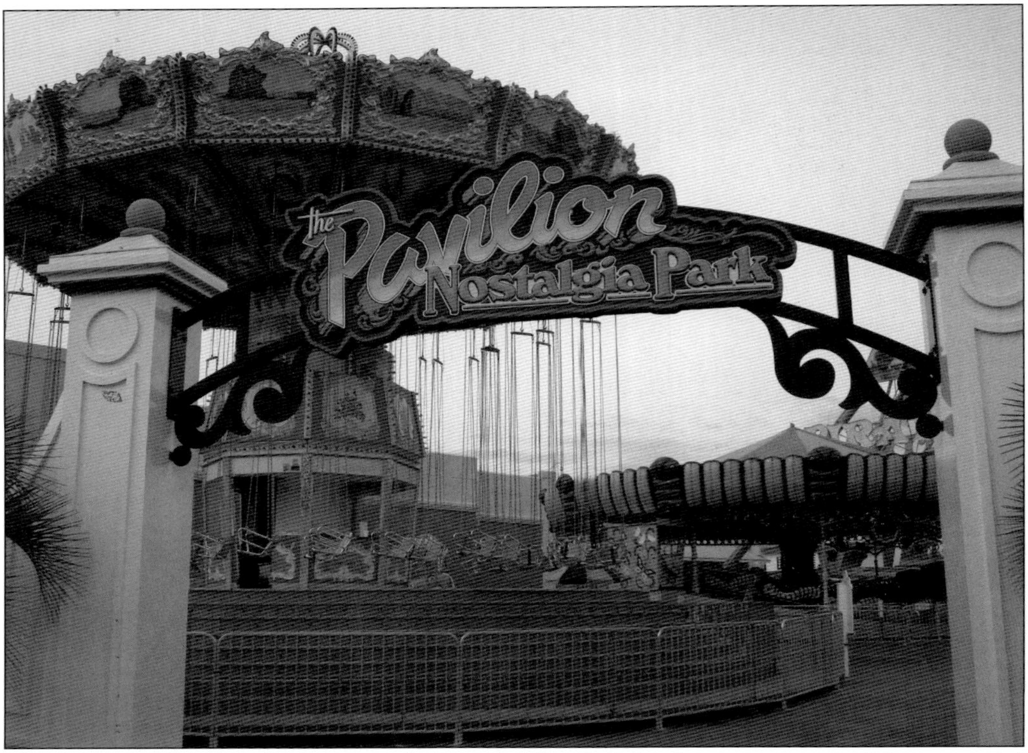

The Pavilion Nostalgia Park at Broadway at the Beach helped preserve some of the perennial favorites of the old park, including several kiddie rides, the Caterpillar, the Wave Swinger, and the Pirate Ship. In addition to the rides, the Baden band organ and the Herschell-Spillman carousel, which were both relocated here. The carousel and organ are both listed on the National Register of Historic Places. Each ride sports a plaque telling when it arrived at the original Pavilion park. Burroughs and Chapin had first tried to move the Pavilion rides to Broadway at the Beach in 1996 but had reconsidered after pressure from the City of Myrtle Beach.

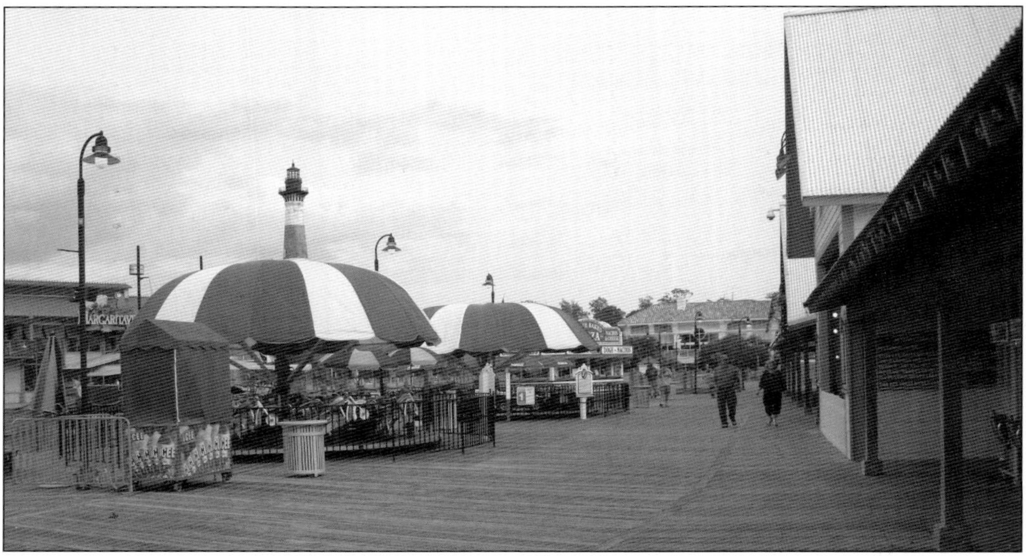

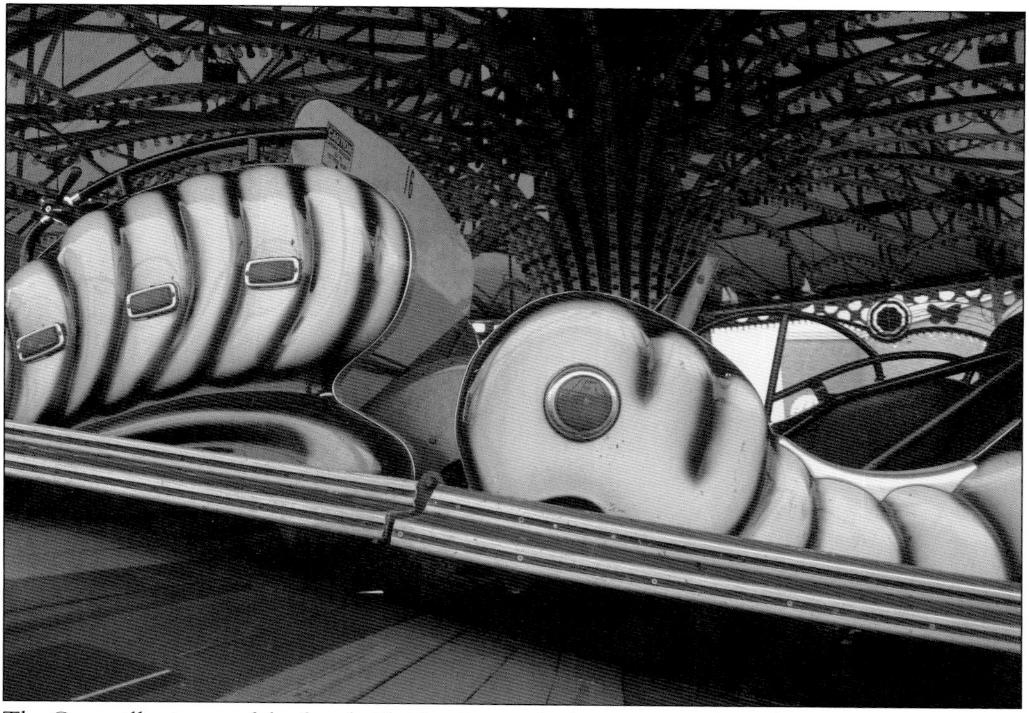

The Caterpillar is one of the few thrill rides that made the transition from the Pavilion Amusement Park to the Pavilion Nostalgia Park. The backwards- and forward-spinning Caterpillar is considered a vintage ride. Allen Herschell, who also helped design and build the historic carousel, designed the mechanisms that run it.

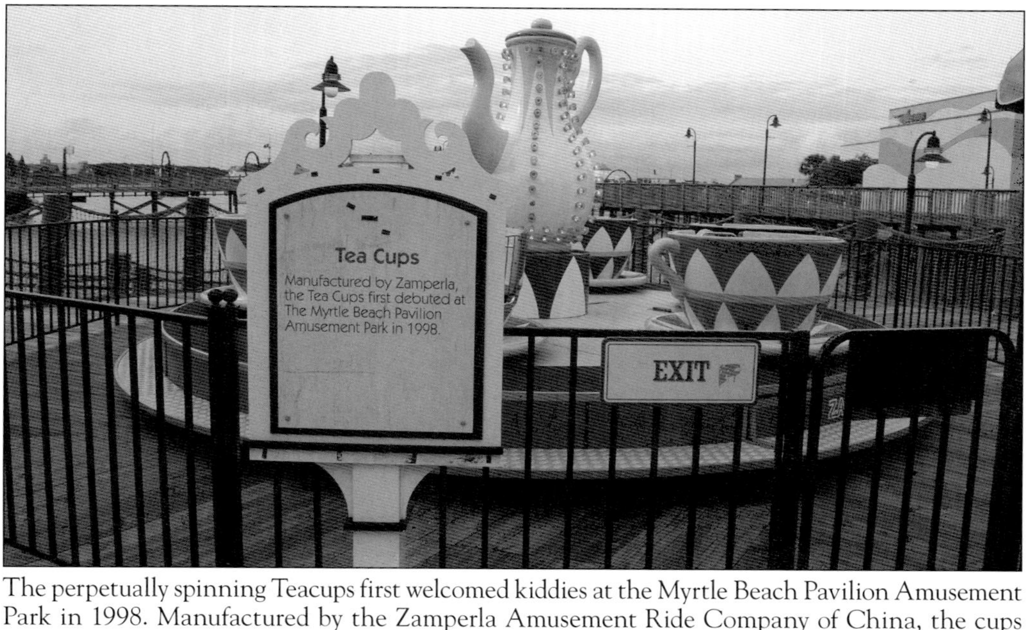

The perpetually spinning Teacups first welcomed kiddies at the Myrtle Beach Pavilion Amusement Park in 1998. Manufactured by the Zamperla Amusement Ride Company of China, the cups were a favorite among youngsters and their parents, who can still take them for a spin on the Broadway at the Beach boardwalk.

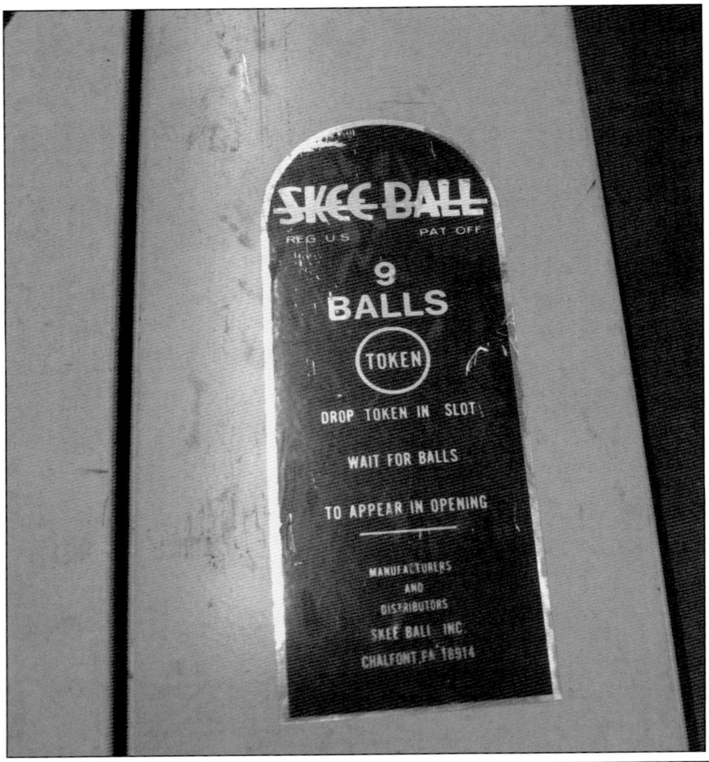

Not only the rides found new life elsewhere; the Pavilion Nostalgia Park contains a small building housing some of the arcade games such as these classic skee ball games. Other attractions include a fortune-telling machine and a few electronic arcade games. It is a place to buy souvenirs and postcards honoring both the old and the new. The building itself is decorated in memorabilia from the original building, including the plaque that adorned the Pavilion building commemorating its dedication in 1948, as well as a plaque in honor of Earl Husted, who served as the Pavilion's general manager for more than 50 years.

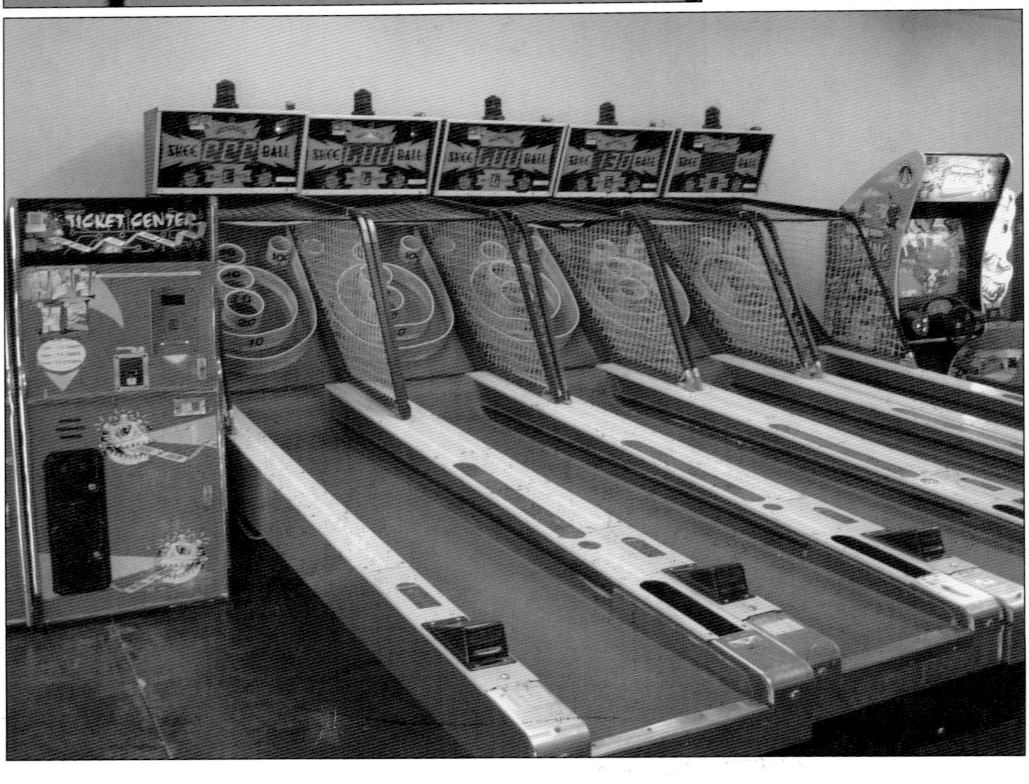

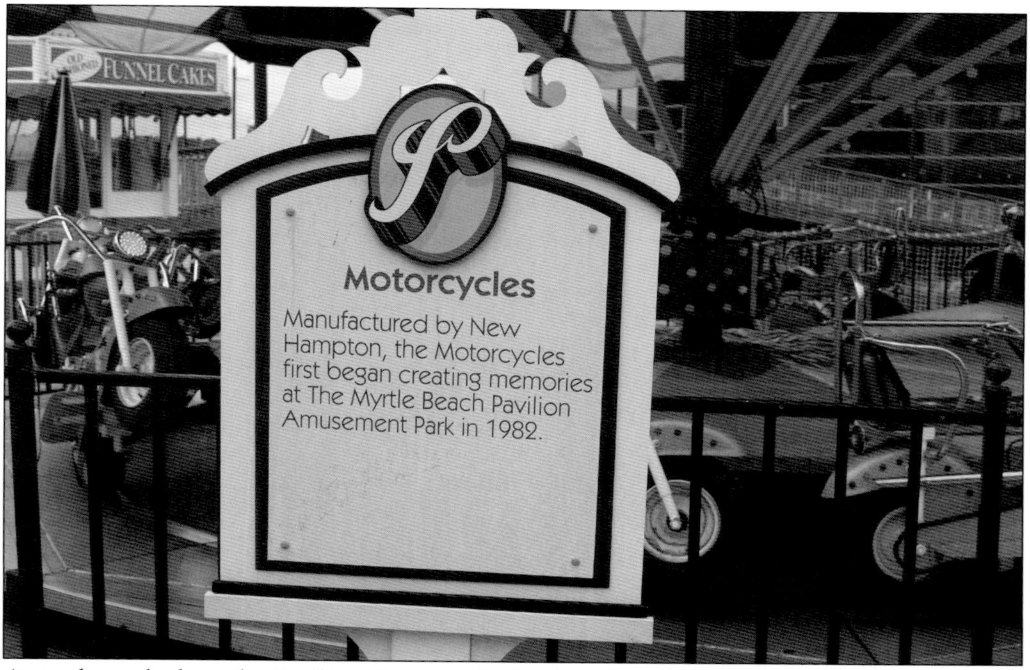

As in the early days, the Pavilion Nostalgia Park sells one ticket per ride. By being relocated to Broadway the Beach, new life was given to the classic rides salvaged from the Pavilion Amusement Park. By being at this shopping and entertainment complex, they were now open to the public every day of the year, except holidays. The Pavilion Amusement Park had long limited its amusements to the summer season.

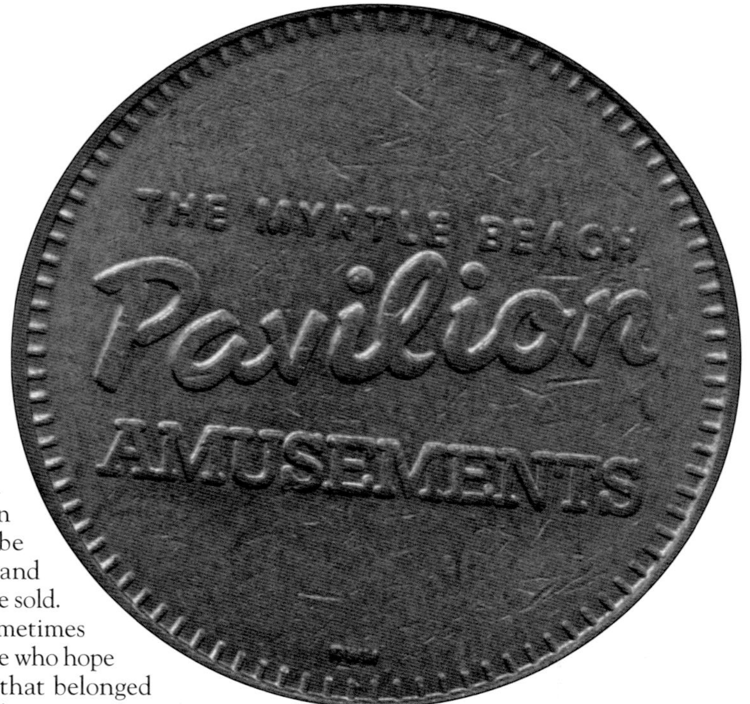

The nostalgia that surrounds the Myrtle Beach Pavilion extends well beyond the Pavilion Nostalgia Park. This token and others like it can be found in online auctions and stores where collectables are sold. These mementoes can sometimes fetch steep prices from those who hope to buy a piece of history that belonged to not just Myrtle Beach but to anyone who visited the landmark.

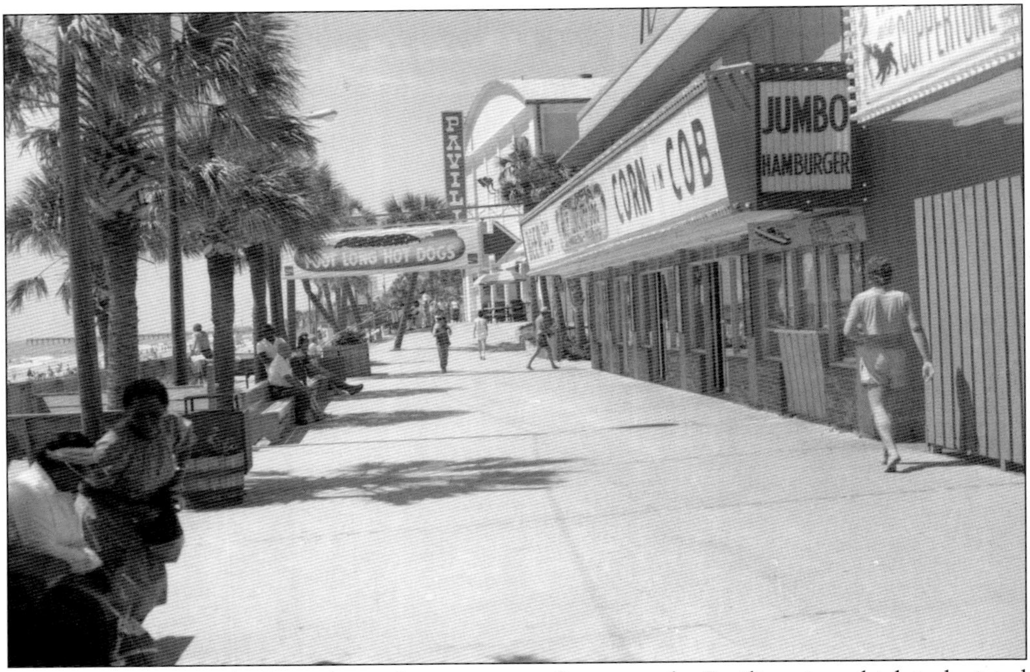

The 1950s photograph above shows the same area adjacent to the Pavilion site, which is depicted in the artist's rendition below, released in 2009. Coming in September 2009 and three years after the Pavilion's closing, the City of Myrtle Beach launched a $6-million boardwalk development designed to revitalize the 11-acre area in the heart of the city left vacant by the demise of the Pavilion. For some, the construction brought Myrtle Beach full circle. A boardwalk had been as much a part of Myrtle Beach's identity as the Pavilion. The earliest days of the city's development had centered on a boardwalk that connected the first Pavilion and hotels to cottages in the area.

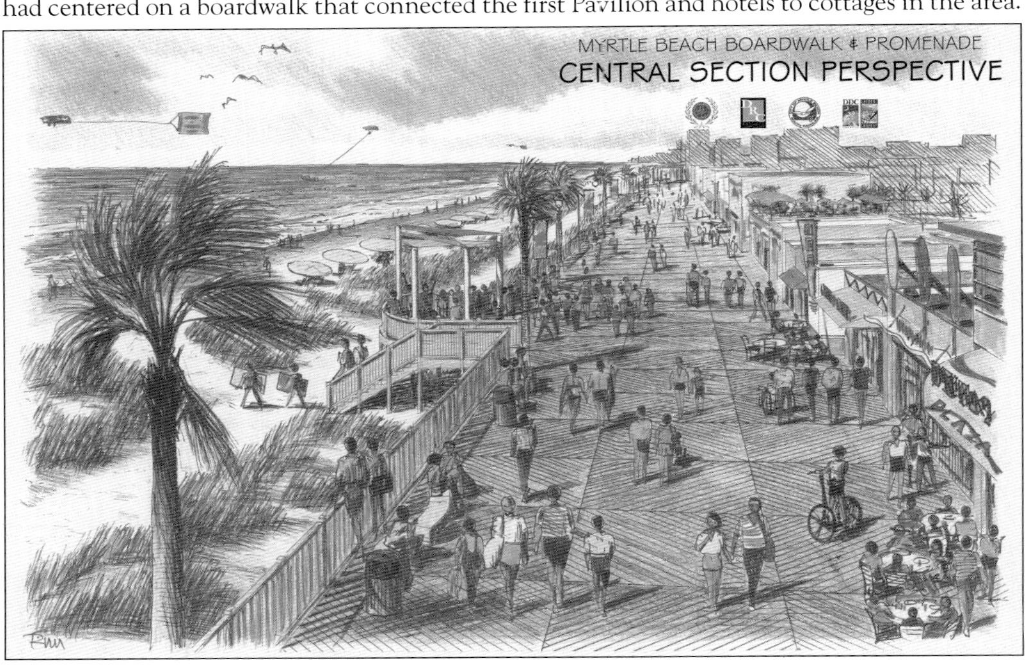

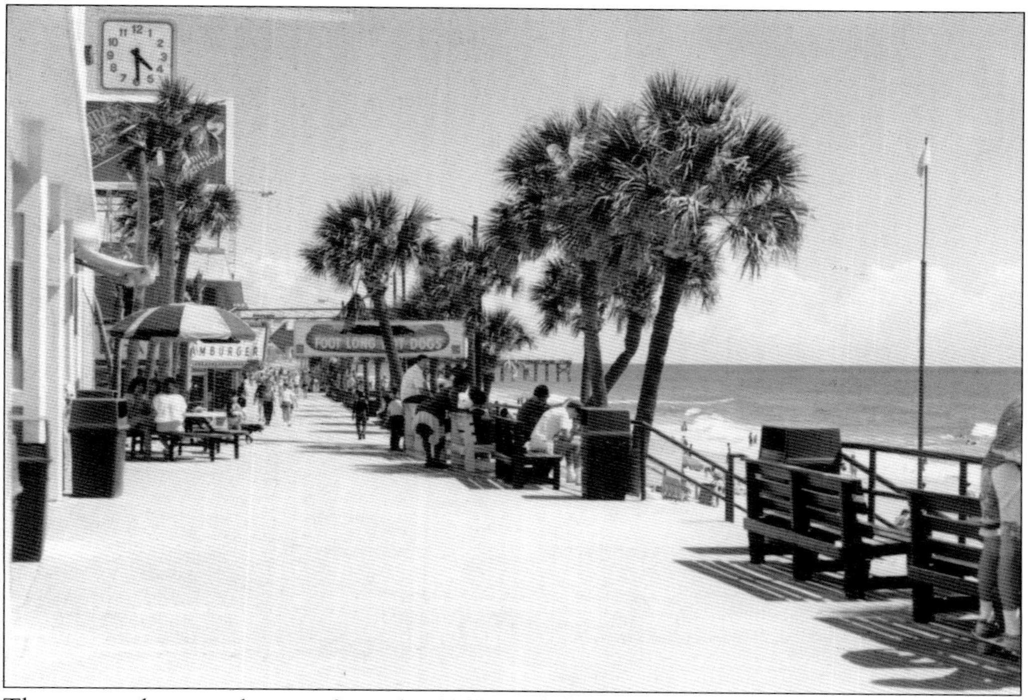

These two photographs, one from the 1960s and the other from 2009, were taken from the same vantage point looking northward. At the time the second photograph was taken, the new boardwalk had been under construction for two months. It was completed in May 2010. The new promenade was designed to reconnect all the businesses on either side of the old Pavilion location, stretching from the Fourteenth Avenue Pier in the north to the Second Avenue Pier in the south.

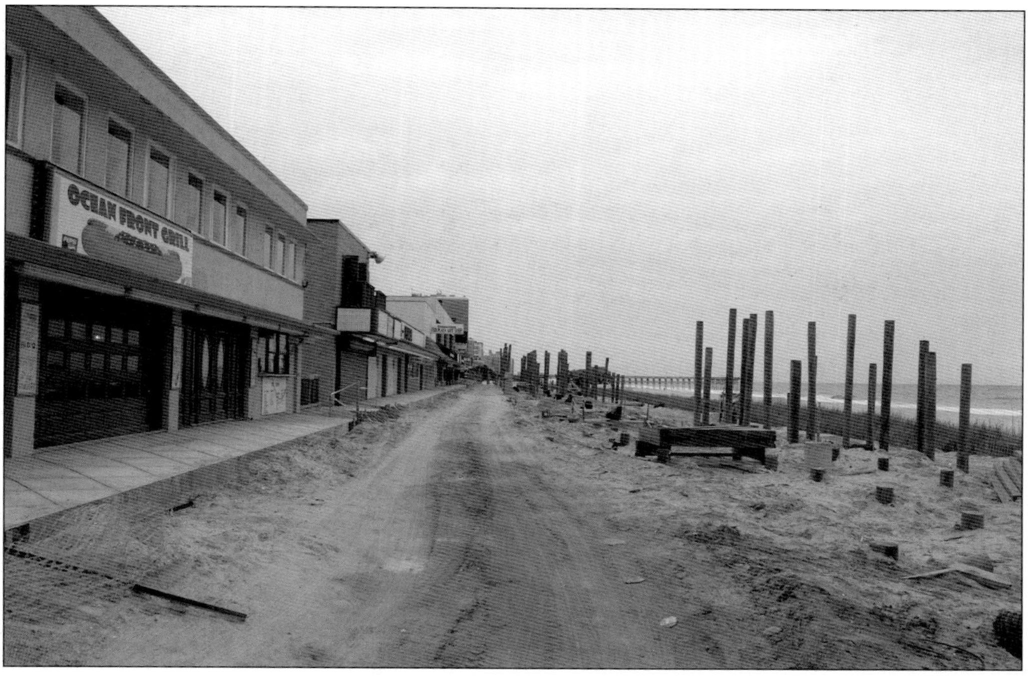

BIBLIOGRAPHY

Edgar, Walter, ed. *The South Carolina Encyclopedia.* Columbia, SC: The University of South Carolina Press, 2006.

Gragg, Rod. *The Illustrated History of Horry County.* Myrtle Beach, SC: Burroughs and Chapin Company, Inc., 1994.

———. *Pirates, Planters, and Patriots: Historical tales From the South Carolina Grand Strand.* Winston-Salem, NC: Peace Hill Publishers, 1984.

Horry Herald. Conway, SC. Selected issues, 1900–1929.

Independent Republic Weekly, Vol. 3, No. 3 (July 1969), 9–18.

Merrill, Adeline Godfrey Pringle, ed. *A Personal History of the F. G. Burroughs Family.* Privately published, 2003.

Milliken, Helen. *From the Beginning: A History of Burroughs and Chapin Company.* Myrtle Beach, SC: Sheriar Press, 2004.

Rhyne, Nancy. *Touring the Coastal South Carolina Backroads.* Winston-Salem, NC: John F. Blair Publisher, 1992.

———. *The Grand Strand: An Uncommon Guide to Myrtle Beach and Its Surroundings.* Winston-Salem, NC: East Wood Press, 1981.

Stokes, Barbara J. *Greetings from Myrtle Beach, A History, 1900–1980.* Columbia, SC: The University of South Carolina Press, 2007.

Sun News. Myrtle Beach, SC. Selected issues, 1985–2008.

INDEX